PHPUnit Essentials

Get started with PHPUnit and learn how to write
and test code using advanced technologies

Zdenek Machek

open source
community experience distilled

PACKT PUBLISHING

BIRMINGHAM - MUMBAI

PHPUnit Essentials

First published: May 2014

Production Reference: 1190514

Published by Packt Publishing Ltd.
Livery Place
35 Livery Street
Birmingham B3 2PB, UK.

ISBN 978-1-78328-343-9

www.packtpub.com

Cover Image by Asher Wishkerman (wishkerman@hotmail.com)

Credits

Author

Zdenek Machek

Reviewers

R. Rajesh Jeba Anbiah

Azizur Rahman

Mauro Takeda

Jakub Tománek

M. A. Hossain Tonu

Aaron Saray

Dmytro Zavalkin

Commissioning Editors

Amarabha Banerjee

Usha Iyer

Acquisition Editor

Amarabha Banerjee

Content Development Editor

Arvind Koul

Technical Editors

Shweta S. Pant

Ritika Singh

Copy Editors

Sarang Chari

Janbal Dharmaraj

Mradula Hegde

Deepa Nambiar

Alfida Paiva

Adithi Shetty

Project Coordinator

Kranti Berde

Proofreaders

Simran Bhogal

Maria Gould

Linda Morris

Indexer

Mehreen Deshmukh

Production Coordinator

Manu Joseph

Cover Work

Manu Joseph

About the Author

Zdenek Machek is an experienced PHP developer, who has been working with PHP since the year 2000 and PHP3 days. He introduced software testing and PHPUnit to various companies, and used them on various small as well as large scale projects.

Zdenek wrote several articles and blog posts focused on Continuous Integration processes during PHP application development.

Currently, Zdenek leads technology standards and values across the organization, and also handles analysis, planning, and technical delivery of large scale, critical, and high performance systems for our most complex projects.

First and foremost, I would like to thank all the people who invest their time and energy in open source software—people writing code, documentation, reporting and fixing bugs, and organizing meetings. They allowed PHP to become so popular and widely used. The same can be said about PHPUnit and all other related projects, which really transformed the way developers work and probably how the Internet looks and works today.

I would like to thank all the people who helped me and supported me through all my life. Especially, I would like to thank my family for their patience for all the hours, days, and years that I have spent in front of a computer screen.

I would also like to thank the people at Packt Publishing, who have been working on this project, for their valuable feedback and professional approach, as well as the reviewers who helped to improve the book with their excellent comments and suggestions.

About the Reviewers

R. Rajesh Jeba Anbiah has been into programming since 1998 with C, Visual Basic, Delphi, Perl, PHP, ASP.NET MVC, and Play. He currently heads the project division in Agriya (http://www.agriya.com/), where he oversees challenging web and mobile development projects, web software products, and lab initiatives. These days, he's more passionate about topics related to machine learning and REST-based SPA using Node.js, AngularJS, and upcoming frameworks.

So far he has authored two books:

- *A to Z of C, Packt Publishing*
- *PHP Ajax Cookbook, Packt Publishing*

When he's not in the office, he is mostly available at home nagging his wife and two children.

Azizur Rahman is a senior web developer at the BBC. Currently, he's working on the BBC Homepage project. He has a BSc (Hons) Artificial Intelligence degree from the University of Westminster, UK.

He joined BBC in late 2011 as a web application developer within the Future Media Knowledge and Learning department. While working on the Knowledge & Learning project (http://www.bbc.co.uk/education), he put his knowledge of Test-Driven Development (TDD) using PHPUnit into practice. In this large scale project, the development team also used Ruby and Cucumber for fully automated acceptance testing.

The Knowledge & Learning project's purpose was to bring together factual and learning content from over 100 existing BBC websites, from Bitesize, Food, Science to History, and place them into a single consistent user experience designed to make learning feel effortless and delightful.

After the successful launch of the Knowledge & Learning project, he moved to the Interactive Guides project (http://www.bbc.co.uk/guides). While developing Interactive Guides, he solidified and advanced his knowledge of TDD and Behavior-Driven Development (BDD).

The Interactive Guides project took a different approach to presenting content compared to traditional web articles of TV and radio programs online. They organize video and audio, rich infographics, written summaries, and activities into stories that make the most out of BBC's interactive medium. Interactive Guides takes the audience through a series of steps that ask them to look at multiple perspectives of intriguing questions, always with the chance to reflect on the significance of the story at the end.

A firm believer in philanthropy, Azizur spends his spare time supporting philanthropic causes using his knowledge and expertise of open source technologies.

He serves as a senior web developer / IT advisor to ProductiveMuslim.com — a website dedicated to Islam and productivity. A global team of volunteers with the sole aim to help the Ummah ("nation" or "community") become productive again!

The following is a quote by Prophet Muhammad (PBUH) taken from http://sunnah.com/urn/1252420:

> *"The best of charity is when a [Muslim] man gains knowledge, then he teaches it to his [Muslim] brother."*

In April 2014, he became an ambassador of STEMNET. As an ambassador, he uses his enthusiasm and commitment to encourage young people to enjoy science, technology, engineering, and mathematics. You can read more about STEMNET at http://www.stemnet.org.uk.

Along with technically reviewing this book, he has also technically reviewed *PHP Application Development with NetBeans: Beginner's Guide, Packt Publishing*.

His keen interest in open source software makes him a regular attendee at local technology user groups and wider open source community events.

Mauro Takeda has been working in the IT industry since 1999 when he faced his first legacy problem: the Y2K bug. Since then, he has worked with several programming languages, such as COBOL, Dataflex, C, Visual Basic, Delphi, Pascal, Lisp, Prolog, and Java with whom he has a relationship of over 10 years. His newer passion is functional programming.

In the last five years, he has worked in CI&T (www.ciandt.com), a global IT company headquartered in Campinas, Brazil (a prominent tech center considered as the Brazilian Silicon Valley) with strategic locations across Latin America, North America, Europe, and the Asia-Pacific. Nowadays, as a systems architect, he is responsible for people and software development, mainly in PHP and Drupal.

> For Helena, Henrique, and Márcia, whose smiles make me happy even when nothing else does.

Jakub Tománek is a seasoned (more than eight years' experience) PHP developer. After having started working on regular websites, he quickly focused on complex web applications, including creating APIs, background jobs, vast databases, and fixing untraceable bugs.

He currently works as a Senior Software Development Engineer in Microsoft, where his team maintains and improves Skype's website.

> I'd like to thank my parents for all they've done for me in the past. I wouldn't be where I am without their support. I also want to thank all my current and past colleagues from whom I had the opportunity to learn so much.

M. A. Hossain Tonu, the author of the book *PHP Application Development with NetBeans: Beginner's Guide, Packt Publishing*, graduated in Computer Science and Engineering from the Dhaka University of Engineering and Technology (DUET) in Bangladesh.

He is working at Vantage, Dhaka (`http://www.vantage.com/`), where he is leading and maintaining a highly available SAAS platform Vantage CRM that is the single most intuitive and easy-to-use Customer Relationship Management system (`http://www.vantageip.com/products-services/vantage-crm/`) on the market.

He has been a passionate developer for the past eight years, and has developed a series of web applications, services, and solutions for leading software companies in the country, such as somewherein and Improsys.

You can reach Tonu at `mahtonu@vantage.com` and at his tech blog at `http://mahtonu.wordpress.com`.

Aaron Saray knows exactly what it's like to have code under the microscope. PHP conference presentations, open source contributions, and managing a team that now works in his old code, are things that have made him used to the constant code reviews. While he enjoys learning the newest in web technologies, more than a decade later, his true passion is still the core and basics of PHP programming, testing, and best practices. He reflects this in his WROX book *Professional PHP Design Patterns* and his technical blog at `aaronsaray.com/blog`. Additionally, he can be found as a technical editor of many books encompassing PHP, JavaScript, and Internet technologies.

Dmytro Zavalkin has around seven years of experience in the field of Web Development using LAMP stack. For the last three years, he has been using PHPUnit in his everyday work. Currently, he works as a PHP/Magento developer at AOE GmbH, Wiesbaden, Germany. Before relocating to Germany, he worked at Magento, an eBay Inc. company in Donetsk, Ukraine.

www.PacktPub.com

Support files, eBooks, discount offers, and more

You might want to visit www.PacktPub.com for support files and downloads related to your book.

Did you know that Packt offers eBook versions of every book published, with PDF and ePub files available? You can upgrade to the eBook version at www.PacktPub.com and as a print book customer, you are entitled to a discount on the eBook copy. Get in touch with us at service@packtpub.com for more details.

At www.PacktPub.com, you can also read a collection of free technical articles, sign up for a range of free newsletters and receive exclusive discounts and offers on Packt books and eBooks.

http://PacktLib.PacktPub.com

Do you need instant solutions to your IT questions? PacktLib is Packt's online digital book library. Here, you can access, read and search across Packt's entire library of books.

Why subscribe?

- Fully searchable across every book published by Packt
- Copy and paste, print and bookmark content
- On demand and accessible via web browser

Free access for Packt account holders

If you have an account with Packt at www.PacktPub.com, you can use this to access PacktLib today and view nine entirely free books. Simply use your login credentials for immediate access.

Table of Contents

Preface

In the last ten years, PHP as a programming language has made great progress. It has evolved from a simple scripting language to a powerful platform, powering some of the busiest websites on the Internet, such as Wikipedia and Facebook. It has grown from an ugly duckling to a beautiful swan, and some statistics say that 75 percent of the Internet these days is powered by PHP.

Many sites began as simple PHP scripts, which were successful and grew—more users and transactions. Yet a simple scripting language wasn't enough. For example, object-oriented programming was introduced in PHP 4, which was completely rewritten in PHP 5 with the usage of design patterns such as MVC (Model-View-Controller), event-driven programming, and much more. Things are not simple anymore; everything became more complex and also more difficult to understand. However, applications have become quicker to build by reusing already existing components without the need to reinvent the wheel again and again. Also, the developers are able to work with the code that they haven't seen before, and they are able to extend and modify this code.

What seems to be simple on paper is not simple in the real world. There exists complexity and dependency in the code, and this is exactly where the problem lies. The more complex the code, the bigger the chance it will break. This even has a name CRAP (Change Risk Analysis and Predictions) index. The CRAP index shows how difficult it will be to maintain and extend a certain code and how likely it is that new bugs can occur.

So what can you do to minimize the possible problems? The answer is unit testing. Simply, try to split your code into units (such as cells), which you can test independently, then test that every small bit for its desired actions. In the PHP world, it has become standard to have a PHPUnit, library, and framework written by Sebastian Bergmann for PHP code automated testing. The API is very similar to any other xUnit framework, such as the JUnit in Java world or NUnit in the .NET world.

What this book tries to show and teach you is how to write better and more predictable code, and PHPUnit and automated testing is great way to start.

But this book is not theoretical. The focus is on practical PHPUnit usage. While the PHPUnit is a great cornerstone, a cornerstone is not enough to build a house. This book helps you learn what a PHPUnit is and to write unit tests, but with real-world examples and not just isolated theoretical ones. Automated testing is really useful when it works, and this is something that is missing in many similar books—a style where the topic is in the real world and in the everyday developer's work context. Thus, the book covers all aspects, from the very beginning on how to install and use the PHPUnit, to how to run tests and, of course, how to write tests. But the question is why should we write tests?

As mentioned earlier, it's a way to write better code. It's a way to guarantee the quality of produced code, thus minimizing the number of bugs. Every developer wants to minimize these mistakes. But then question arises, who will pay for the tests? It's extra code that needs to be written, which will cost us extra time. The answer to this question is simple. Do you care about the work that you are doing, the code that you write, or don't you?

Writing tests and setting up automated testing should be a part of any bigger project and also part of the budget.

Quickly developing a project, sticking to a very tight budget and deadline, and sacrificing all procedures, including testing is a straight way to hell. When the project is delivered, more and more bugs will be found, and any refactoring or changes in application will be problematic and expensive. These extra costs will very quickly become much more than the initial investment in automated testing and writing testable code. But the worst case is that these costs could be completely unpredictable because even a simple change in an application might return as a boomerang again and again as more and more problems are reported by customers.

Simply writing code without testing is like borrowing money on a credit card—one day you have to pay it back, and you pay it back with interest. Not investing in development procedures and quality assurance is very shortsighted and sooner or later will lead to disaster. Writing PHPUnit tests and better code is the way to make your projects and business successful.

What this book covers

Chapter 1, Installing PHPUnit, introduces you to various PHPUnit installation methods. A simple thing such as PHPUnit installation is something where many users really struggle. It is easy, but it's worth considering different options and installation methods.

Chapter 2, PHPUnit Support in IDEs, shows how to configure and use four of the most popular PHP IDEs used for writing and running PHPUnit tests.

Chapter 3, Tests and What They're All About, gives a gentle introduction to unit testing and why and when to write tests.

Chapter 4, Testing Dependencies and Exceptions, will demonstrate how to write the code in a way that can be tested because one of the biggest nightmares in testing is to test dependencies.

Chapter 5, Running Tests from the Command Line, explains how to execute tests by using the command-line test runner. Running tests from the command line is a basic yet powerful way to run tests and get good test results.

Chapter 6, Test Isolation and Interaction, describes fixtures of the tests, which are steps to create a consistent known environment where tests will behave in an expected way or will highlight any lapses from expected behavior.

Chapter 7, Organizing Tests, will describe how to organize tests, where and how to store tests, and group tests to test suites.

Chapter 8, Using Test Doubles, explains how test doubles are a really useful way to replace dependencies. There are several techniques on how to achieve an expected behavior. You can easily replace a tested object or its part through doubles.

Chapter 9, Database Testing, explains techniques that allow to test code using a database.

Chapter 10, Testing APIs, describes that the best way to implement a third-party API into your own application is to first write integration tests to see whether the API works and how.

Chapter 11, Testing Legacy Code, will show several techniques on how to test a legacy code to be able maintain and extend it. But without tests, there is no refactoring.

Chapter 12, Functional Tests in the Web Browser Using Selenium, shows how to write PHPUnit Selenium functional tests. Over the years, Selenium has become standard in functional tests, running in a web browser by imitating user's behavior. Selenium tests are just extended PHPUnit tests and definitely are an important jigsaw in the testing puzzle.

Chapter 13, Continuous Integration, describes three popular open source projects that can host and run PHPUnit tests.

Chapter 14, PHPUnit Alternatives, Extensions, Relatives, and BDD, describes several interesting projects and alternatives of PHPUnit, their differences, and advantages in comparison to PHPUnit.

What you need for this book

PHP CLI (PHP Command Line Interface) is required, which can be installed as a package or which comes with packages such as XAMP or WAMP. An installed web server such as Apache or NGINX is also recommended. PHPUnit can be installed, and it works on Linux, Mac OS X, or Windows.

The first chapter covers various PHPUnit installation methods and the reader can choose, if he or she prefers, PEAR, Composer, GIT, or manual installation.

Who this book is for

PHPUnit Essentials is a book for PHP developers. The book helps with the first steps of the unit-testing world, and teaches readers how to install and use PHPUnit. It also gives developers, who have previous experience with PHPUnit, a detailed overview about testing in the context of the continuous integration process.

Testing is definitely a skill that every good developer should master, and the book helps you understand the point of testing by using simple everyday examples and by offering practical solutions to problems that developers face every day.

Conventions

In this book, you will find a number of styles of text that distinguish between different kinds of information. Here are some examples of these styles, and an explanation of their meaning.

Code words in text, database table names, folder names, filenames, file extensions, pathnames, dummy URLs, user input, and Twitter handles are shown as follows: "CLI may use a different `php.ini` configuration file than the one your web server uses."

The book uses a straightforward approach. Usually the problem is described and then presented in a code similar to the following:

```php
<?php

class FistTest extends PHPUnit_Framework_TestCase {

    public function testAddition(){
        $this->assertEquals(2, 1 + 1);
    }

    public function testSubtraction(){
```

```
        $this->assertTrue(1 == (2 - 1));
    }
```

Any command-line input or output is written as follows:

```
> php -r "echo 'Hello, World!';"
```

Other code like Composer JSON configuration files are displayed in the same way as code:

```
{
    "require": {
        "phpunit/phpunit": "3.7.*"
    },
    "config": {
        "bin-dir": "/usr/local/bin/"
    }
}
```

New terms and **important** words are shown in bold. Words that you see on the screen, in menus or dialog boxes for example, appear in the text like this: "As a first step, create a new project as PHP application by navigating to the **File | New Project** menu."

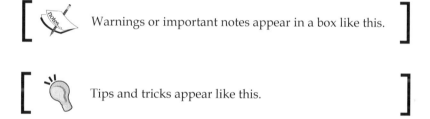

Warnings or important notes appear in a box like this.

Tips and tricks appear like this.

Reader feedback

Feedback from our readers is always welcome. Let us know what you think about this book—what you liked or may have disliked. Reader feedback is important for us to develop titles that you really get the most out of.

To send us general feedback, simply send an e-mail to feedback@packtpub.com, and mention the book title via the subject of your message.

If there is a topic that you have expertise in and you are interested in either writing or contributing to a book, see our author guide on www.packtpub.com/authors.

Customer support

Now that you are the proud owner of a Packt book, we have a number of things to help you to get the most from your purchase.

Downloading the example code

You can download the example code files for all Packt books you have purchased from your account at `http://www.packtpub.com`. If you purchased this book elsewhere, you can visit `http://www.packtpub.com/support` and register to have the files e-mailed directly to you.

Downloading the color images of this book

We also provide you a PDF file that has color images of the screenshots/diagrams used in this book. The color images will help you better understand the changes in the output. You can download this file from `https://www.packtpub.com/sites/default/files/downloads/3439OS_ColoredImages.pdf`.

Errata

Although we have taken every care to ensure the accuracy of our content, mistakes do happen. If you find a mistake in one of our books—maybe a mistake in the text or the code—we would be grateful if you would report this to us. By doing so, you can save other readers from frustration and help us improve subsequent versions of this book. If you find any errata, please report them by visiting `http://www.packtpub.com/submit-errata`, selecting your book, clicking on the **errata submission form** link, and entering the details of your errata. Once your errata are verified, your submission will be accepted and the errata will be uploaded on our website, or added to any list of existing errata, under the Errata section of that title. Any existing errata can be viewed by selecting your title from `http://www.packtpub.com/support`.

Piracy

Piracy of copyright material on the Internet is an ongoing problem across all media. At Packt, we take the protection of our copyright and licenses very seriously. If you come across any illegal copies of our works, in any form, on the Internet, please provide us with the location address or website name immediately so that we can pursue a remedy.

Please contact us at `copyright@packtpub.com` with a link to the suspected pirated material.

We appreciate your help in protecting our authors, and our ability to bring you valuable content.

Questions

You can contact us at questions@packtpub.com if you are having a problem with any aspect of the book, and we will do our best to address it.

1
Installing PHPUnit

To be able to write and run PHPUnit tests, PHPUnit has to be installed on the machine. With the right approach, it is not difficult; however, in the past, this was a bit of an issue for many users because they were struggling with the right settings and all of the dependencies that needed to be installed.

Until recently, the recommended installation method for PHPUnit was by using PEAR; however, from PHPUnit 3.7 onwards, there is an option available to use **Composer**. Composer is a tool for dependency management in PHP, which makes PHP tools or libraries' installations much easier. There are a few more options to install PHPUnit, and this chapter describes them step by step.

Apart from what is required for PHPUnit installation, this chapter also describes the Xdebug installation process. This is optional, but this PHP extension really helps with processes such as remote debugging, code coverage analysis, and profiling PHP scripts. Later in the book, how to use Xdebug for debugging and generating code coverage will be explained, and it is more than an option for every PHP developer to have this extension.

This chapter describes how to install PHPUnit, and mentions what is required to be able to run PHPUnit tests; some of these tests are as follows:

- **PHP CLI**: This is a PHP command-line interface to run tests from the command line
- **PHPUnit**: This is a testing framework and tool for unit tests execution
- **Xdebug**: This is a PHP extension for remote debugging, code coverage, and much more

This chapter covers various PHPUnit installation methods, among which the easiest is the Composer or PEAR installation, but there are other installation methods available too. The following are the different PHPUnit installation methods:

- Composer installation
- PEAR installation
- Linux package installation
- Manual installation

As an extra step, it is recommended that you have Xdebug installed. Xdebug is a PHP extension that provides debugging and profiling capabilities and is also used by PHPUnit. Xdebug installation and configuration is described at the end of this chapter.

> On 21st of April, 2014, it was announced end of life for the PEAR installation method. PEAR installation should be available during the entire 2014. However, recommended installation methods are the Composer installation or PHAR archive.

Requirements

A developer who starts with PHPUnit is probably already working with PHP and has already installed the web server with PHP support such as Apache, NGINX, or IIS. It is strongly recommended that you use at least PHP 5.3.3 or higher; older PHP versions are not supported and maintained anymore.

> Information about PHPUnit and downloads and documentation can be found on the official PHPUnit site at http://phpunit.de.

PHPUnit is a unit testing framework written in PHP, but PHPUnit tests are not usually executed on a web server but through the PHP CLI—the PHP command-line interface. Through PHP CLI, the PHP script can be run as any other shell script.

Running PHP from the command line

As mentioned earlier, PHP CLI allows to run any PHP script from the command-line interface. Whichever tool is used to run PHPUnit tests, even if it has used the IDE, which seems to have everything preinstalled, it will always call PHP CLI in the background.

```
root@precise64: /home
root@precise64:/home# php -v
PHP 5.3.10-1ubuntu3.9 with Suhosin-Patch (cli) (built: Dec 12 2013 04:27:25)
Copyright (c) 1997-2012 The PHP Group
Zend Engine v2.3.0, Copyright (c) 1998-2012 Zend Technologies
root@precise64:/home#
```

You can install PHP CLI as a package (PHP5-CLI), or you can find it already installed with the web server package. Even software packages such as WAMP or XAMP have it there, but you might need to specify a path to web server binaries to environment variables to be able to run PHP from the command line anywhere on your machine.

To test if PHP CLI is installed on your machine, run the following command line:

```
> php -r "echo 'Hello, World!';"
```

This is a simple Hello, World! code executed and outputted by the command language interpreter, but it confirms PHP CLI is present and does what is expected. If you see an error message such as command not found, it implies PHP CLI is not installed or the system path is missing—a path to the PHP binary.

> CLI may use a different php.ini configuration file than the one your web server uses. If so, you'll need to configure your PHP extensions and other bits and bobs in there separately. To check this, you can run the following command line:
>
> ```
> > php -i
> ```

It will output a result of the phpinfo() function, but in a text version, where you will be able check configuration settings. If you have problem reading so many lines, try to output it in a text file, which you can open in a text editor, and search for the desired result. The output also can be captured in the text file, which can be easily read with any text editor.

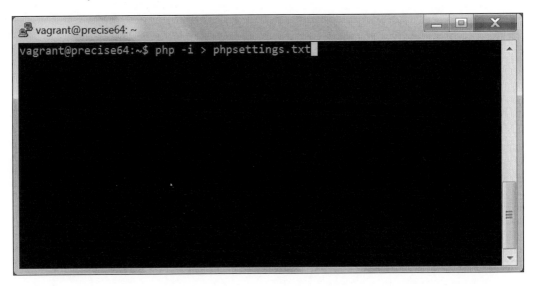

Composer – the dependency manager for PHP

Composer is a tool for dependency management in PHP. It allows you to declare the dependent libraries that the project needs, and it will install them. There is a configuration file called composer.json, which, as the name suggests, is a JSON format file. This is where you set the components/libraries and version your project will be using. When you run Composer, the Composer tool not only downloads all the required libraries, but also all the other required third-party libraries used. It also creates autoloader (the file to load all required classes), and all the hard work is done—everything that is required is ready to be used.

Composer is one of the best tools available for the PHP developers. It really helps and makes your life easier. It is something that was already available in other languages such as Maven for Java or Gems for Ruby and was missing in PHP. The best thing is, in this way, you can not only manage third-party libraries and packages, but also your own libraries.

Installing Composer

The Composer tool is just one file—`composer.phar`. The `.phar` file means a PHP archive (the PHAR file) similar to the JAR files of Java. All PHP files are packed in one archive file. You can download `composer.phar` from `http://getcomposer.org/download/` or by running the following command line:

```
curl -sS https://getcomposer.org/installer | php
```

If you haven't got curl installed, alternatively run the following command line:

```
>php -r "readfile('https://getcomposer.org/installer');" | php
```

As a result, you should see a message that `composer.phar` was downloaded, similar to the message displayed in the following screenshot:

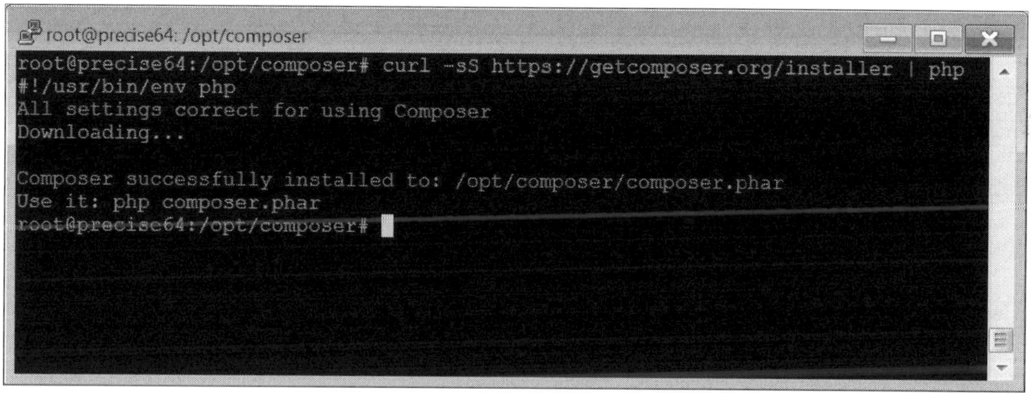

Installation

There are two options that are of the biggest advantage to Composer, compared to other installation methods. Composer gives you the flexibility to specify where to store PHPUnit and also where to store the command-line script so that you can have on your machine as many versions as you want, and by using Composer, you can still maintain and keep them all up to date.

Local installation

Here is one practical example. You can specify and download PHPUnit only for your specific project. This means that when your project was developed and tested, you were working with PHPUnit version 3.5; however, for the new project, you want to use version 3.7. For example, Zend Framework 1 uses PHPUnit version 3.5; however, applications are still developed, extended, and maintained on this system even when Zend Framework 2 is available. This is not a problem as each project will have its own version of PHPUnit with all the dependencies, and there is no need to worry about clashing versions or being stacked with dated versions.

For PHPUnit installation with Composer, you have to create a `composer.json` file. The simplest version could look the following lines of code:

```
{
    "require-dev": {
        "phpunit/phpunit": "3.7.*"
    }
}
```

System-wide installation

The second option is a system-wide installation. Well, basically it is the same thing, except it is created by a shell script / batch file to call PHPUnit from the command line. If a file is stored in a directory set in the system path, then it is available anywhere in your system. The following lines of code represent `composer.json`:

```
{
    "require": {
        "phpunit/phpunit": "3.7.*"
    },
    "config": {
        "bin-dir": "/usr/local/bin/"
    }
}
```

System-wide installation might be easier in the beginning, and allows you to run tests from the command line. It's easier to start with moving `composer.phar` to the project document root—the same place where the `composer.json` file is stored. Then, to install PHPUnit, just run the following command line:

```
> php composer.phar install
```

Composer explores the `composer.json` file and determines all the extra packages that need to be downloaded and installed. This should display a similar result as shown in the following screenshot:

This means PHPUnit was successfully installed, including the required dependencies (YAML) and basic plugins. The line that suggests installing `ext-xdebug` means that you should install the PHP Xdebug extension, because it is a useful thing for development and also PHPUnit uses it to generate code coverage.

Installing PEAR

Another way to install PHPUnit is to use PEAR—the framework and distribution system for reusable PHP components. PEAR has been available since the early PHP 4 days, and more than a framework, it is just a set of useful packages and classes. Also, it is a distribution system for installing and keeping these packages up to date. The first step of installation is to install PEAR. Download the PHP archive file `go-pear.phar` from `http://pear.php.net/go-pear.phar`.

Similar to `composer.phar`, it is a PHP archive file that contains all that you need. Installation is simple, just run the following command line:

```
> php go-pear.phar
```

Follow the PEAR install instructions, hitting *Enter* to accept the default configuration as you go. After installation, you can test it by running PEAR from the command line by just running the following command line:

```
> pear
```

You should see something similar to the following message that will tell you where the PEAR script is stored:

```
The 'pear' command is now at your service at /root/pear/bin/pear
```

If it doesn't work, checking the installation message usually gives a clue as to where the problem is; this is shown in the following message:

```
** The 'pear' command is not currently in your PATH, so you need to
** use '/root/pear/bin/pear' until you have added
** '/root/pear/bin' to your PATH environment variable.
```

PEAR installation has one disadvantage compared to the Composer installation: it is a system-wide installation, which means you have just one version of PEAR—one version of PHPUnit installed in your system.

PHPUnit installation

When PEAR is successfully installed, PHPUnit installation is simple and straightforward, as shown in the following command line:

```
>pear config-set auto_discover 1
>pear install pear.phpunit.de/PHPUnit
```

The first line means that PEAR checks and installs the required dependencies. The sources are called channels that will be automatically discovered and added. With older versions, you had to do it manually; however, it is not necessary anymore with `auto_discover`. The second line then installs the latest stable version of PHPUnit. The result should be similar to the following screenshot:

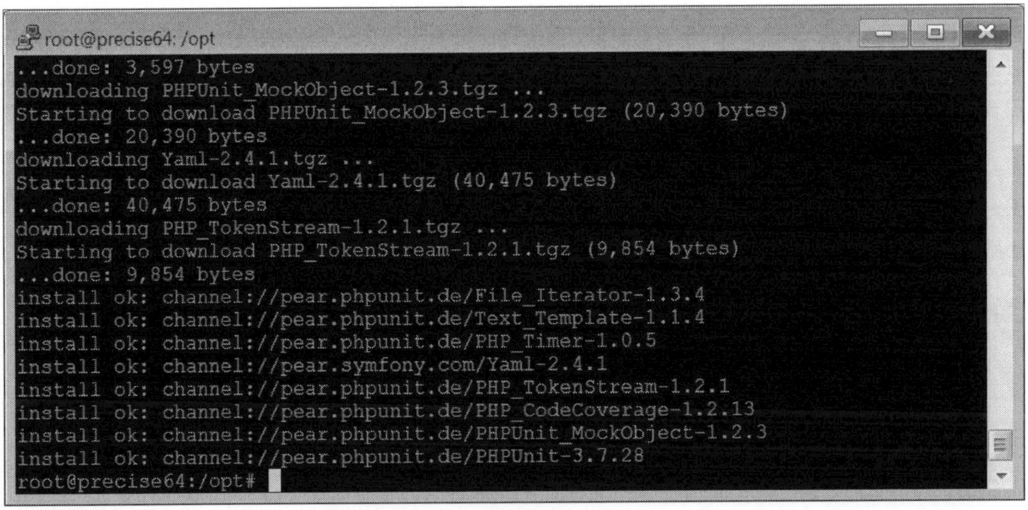

Other installation methods

Along with the two methods that have been mentioned and recommended, there exist another two. It is up to you to choose the installation method that suits you the best (just be careful what you are installing and from where). If there is no specific reason, it's recommended choosing a stable version, and if possible the latest version. The clue could be which version is in the current PHPUnit manual, which can be found at `http://phpunit.de/manual/current/en/index.html`.

Installing the Linux package

For Linux users and users using Linux based virtual machines such as Vagrant and VirtualBox (Mac OS X, Windows), probably the fastest and least painful installation method is to use package manager. It depends on your Linux version, and the package management tool could be yum, apt or aptitude. Run the following command line:

```
>apt-get install phpunit
```

This will install all the required dependencies and libraries, and the result should be similar to the following screenshot:

```
root@precise64: /opt
Setting up autoconf (2.68-1ubuntu2) ...
Setting up autotools-dev (20120210.1ubuntu1) ...
Setting up automake (1:1.11.3-1ubuntu2) ...
update-alternatives: using /usr/bin/automake-1.11 to provide /usr/bin/automake (
automake) in auto mode.
Setting up libltdl-dev (2.4.2-1ubuntu1) ...
Setting up libtool (2.4.2-1ubuntu1) ...
Setting up php-pear (5.3.10-1ubuntu3.9) ...
Setting up php-benchmark (1.2.7-5) ...
Setting up shtool (2.0.8-6) ...
Setting up php5-dev (5.3.10-1ubuntu3.9) ...
update-alternatives: using /usr/bin/php-config5 to provide /usr/bin/php-config (
php-config) in auto mode.
update-alternatives: using /usr/bin/phpize5 to provide /usr/bin/phpize (phpize)
in auto mode.
Setting up phpunit (3.5.5-2) ...
Processing triggers for libc-bin ...
ldconfig deferred processing now taking place
root@precise64:/opt#
```

If this is so easy, why is it not mentioned as the first installation method? Obviously, you can't use it if you are running PHP. It can't be used on Windows or Mac OS X, but there is something else. When this chapter was written, the latest available stable PHPUnit version for Composer and PEAR was 4.0. In comparison, for the Ubuntu Precise Pangolin package 3.5.5-2 version was available, Debian had version 3.6.10-1 for PHPUnit, and EPEL had PHPUnit-3.7.19-1.e16. This is something to watch out for. Some Linux distributions are very mature and very stable, but they stick to the package version that was available when the distribution was released. Then the distribution is supported for the next five years, but the package is never upgraded (just the security fixes are back-ported to the original version). This leads to situations where you have all the updates installed but still see hopelessly old versions of your tool/library.

Manual installation

The final option is manual installation. It is not too bad. There is one option that allows you to get PHPUnit with all that you need but without all the package management hassle. Just download the `phpunit.phar` archive from the PHPUnit site at `https://phar.phpunit.de/phpunit.phar`.

The package contains PHPUnit and all the required dependencies. To test, just run the following command line:

```
>php phpunit.phar –version
```

Or, you can create the `phpunit` executable by running the following commands:

```
>chmod +x phpunit.phar
>mv phpunit.phar /usr/local/bin/phpunit
```

Or, on Windows using `phpunit.bat` from the Git repository, which is also the last option, download PHPUnit source code directly by cloning the Git repository on GitHub by running the following command line:

```
>git clone https://github.com/sebastianbergmann/phpunit/
```

Testing the installation

When PHPUnit is installed, you should be able to run the PHPUnit tool from the following command line:

```
> phpunit
```

And then you should see a list of all the available options like the following list displayed:

```
PHPUnit 3.7.28 by Sebastian Bergmann.


Usage: phpunit [switches] UnitTest [UnitTest.php]
       phpunit [switches] <directory>
```

If it doesn't work, don't panic; try to think what might be wrong. Is the PHPUnit script on the system path? Have you installed it as user or root?

In the worst case scenario, you can try alternative installation methods or install it as a local installation just for one user. This means that all the files are going to be stored in the user home directory, and when you want to run PHPUnit, just go to `phpunit/bin` and there is the script. The difference with the system-wide installation is just that the files are stored in different places and PHPUnit is not added to the system path.

Anyway, now we would like to see a bit more. So, let's create our first tests and run it by using the freshly installed PHPUnit.

The best way to try PHPUnit is to create a simple unit test and execute it by using the freshly installed PHPUnit. Let's try basic mathematical operations to see if PHP counts correctly. Later, we will talk about tests syntax, but for now, let's not worry about it. There are just a few extra lines of wrapping code in class and test methods, as shown in the following code snippet:

```php
<?php

class FirstTest extends PHPUnit_Framework_TestCase {

    public function testAddition(){
        $this->assertEquals(2, 1 + 1);
    }
public function testSubtraction(){
        $this->assertEquals(0.17, (1- 0.83))
    }

    public function testMultiplication(){
        $this->assertEquals(10, 2 * 5);
    }
public function testDivision(){
        $this->assertTrue(2 == (10 / 5));
    }

}
```

Let's save it into `FirstTest.php` and then run it using the following command line:

```
> phpunit FirstTest.php
```

And then we see the result as shown in the following screenshot:

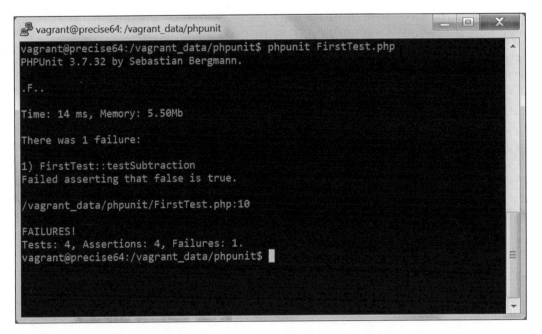

Brilliant, it works!

Works, but it says one failure? And it's correct. This example shows you why it is important to run tests. Even things that seem obvious and appear to have no reason to be tested might not be as straightforward as you think.

Let's change the problematic line 10 with the following line of code:

```
$this->assertEquals(0.17, 1 - 0.83);
```

Now run the test again. The result now should be as shown in the following command line:

```
OK (4 tests, 4 assertions)
```

If you wonder why the previous test failed, it was that type float and floating point numbers have limited precision, so they are not exactly equal. The second number is approximately 0.1699999999999, but when the assertion method was changed to equals, PHPUnit is able to detect and handle it correctly.

Xdebug

As mentioned earlier, Xdebug is not required, but it is really recommended that for development and for running PHPUnit tests, you should install this brilliant PHP extension created by Derick Rethans. The following are killer features of Xdebug:

- **Remote debugging**: This allows to stop code execution, step line by line through the code execution, watch variables, and much more.

- **Code coverage analysis**: This tells you which lines were executed. This is important for testing to know if all code is covered by tests or how much is missing.

- **Code profiling**: During the code execution, it is measured how much time and how much resource each class, method, and function needs. This is handy when you need to identify bottlenecks in your application.

Another similar option is Zend Debugger that is pre-installed in Zend Server, but Xdebug provides better support for code coverage, profiling, and so on.

Installation is the same as any other PHP extension. If you are not using package manager, the tricky bit could be to figure out which one is the right one for you. On the other hand, if you have installed the web server bundle, it might be already there; check the extension directory or `phpinfo()` output.

Installing Xdebug

If Xdebug is not installed, the following are three installation options available for it:

- Use the precompiled binary version of Xdebug. This version needs to match your PHP version. The `http://xdebug.org/download.php` link contains lots of Windows binaries. It is necessary to have the correct PHP version, the compiler that was used for your installation (VC6, VC9, VC11), and if you have it, the thread-safe installation. You can see all of these things in `phpinfo()` output. On Linux, it is much easier to install if you use your package manager. For example, run the following command line:

```
>apt-get install php5-xdebug
```

- PECL installation (for instructions on how to install PECL, see the *PEAR installation* section discussed earlier). If you have PECL installed, just run the following command line:

```
pecl install xdebug
```

- Use compiling extension from the source code to install Xdebug. This method is only recommended for experienced users.

To enable the extension, you have to add the following extra line to the configuration file:

```
zend_extension="/usr/local/php/modules/xdebug.so"
```

 The path in the configuration file needs to be an absolute path, not a relative one as it is for other PHP extensions.

To check whether the extension is installed correctly and loaded by PHP, just run the following command line:

```
>php --version
```

If extension is loaded, you should see an output similar to the following screenshot:

```
vagrant@precise64: /vagrant_data/phpunit

vagrant@precise64:/vagrant_data/phpunit$ php --version
PHP 5.3.10-1ubuntu3.10 with Suhosin-Patch (cli) (built: Feb 28 2014 23:14:25)
Copyright (c) 1997-2012 The PHP Group
Zend Engine v2.3.0, Copyright (c) 1998-2012 Zend Technologies
    with Xdebug v2.1.0, Copyright (c) 2002-2010, by Derick Rethans
vagrant@precise64:/vagrant_data/phpunit$
```

Summary

There are several ways to install PHPUnit. This chapter showed all the available options. The Composer and PEAR installation methods are recommended as they can handle all the required dependencies and allow to keep PHPUnit and the required libraries up to date. PHPUnit installation is not difficult if the right path is followed. Xdebug extension is optional, but it is strongly recommended that you install it as we will need extra features such as remote debugging and code coverage later.

When writing and running PHPUnit tests, it's really important to have a good **IDE (Integrated Development Environment)**. All modern IDEs have good PHPUnit support. The next chapter will show the four most popular IDEs in PHP world. We will also see how to configure them, how to execute tests, and how to debug tests. Good support for PHPUnit and PHP in general is something that makes a developer's life much easier, and he/she is able to produce good code much faster than using an ordinary text editor.

To have PHPUnit installed is the first good step. In the next chapter, before jumping to writing tests, it's good to have a look at how to run and debug PHPUnit tests in IDE such as Zend Studio and NetBeans.

2
PHPUnit Support in IDEs

The first chapter was about how to install PHPUnit. The next step before writing tests is to prepare the development environment for testing.

A good IDE helps to write unit tests and integrate them with the code, of course, there are many options. There are advanced editors available such as vi or vim, emacs, TextMate, and Notepad++, but IDE makes the developer's life much easier by assisting when you write the code, helping to debug and highlight errors, and much more. As a developer, it's the first thing that you start in the morning and the last thing that you switch off in the evening. A good IDE is like a Swiss army knife, offering everything that is needed in one application. Of course, it's every developer's choice, but this chapter shows what can be done with the four most popular IDEs in the PHP world when writing, running, and debugging tests.

Different IDEs offer different features, but you always need an IDE to run and debug PHPUnit tests. This chapter describes PHPUnit support in two open source products and two commercial, but exceptional, products. All products are Java applications, which means they are cross-platform applications working on Windows, Mac OS X, and Linux. These IDEs have very good integration support for PHPUnit, which is not just for launching PHPUnit as an external tool. This is important when you want to use remote debugging to step through the code, and be able to see exactly what's going on when tests are failing and you are not sure why. Even if you are using different IDEs, a good one has very similar features but maybe in different places.

We chose the following four IDEs mainly because they provide the best features or are the most used:

- NetBeans
- Zend Studio
- Eclipse PDT
- PhpStorm

The following sections not only describe how each of the IDEs support PHPUnit, how to run tests from IDE and get results, but also how to use remote debugging and step through the code execution. Debugging in IDE is a very useful thing, but many PHP developers still use only `var_dump()` and `die()` as their main debugging techniques. It is really bad to commit them to the repository and release to production servers. It not only looks really bad and possibly will break an application, but it might also be a serious security risk when exposing application internals.

> This chapter describes IDE's integration with PHPUnit Version 3.7. PHPUnit Version 4 is distributed as a PHAR file (PHP archive), and at the time of writing this chapter, it was not supported by IDEs. However, as soon as updated versions are available, functionality and configuration should be very similar to the following section.

IDEs and PHPUnit

What is required is to have an already installed web server with PHP support, PHP-CLI and PHPUnit, even if some IDE's might have built-in PHP or PHPUnit support.

In all IDEs, PHPUnit support is very similar, and to be fair, it should be done the same way. You write a test, which is PHP code extending `PHPUnit_Framework_TestCase`. IDEs help to validate code, and show all assertions that can be used and their parameters by parsing PHPDoc comments in the code. A good developer writes comments, and in PHP, which is a weakly typed language, you can use it as a helper to notify the IDE about object types when it's not able to detect them from input parameters.

Before looking at how to configure and run tests, it would be good to mention the following two files that are used when executing tests:

- `bootstrap.php`: This is the file that is run before tests. This file is usually used for autoloading classes, so it's not necessary to run `require_once` for every file that needs to be loaded.
- `phpunit.xml`: This is the XML configuration file for tests.

These files are going to be described later in this book; for now it is enough to know what they are because they are mentioned in some of the configuration dialogs.

When PHPUnit is installed, its classes can be used in our project. Before being able to utilize PHPUnit support, usually a bit of configuration is necessary. It doesn't matter which IDE is used, but the following steps might be required:

1. Set which PHP interpreter is used, that is, point it where PHP binary is stored.
2. Set the path to PHPUnit script.
3. Set the include path to PHPUnit classes.
4. Set which debugger is used, for example, Xdebug on standard port 9000.

To be able to run PHPUnit tests, usually, IDE needs to know which PHP interpreter is used, where PHP binary is stored, where PHPUnit classes are, and possibly where PHPUnit script is stored. This is good to know because then you can tweak the configuration to be able to choose any environment/version you need for each project. Another option is to use IDE that has built-in support for everything, such as Zend Studio. The advantage is that you can immediately start writing and running tests without any configuration changes, but the disadvantage is that you haven't got full control over which version is used. Usually, it is good to have matching configuration for the development environment and production servers.

NetBeans

NetBeans is a very well known IDE in the Java world. It was bought by Sun Microsystems and released as open source and is now supported by Oracle. A few years ago, this proved to be an added support for PHP, and NetBeans became a good IDE for PHP developers. It is popular among beginners because the user interface is simpler to use than Eclipse-based IDEs and also more user friendly. NetBeans can be downloaded from `https://netbeans.org`.

To test what can be done with the PHPUnit, let's create a project and use tests that we used for validating installation by performing the following steps:

1. As a first step, create a new project as a PHP application by navigating to the **File | New Project** menu.

2. Then, for configuration, set the path to the PHP interpreter and PHPUnit. Navigate to **Tools | Options** and there click on the **PHP** tab. The following screenshot shows the **Options** window:

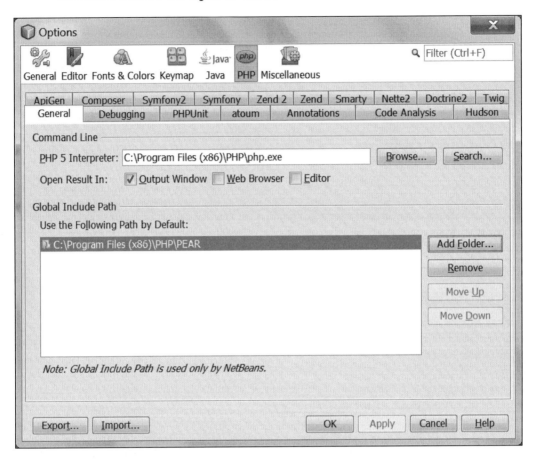

Here, PHP binary needs to be set in the **PHP 5 Interpreter** field.

3. Then, add PHPUnit path to **Global Include Path** as you can see in the preceding screenshot. Of course, depending on your operating system and PHP installation, the location is going to be different. We are doing this because we are extending PHPUnit_Framework_TestCase, and we need to inform the IDE where to look for PHPUnit classes.

4. The last thing that we need to change is on **PHPUnit** under the **Testing** section; set the path to the PHPUnit script.

   To simplify things, there is going to be just the `FirstTest.php` file in the project. We can change project properties in the PHPUnit section under **Testing** by clicking **Run All *Test Files using PHPUnit**, all files with filename ending with `*Test.php` will be executed by PHPUnit.

5. In the latest version of NetBeans, you have to enable **PHPUnit** as **Testing Providers** as shown in the following screenshot:

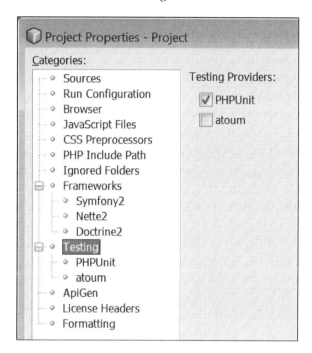

   After configuring IDE, it's time to create the first test suite. Create a new PHP class and name it `FirstTest`.

6. When the file is created, copy the source code for `FirstTest` from *Chapter 1, Installing PHPUnit*, and save the file. To run tests, just click on **Run file** or press *Shift + F6*. Since all test files end with `Test.php`, NetBeans detects its PHPUnit test and runs it as a unit test.

Then you should see similar output saying that all tests are passed as shown in the following screenshot:

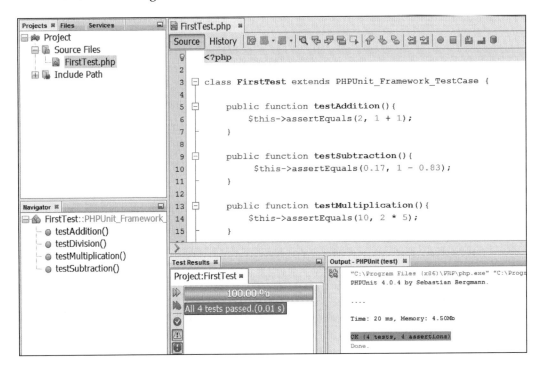

7. To debug tests, just put the breakpoint in the place where you want to stop execution by clicking on the row number.

Debugging can be done by clicking on **Debug** or pressing *Ctrl + Shift + F5*. The code is executed, and then it stops on the breakpoint.

In the toolbar, now you can see extra buttons: the debug toolbar for stepping over, stepping in, or stopping debugging. Under the code windows, you have a couple of extra windows for seeing **Variables**, **Call Stack**, and **Breakpoints**, as shown in the following screenshot:

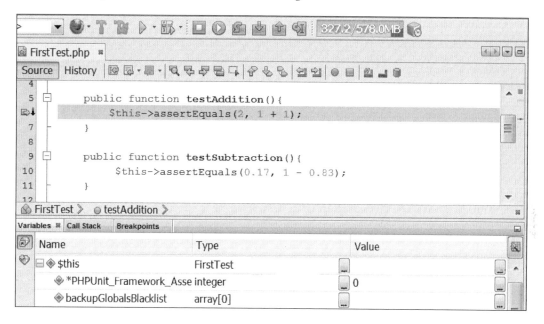

NetBeans is really easy to configure and use, and it gives you very nice and smooth PHPUnit support.

Zend Studio

Zend Studio is a commercial product from Zend. It is a very mature, advanced IDE-based on Eclipse, which is a platform developed by IBM, originally as IDE for Java development, but later adopted as a platform for IDEs for many programming languages.

Eclipse is a heavyweight champion, so it might take a little while to get used to it, but then you will see how advanced and flexible a platform it is.

Zend Studio can be downloaded from `http://www.zend.com/en/products/studio`.

To see Zend Studio PHPUnit support, let's use `FirstTest` from *Chapter 1, Installing PHPUnit*. Zend Studio configuration is very easy and straightforward as shown in the following steps:

1. As a first step, we need to create a new project. Navigate to **File** | **New** and select **Local PHP Project**, as shown in the following screenshot:

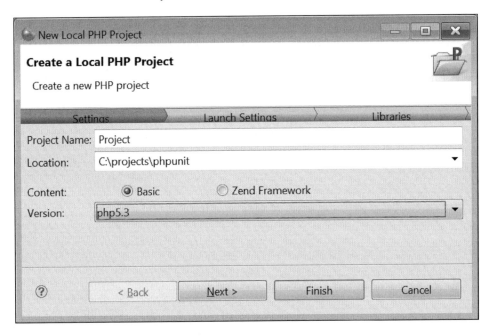

2. Click on **Next** and select **Launch CLI Application**, and then click on the **Next** button.

3. In the **Libraries** tab, select the **PHPUnit [built-in]** library option. Then, click on the **Finish** button. This will create a new project. Now, add PHPUnit to **PHP Include Path**.

> PHPUnit in Zend Studio is not your installed PHPUnit, but the one shipped with Zend Studio. If you want to change it, go to project properties, remove this library, and add a location where your PHPUnit is stored.

4. To create our test case, right click on the **Project**, navigate to **New**, and select **PHPUnit Test Case**.

5. Replace the content of the generated class with that of our `FirstTest.php`. Then to run test, just right-click in the code, and select **Run As** and then **PHPUnit Test** or press *Alt + Shift + X*, and then select **PHPUnit test**. Then you should see a similar result as shown in the following screenshot:

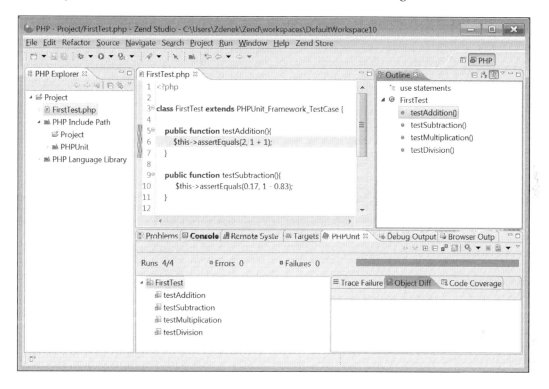

6. To be able to debug tests, put the breakpoint next to line number by double clicking there.

7. To debug the test, right-click anywhere in the code and select **Debug As** and then **PHPUnit Test** or press *Alt + Shift + D*, and then select **PHPUnit test**.

8. Then, confirm switch to the debug perspective, and execution is stopped on the breakpoint. Now you can go step by step through code execution as shown in the following screenshot:

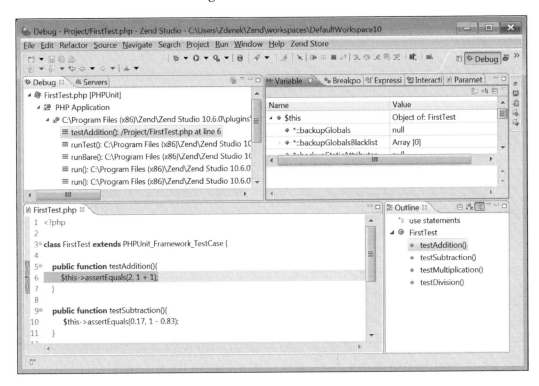

Zend Studio comes with everything that you need. It is even shifted with its own bundled PHP and the PHPUnit version so that you don't have to worry about the configuration too much. But if you want to use your own libraries and configuration, then you have to do some configuration changes. PHPUnit support is very good and easy to use.

Eclipse PDT

PDT means PHP Development Tools. It is an open source version of Zend Studio and can be downloaded as an all-in-one package from `http://www.zend.com/en/company/community/pdt/downloads` or installed as a plugin to Eclipse. As compared to Zend Studio, it has lesser features, but by using Eclipse plugins, you can add most of the functionality, which Zend Studio has built in. One of the features is support for PHPUnit. A brilliant Eclipse plugin called **MakeGood** is available. You can find out more about this project on the project wiki page at `http://piece-framework.com/projects/makegood/wiki`.

There is one interesting thing about Eclipse that hasn't been mentioned earlier in this chapter. Besides being IDE for many languages and platforms, Google chose Eclipse as the official platform for Android application development through **Android Development Tools (ADT)**. So, if you tried building something for Android or you are planning to, knowing Eclipse really helps.

When you have Eclipse PDT installed, a few configuration tweaks are needed. You also need to install MakeGood because it's not installed by default.

Installing MakeGood

Perform the following steps to install MakeGood:

1. Navigate to **Help | Install New Software...**, and then click on **Add...** to add from where to download the plugin (`http://eclipse.piece-framework.com`), as shown in the following screenshot:

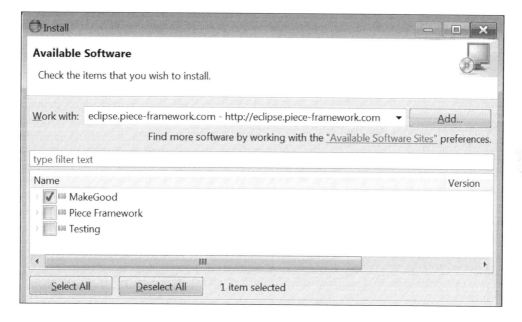

2. Select **MakeGood**, and then click on **Next**. Go through the installation wizard and install the plugin. After successful installation, you will be asked to restart Eclipse. If you are having problems with installation, try cleaning PDT's all-in-one installation, and before installing the plugin, check for updates and install all available updates.

 After installing PDT with brilliant support for PHPUnit, the same way you can find and install additional plugins such as support for GIS or SVN.

3. Now a few configuration changes need to be done. Go to **Window** and select **Preferences**.

4. Under the **PHP** section, select **PHP Executables**, and point it to the location where your PHP binary is stored. It is safer to manually point it to the location where PHPUnit is stored, instead of using the search functionality. Also, switch the debugger option to **Xdebug** as shown in the following screenshot:

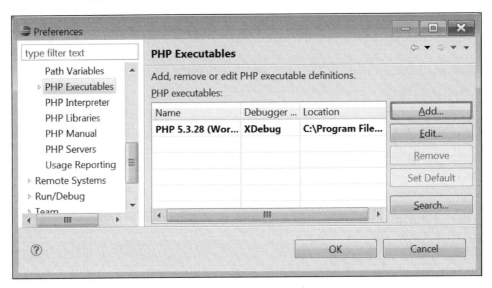

5. Now, select the **Debug** option. In the **PHP Debug** section, set **PHP Debugger** to **Xdebug** and select your configured PHP executable. Also, check **Enable CLI Debug**, as shown in the following screenshot:

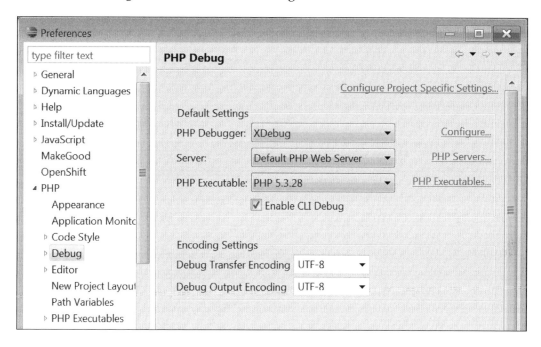

6. Now add **PHPUnit** to **PHP Libraries**, that is, two options below **PHP Executables**.

7. Click on **New**, and then add an external folder. Point to the location where the PHPUnit classes are stored, as shown in the following screenshot:

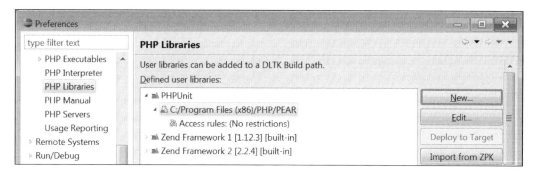

8. Now configuration is done, and you can create a project. Go to **File** and select **New** project. The project needs to be of the type Local PHP project. If you can't see it in the menu, click on **Other** and scroll to the **PHP** section.

9. Click on **Next** and select **Launch CLI Application**, and then click on the **Next** button. In the **Libraries** tab, select the **PHPUnit** library option, as shown in the following screenshot:

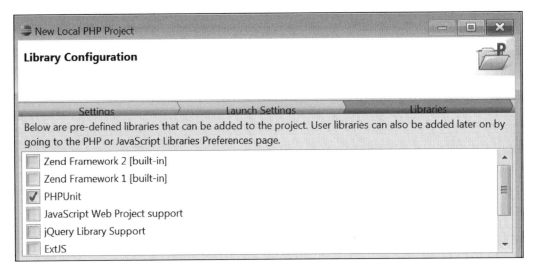

10. Now click on **Finish** and switch to the PHP perspective.

Perspectives and views are very important things in Eclipse. In every window, view can be fully customized. This can sometimes cause problems for beginners; it might be quite easy to get lost. For PHP, there are two most important perspectives: PHP for writing code and PHP debug for debugging code.

PDT is now configured to have a full built-in support for PHPUnit.

Creating your FirstTest

For creating your `FirstTest.php`, perform the following steps:

1. To create your `FirstTest.php` file, right-click on project and select **New PHP file**.

2. In the newly created file, copy the code from `FirstTest`, which we used in *Chapter 1*, *Installing PHPUnit*. To run all tests, right-click anywhere in the code and select **Run Tests In File** or **Class**, or press *Alt + M* to see run options. After selecting **Run Tests In Class**, you should see a similar output to that shown in the following screenshot:

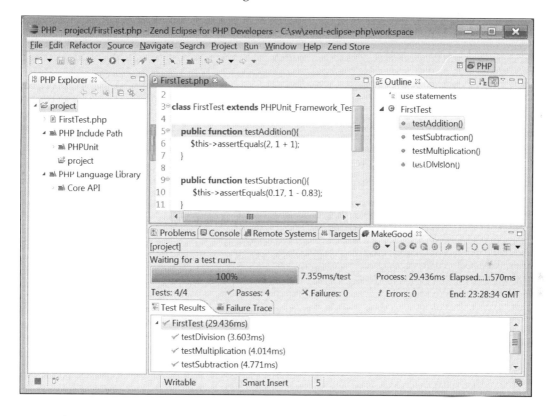

3. There might be something different on your screen. If you can't see the **MakeGood** tab, navigate to **Window** | **Show View** | **Other** and select **MakeGood**.

4. Debugging is very easy now. Double-click in the column next to row number to toggle breakpoints. To switch **MakeGood** to debug mode, click on the bug icon in the **MakeGood** view.

5. When you run the test again, you will be asked to switch to the debug perspective. Execution is going to be stopped where you put a breakpoint, and you can step through the execution line by line, as shown in the following screenshot:

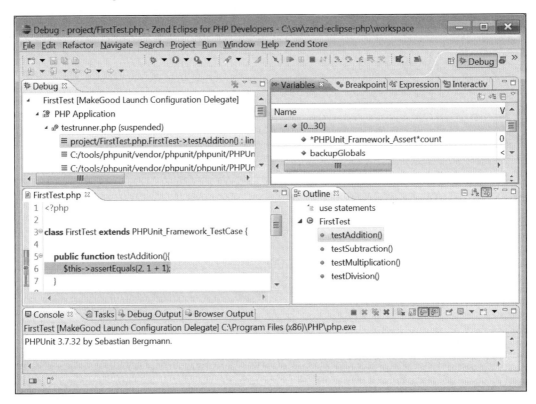

Eclipse PDT with MakeGood is a very good IDE. But you have to do a few configuration tweaks before you can use it. An advantage is that you can fully customize it to your needs and configuration. Then it's a very interesting and free alternative.

PhpStorm

PhpStorm is an advanced IDE based on InteliiJ, a very popular IDE in the Java world. It has support for almost everything that you need for web development, but more importantly, very good support for PHP and PHPUnit. It is similar to Zend Studio in its features, and seems to be faster than Eclipse-based products.

PhpStorm is a commercial application and can be downloaded from `http://www.jetbrains.com/phpstorm`. PHPUnit configuration in PhpStorm is not difficult. Perform the following steps for installation:

1. As a first step, you need to create a new project. Go to **File** and select **New Project...**.

2. Now in this project, you need to configure where the PHP interpreter is installed. Go to **File** and select **Settings...**, and there select **PHP**. Now you need to choose which version of PHP you are using and where PHP binary files are stored. Also, you should have installed Xdebug, so select **Xdebug** in the **Debugger** field, as shown in the following screenshot:

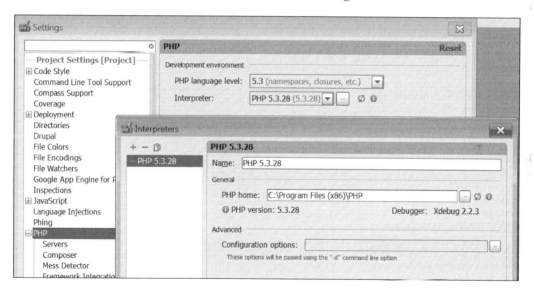

3. The next thing that we have to do is set the path to the location where PHPUnit is installed. Navigate to **File | Settings | PHP | PHPUnit**, and here you have multiple options. For PHPUnit 3.7, it is best to select **Load from include path** and point it to where PHPUnit is installed, for example, C:\Program Files (x86)\PHP\PEAR. For PHPUnit 4, you will need PHPStorm 8 or a higher version; select **Path to phpunit.phar**, as shown in the following screenshot:

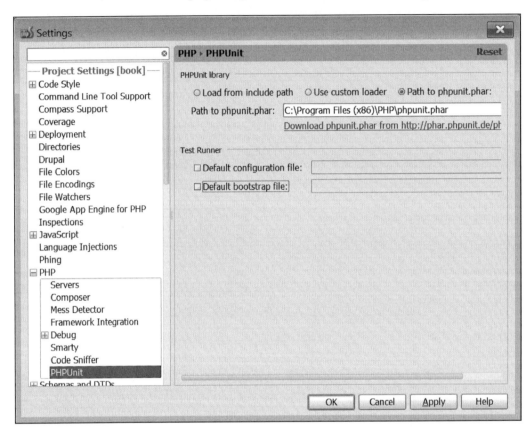

4. Now PhpStorm is configured to be able to write and run tests. Let's use our first test. To create file and test class, right-click on your project and navigate to **New | PHPUnit | PHPUnit Test**. Give it the name `FirstTest` and namespace `Tests`.

5. Now, you will have an empty class extending `PHPUnit_Framework_TestCase`. Let's copy the test methods that were used for testing installation in the previous chapter. Then, if you right-click anywhere in the code, or you go to Run item in the menu, or if you press *Alt + Shift + F10*, you run all tests in the test class and should see an output similar to the following screenshot:

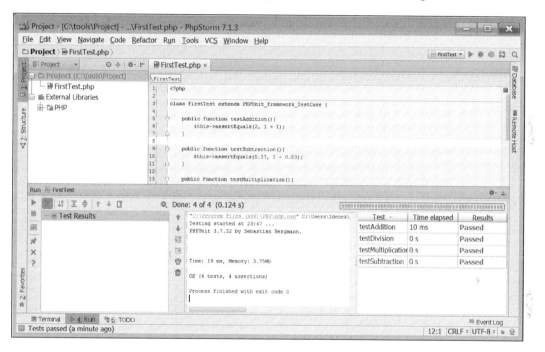

6. Now if you click between line number and code, you can put the breakpoint there. When you run test in debug mode, execution will be stopped. IDE brings debug view, where you can see all the variables; you can step through the code, and see code execution step by step. You start debugging the same way as running tests; just select **Debug** instead of **Run**. If you run debug and the breakpoint is in the right place, you should see a result similar to the following screenshot:

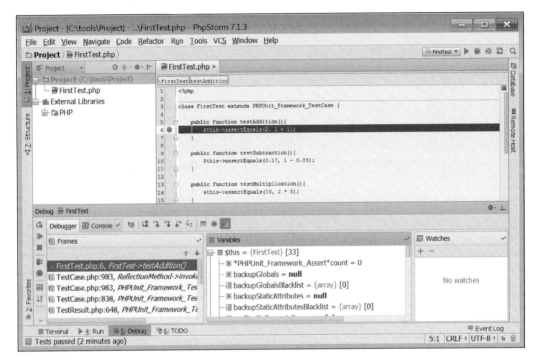

PhpStorm requires a bit of configuration to be able to run the PHPUnit tests. But otherwise, it's a brilliant IDE, and to run and debug tests is really easy.

Summary

To be able to use PHPUnit effectively, it is important to have good tools available. Most advanced IDEs have good PHPUnit support. Configuration could be a bit tricky, but it's an investment that pays off later. Good IDE must support PHPUnit test execution and debugging as basic, must-have features. Many of them support more features such as generating and displaying code coverage, but the developer always needs the basic features mentioned in this chapter and advanced features for later use.

In this chapter, we described four IDEs, but any other good IDE will have similar configuration and PHPUnit support, and it is up to the developer to choose the one that suits him/her best. After the two introductory chapters, the next chapter will explain what are unit tests and when and why to write them.

3
Tests and What They're All About

In the first two introductory chapters, we installed PHPUnit and set up IDE to be able to write and run tests. Now it's time to jump into the unit testing swimming pool and swim. Lots of theory has been written about unit testing, test-driven development, behavior-driven development, and many more clever things. But the developer needs to be able to use technology as quickly as possible and see results, and this is what we try. You will see step by step how you can use it: how to write code that can be tested and code that can't be tested. As PHP is the language used by web developers, the focus of unit testing is going to be web applications. It's important to understand the structure of the application or framework that you are using. Good design patterns especially MVC are something that really help to write robust and maintainable code and also help a lot when you are writing tests. Simply put, testable code is very often better code.

In this chapter, we are going to look at the following topics that not only include basic PHPUnit tests, but also writing and running tests in the web application context:

- Understanding unit testing
- The anatomy of a PHPUnit test
- Testing functions
- Testing methods
- MVC application architecture and tests
- Testing controllers

Understanding unit testing

Before looking at code, it would be good to mention some basic information and rules for writing unit tests and using unit testing. It's really important to remember these few basic rules and understand the point of unit testing. Unit tests are not just a nice feature, but are an absolutely necessary part of any decent software project.

What is a unit test?

A simple question is what is a unit test? A unit test is code that executes another piece of code (function/method) in a known context with known inputs, and compares the output to the expected values. This is also called an assertion. The following code snippet is the simplest assertion verifying that one plus one equals two and if function sum works:

```
function sum($a, $b)
{
    return $a + $b;
}


$this->assertEquals(2, sum(1, 1));
```

Assertions

An assertion is the heart and soul of unit testing. An assertion comes together with constraint. Your assertThat value suits constraint. A good example of how this works is the simplest assertion available in PHPUnit assertTrue(), as shown in the following code snippet:

```
public static function assertTrue($condition, $message = '')
    {
        self::assertThat($condition, self::isTrue(), $message);
    }
```

The following are basic and the most used assertions:

- assertTrue(): This verifies that a condition is true
- assertFalse(): This verifies that a condition is false
- assertEquals(): This verifies that expected and actual values are equal, the same way as the PHP comparison operator ==
- assertSame(): This is similar to assertEquals(), but it checks whether values are identical, the same way as the === operator

- assertNull(): This verifies that value is null
- assertEmpty(): This verifies that value is empty, but it uses the PHP function empty(), which means empty can be false, null, '', array()

But PHPUnit has many different built-in assertions. You can find a complete list of these assertions in official documentation at http://phpunit.de/manual/3.7/en/appendixes.assertions.html.

But if you need more, you can create your own assertion by extending the PHPUnit_Framework_Constraint class.

The importance of unit testing

Unit tests give us confidence that written code works as expected and it's a solid piece on which a developer can rely. Breaking code into small independent units reduces the risk of introducing bugs when the code interacts with another piece of code. It's the best investment available if you need to expend and modify an application without worrying about any unexpected consequences of your changes.

It can also be a very good piece of documentation to describe how code was designed and what it's supposed to do. Another reason is refactoring. Changing complex code without testing is like stepping into the mine field.

Testing all possible scenarios

It would be nice to test all possible scenarios but consider a function as shown in the following code snippet:

```
function plusOne($a)
{
return 1 + $a;
}
```

PHP is a loosely typed language, and you can have many scenarios. But it is usually enough to cover the most expected or the most important scenarios and also a couple of unexpected ones (in our case, for example, $a can be NULL or FALSE).

But what you should try is to test as much code as possible, hitting all if else or case statements. Try to assume the worst by testing edge cases. It is important to test not only positive cases, getting expected results, but also negative cases to verify that code wouldn't break when unexpected inputs or exception is thrown.

What makes a good test?

The following are some generic rules that are valid for any unit test and not just PHPUnit:

- **Independent**: Each test needs to run independently from other tests and environments.

- **Fast**: To have useful tests and be able to run them as often as possible (for example, as pre- or post-commit hooks), tests need to be fast.

- **Repeatable**: You should be able to run a test as many times as you want with the same result.

- **Up to date**: Tests are written once, but code can be changed or extended. If you are not going to keep tests up to date, the initial investment in tests will be just a waste of time and money. The rule is, whoever breaks the test, fixes the test.

- **Short**: Tests should be just a few lines—easy to read and understand.

- **Resilient**: Once written, tests shouldn't change till the behavior of tested class/method changes.

When to write tests

It would be nice to have 100 percent code coverage (the amount of code tested, but not necessarily 100 percent code coverage also means all possibilities tested). Usually, better coverage means a better quality project. Check several open source projects on GitHub to see how many tests they have, and this gives you a clue about the quality of these projects, and it doesn't matter how often these projects are used. A widespread system doesn't automatically mean high quality code.

But what is more important is to get into the habit of writing tests. You can try the test-driven development approach, where you can imagine your class like an interface with no implementation, just saying how each method should work. You then write tests describing exactly what you expect, and then you implement the interface— writing the required functionality and the test will verify that it does what you expect.

A second way is to write the class or function and then test it with written tests to verify functionality. The rule should be that you write the test the same day as you wrote the code, because later you are not going to do it as you will be focusing on something else.

It is absolutely necessary to have the entire core functionality covered by unit tests. This is a must-have feature.

Anatomy of a PHPUnit test

Now, let's have a closer look at what the test structure looks like. Let's start with a simple test case, which will show the basic PHPUnit test structure. The following code snippet is a very basic example testing two PHP functions used for sorting arrays: `asort()` is used to sort an array and maintaining the indexes, and `ksort()` is used to sort the array by key. To start with, we have an array of vegetables, where name is the key and price is the value:

```php
<?php

class SecondTest extends PHPUnit_Framework_TestCase
{
    public function testAsort()
    {
        $vegetablesArray = array('carrot' => 1, 'broccoli' => 2.99,
'garlic' => 3.98, 'swede' => 1.75);
        $sortedArray = array('carrot' => 1, 'swede' => 1.75,
'broccoli' => 2.99, 'garlic' => 3.98);
        asort($vegetablesArray, SORT_NUMERIC);
        $this->assertSame($sortedArray, $vegetablesArray);
    }


    public function testKsort()
    {
        $fruitsArray = array('oranges' => 1.75, 'apples' => 2.05,
'bananas' => 0.68, 'pear' => 2.75);
        $sortedArray = array('apples' => 2.05, 'bananas' => 0.68,
'oranges' => 1.75, 'pear' => 2.75);
        ksort($fruitsArray, SORT_STRING);
        $this->assertSame($sortedArray, $fruitsArray);
    }
}
```

 You might be tempted to put in the code print statement or use `var_dump()`. This might also be the moment to write the test, to understand what the code is doing, and verify the functionality without needing to open a browser page. Tests are a good way of learning about your code.

As you can see, every test case is a class. The class name should end with `Test`. This is because when you test your classes, the test class should mirror tested class, and the difference between the tested class and the test suite is Test added to the name:

```
.
|-- src
|    '-- library
|         '-- Util
|              '-- File.php
'-- tests
     '-- library
          '-- Util
               '-- FileTest.php
```

Every test class also called test suite extends the `PHPUnit_Framework_TestCase` class. Of course, you can write your own modified or extended `PHPUnit_Framework_TestCase` and call it, for example, `MyTestCase`, but again this parent class should extend the original PHPUnit class. This can be seen in the following class definition:

```
abstract class PHPUnit_Framework_TestCase extends
    PHPUnit_Framework_Assert implements PHPUnit_Framework_Test,
    PHPUnit_Framework_SelfDescribing
```

And the following tells you what the preceding class definition does:

- `abstract`: This is used because you always extend the `PHPUnit_Framework_TestCase` class and do not execute this class directly

- `extends PHPUnit_Framework_Assert`: This is the class providing a set of assert methods such as `assertTrue()` and `assertEquals()`

- `implements PHPUnit_Framework_Test`: This is a simple interface containing just one method, `run()`, to execute the test

- `implements PHPUnit_Framework_SelfDescribing`: This is another simple interface containing just one method `toString()`

PHPUnit doesn't use namespaces, which have been introduced to PHP 5.3. Mainly for backwards compatibility, PHPUnit uses underscores in class names to match the class location in a filesystem.

Defining test methods

Each test method name should start with `test`. Then the name is up to you. You can mirror their testing class methods, but you will probably need more tests. Each test method should have an explanatory name, meaning you should be able to say what you are testing just from the name, for example, `testChangePassword()` or `testChangePasswordForLockedAcoounts()`.

Testing functions

That was a bit of theory, now let's have a look at a specific real-life example. Let's use the following question that developers can get during a job interview, and with this example see how PHPUnit can help us to solve the problem or make us confident that we have found right solution.

The task is to write a function in PHP that returns the largest sum of contiguous integers in an ordered array.

For example, if the input is [0, 1, 2, 3, 6, 7, 8, 9, 11, 12, 14] the largest sum is 6 + 7 + 8 + 9 = 30.

As you can see, it doesn't look particularly difficult. You can take several different approaches. Write something really clever, use brute force and a traverse array, but anything that works is the right answer.

Now, let's have a look at how PHPUnit can help to solve this problem. Firstly, you have to stop and think about what you are doing—not just start writing code, and after a while becoming lost, not knowing what you wanted to achieve.

So how do you solve this problem?

The following steps would be the best approach:

1. Use the PHP function `usort()` to sort an array by values using a user-defined comparison function.

2. Then return the last element of the sorted array, which is going to be the largest group.

This is the important bit for figuring out strategy. Now, let's translate it into a function without writing the implementation yet. Consider the following code snippet:

```
/**
 * Returns largest sum of contiguous integers
 * @param array $inputArray
 * @return array
```

```
 */
function sumFinder(array $inputArray){}
/**
 * Custom array comparison method
 * @param array $a
 * @param array $b
 * @return int
 */
function compareArrays(array $a, array $b){}
```

Now you have two functions. The first function takes array as the input by using the PHP function usort(), and second function, compareArrays(), sorts the arrays by groups. The first function then returns an array with the group name and sum.

Now you know what the functions will look like. Let's write tests for them that will describe how they will behave, as shown in the following code snippet:

```php
<?php

require_once 'SumFinder.php';

class SumFinderTest extends PHPUnit_Framework_TestCase
{
    public function testSumFinder()
    {
        $input = array(0, 1, 2, 3, 6, 7, 8, 9, 11, 12, 14);
        $result = array('group'=>'6, 7, 8, 9', 'sum'=> 30);
        $this->assertEquals($result, sumFinder($input));
    }

    public function testCompareArrays()
    {
        $array1 = array(0,1,2,3);
        $array2 = array(6,7,8,9);

        // $array2 > $array1
        $this->assertEquals(-1,compareArrays($array1,$array2));
        // $array1 < $array2
        $this->assertEquals(1,compareArrays($array2,$array1));
        // $array2 = $array2
        $this->assertEquals(0,compareArrays($array2,$array2));
    }
}
```

As you can see, there are two simple tests for each function. The first test, `testSumFinder()`, verifies the main `sumFinder()` function, and the second test, `testCompareArrays()`, verifies that arrays are going to be sorted correctly when `usort()` is used. Now you can run them and see the following results:

FAILURES!

Tests: 2, Assertions: 2, Failures: 2.

Brilliant! This is what we want: it's failing because we have to write an implementation. Let's start with the `compareArrays()` function as shown in the following code snippet:

```
/**
 * Custom array comparison method
 * @param array $a
 * @param array $b
 * @return int
 */
function compareArrays(array $a, array $b)
{
    $sumA = array_sum($a);
    $sumB = array_sum($b);

    if ($sumA == $sumB ){
        return 0;
    }
    elseif ($sumA > $sumB){
        return 1;
    }
    else {
        return -1;
    }
}
```

Then you can run `testCompareArrays()`, and great, it works as shown in the following output:

OK (1 test, 3 assertions)

Now we can move on to `sumFinder()` implementation as shown in the following code snippet:

```
/**
 * Returns largest sum of contiguous integers
 * @param array $inputArray
 * @return array
```

```
 */
function sumFinder(array $inputArray)
{
    $arrayGroups = array();

    foreach ($inputArray as $element) {
        //initial settings
        if (!isset($previousElement)) {
            $previousElement = $element;
            $arrayGroupNumber = 0;
        }

        if (($previousElement + 1) != $element){
            $arrayGroupNumber += 1;
        }

        $arrayGroups[$arrayGroupNumber][] = $element;
        $previousElement = $element;
    }

    usort($arrayGroups,'compareArrays');
    $highestGroup = array_pop($arrayGroups);

    return(array('group'=> implode(', ',
        $highestGroup),'sum'=>array_sum($highestGroup)));
}
```

When you run the preceding code snippet, you will get the following result:

OK (1 test, 1 assertion)

And this is the solution. Here you should see one of the biggest advantages of unit testing; it forces you to think about what you are doing and to have a clear idea before you start to write code or clarify it before implementation.

Testing methods

Testing methods are very similar to testing functions, but you can do much more. There is nothing wrong with procedural programming, but there are very good reasons to use **Object Oriented Programming (OOP)**. PHP is strictly not an OOP language such as Java or C#, but this doesn't mean you can't use OOP. Of course you can, and PHP has a very good object model. It's a solid implementation with all the main features you would expect. Where OOP really helps is in organizing your code with all the OOP advantages, and it also helps when you are writing tests.

PHPUnit has strong support for testing classes and objects. The real strength of PHPUnit and unit testing comes when you are testing classes. Not only can you test every method, but when necessary, you can replace part of the class with your implementation just for testing, for example, to avoid storing data in the database. This is called test doubles and these techniques are going to be described later in this book.

When testing class methods, it is recommended to test just public methods. This might sound a bit strange after it was said as much code as possible should be tested. Why not write a test for private or protected methods? The reason is that you should test just public methods; everything else is just internal implementation that you shouldn't worry about, and even if it changes, public methods should still behave in the same way. If private/protected methods are too complex, it might suggest that they deserve their own class, or you can use PHP Reflection and change accessibility on the fly.

As an example of how to test methods, let's use the example that we used for testing functions and adapt it to classes.

So the following task is the same as mentioned earlier.

The task is to write a function in PHP that returns the largest sum of contiguous integers in an ordered array.

For example, if the input is [0, 1, 2, 3, 6, 7, 8, 9, 11, 12, 14] the largest sum is 6 + 7 + 8 + 9 = 30.

Again, it would be good to start with a class that looks almost like an interface, or if you want, you can create an interface, as shown in the following code snippet:

```php
class SumFinderClass
{

    private $inputArray;

    /**
     * @param array $inputArray
     */
    public function __construct($inputArray = null){}

    /**
     * Returns largest sum of contiguous integers
     * @return array
     */
    public function findSum(){}
```

```
/**
 * Custom array comparison method to sort by sum of contiguous
integers
 * @param  array $a
 * @param  array $b
 * @return int
 */
public function compareArrays(array $a, array $b){}}
```

The difference with procedural implementation, in this case, is that it just encapsulates all functionality into one class that can be extended and modified if necessary. In this case, you could be tempted to set the compareArrays() method as private, but in order to test it easily, let's leave it as public for now. Now we have a class skeleton, let's write tests as shown in the following code snippet:

```php
<?php
require_once 'SumFinderClass.php';

class SumFinderClassTest extends PHPUnit_Framework_TestCase
{
    public function testFindSum()
    {
        $input = array(0, 1, 2, 3, 6, 7, 8, 9, 11, 12, 14);
        $result = array('group'=>'6, 7, 8, 9', 'sum'=> 30);

        $sumFinder = new SumFinderClass($input);
        $this->assertEquals($result, $sumFinder->findSum());
    }

    public function testCompareArrays()
    {
        $array1 = array(0,1,2,3);
        $array2 = array(6,7,8,9);

        $sumFinder = new SumFinderClass();

        // $array2 > $array1
        $this->assertEquals(-1,
          $sumFinder->compareArrays($array1,$array2));
        // $array1 < $array2
        $this->assertEquals(1,
          $sumFinder->compareArrays($array2,$array1));
        // $array2 = $array2
        $this->assertEquals(0, $sumFinder->compareArrays($array2,
          $array2));
    }
}
```

We have two test methods: `testFindSum()` and `testCompareArrays()`, which are testing two public methods in this class. The `testCompareArrays()` method doesn't require any dependency, and we are just passing test data there to verify that the compare method works as expected. The `testFindSum()` method does a full check, of course, internally it's covering even `compareArrays()`. So in this case, we could really leave `compareArrays()` as private and write just one test. On the other hand, there is no harm in leaving this method public. It helps to have tests to verify that the array comparison works as expected, because it's used as callback for `usort()` and it could be difficult to debug it when we are getting unexpected/unwanted results.

Then the complete implementation looks like the following code snippet:

```php
<?php
/**
 * Class SumFinderClass
 */
class SumFinderClass
{
    private $inputArray;

    /**
     * @param $inputArray
     */
    public function __construct($inputArray = null)
    {
        $this->inputArray = $inputArray;
    }

    /**
     * Returns largest sum of contiguous integers
     * @return array
     */
    public function findSum()
    {
        $arrayGroups = array();

        foreach ($this->inputArray as $element) {
            //initial settings
            if (!isset($previousElement)) {
                $previousElement = $element;
                $arrayGroupNumber = 0;
            }

            if(($previousElement + 1) != $element)
```

```
                    $arrayGroupNumber += 1;

            $arrayGroups[$arrayGroupNumber][] = $element;
            $previousElement = $element;
        }

        usort($arrayGroups,array($this,'compareArrays'));
        $highestGroup = array_pop($arrayGroups);

        return $this->extractResult($highestGroup);
    }

    /**
     * Custom array comparison method to sort by sum of contiguous
integers
     * @param  array $a
     * @param  array $b
     * @return int
     */
    public function compareArrays(array $a, array $b)
    {
        $sumA = array_sum($a);
        $sumB = array_sum($b);

        if($sumA == $sumB ) return 0;
        elseif($sumA > $sumB) return 1;
        else return -1;

    }

    /**
     * @return array|bool
     */
    private function extractResult(array $highestGroup)
    {
        if(!$highestGroup || !is_array($highestGroup))

            return false;

        $group = implode(', ', $highestGroup);
        $groupSum = array_sum($highestGroup);

        return(array('group'=> $group,'sum'=>$groupSum));
    }
}
```

When you run our test for this class, the following result must be the output:

```
OK (2 tests, 4 assertions)
```

As you can see, there is one extra `private` method `extractResult()`, but because it's an internal implementation inside the class, we are not writing extra tests for this method as it's covered by `testFindSum()`.

The MVC application architecture and tests

After looking at how to test a single piece of functionality, you may ask, what about the whole web application? As mentioned earlier, there are the following levels of testing:

- Unit testing
- Integration testing
- Functional testing

It is important to consider this when you start writing tests. There may be other types of testing, but let's focus on these three for now. When talking about web applications, you will need all of them but different ones in different scenarios.

As you probably know, the design pattern of MVC is used by many web applications and frameworks.

The model is the part where all the business (main) logic is stored. You should definitely have covered with unit tests the main business logic, possibly without database interaction or API calls. This is sometimes a problem with PHP applications; businesses logic equals database access, which is not always right. A bit of abstraction is not a bad idea, things such as **Object Relational Mapping (ORM)** and systems such as Doctrine ORM or Propel really help when it comes to testing.

As a starting point, you should write plain PHPUnit tests with no database interaction, just to cover the main business logic (for example, VAT calculation).

The next thing we are going to explore in detail is integration testing. When you are accessing a database or calling API, it is good to know how your code will interact with another system, and if your implementation is matching, what is happening on the other side.

Compared with unit tests, integration tests could be slow — you probably can't run them as often as unit tests. If you are working with a database, then it depends how you set your test. If you are working on a known dataset and database structure, the database structure can change without your knowledge (then it might be good that the test fails as a changed database structure and not updated code could be a very serious problem). If you work directly with a third-party API, you never know when it might go down or it changes. But again, it could be good to know immediately that something is not quite right.

Controllers shouldn't contain any business logic. If they do, it's usually very ugly spaghetti code, where the code is duplicated, inconsistent, and maybe even full of bugs. A controller should just handle (dispatch) requests and send responses. In theory, you can write unit tests for them, but usually, you use unit testing support provided by MVC frameworks. As you could be launching a whole application, to be able to test controller functionality, you need functional testing. Hundreds or possibly thousands of lines of code are executed to test even simple requests/responses.

And last but not least is a view. A view should just process and display output; nothing else. To keep a strict MVC structure and divide work between the frontend and backend developers, it is good to use a templating system such as Twig or Smarty for the view. With plain PHP, it is very tempting to do more than is necessary. Even view can be tested but usually just by functional tests through controller or by tools such as Selenium when you run black box testing directly in the browser.

The conclusion, when talking about the MVC design pattern, should be that unit testing should focus on a model and a more strict MVC pattern should be applied. The code is going to be of better quality, more easily tested, and possibly will contain less bugs than nasty spaghetti code, where a controller is the master of everything. But you can test controllers, and modern frameworks usually have helpers to allow you to test controllers.

Testing controllers

To see how you can test controllers, let's have a look at what some of the best known PHP MVC frameworks provide. This is just a short overview; you might need the official documentation to see exactly what each framework provides.

 The following code snippets show how to tests controllers in some popular MVC framewroks, but they won't work without installed and configured frameworks.

The given example is an `IndexController` test, which returns in the `h1` node text `Hello World!`.

The test for Zend Framework 1 can appear as shown in the following code snippet:

```php
<?php
class Zf1Test extends Zend_Test_PHPUnit_ControllerTestCase
{
    public function setUp()
    {
        $this->bootstrap = array($this, 'appBootstrap');
        parent::setUp();
    }

    public function testIndexActionShouldContainLoginForm()
    {
        $this->dispatch('/');
        $this->assertAction('index');
        $this->assertResponseCode(200);
        $this->assertQueryContentContains('h1','Hello World!');
    }
}
```

The test for Zend Framework 2 can be shown as the following code snippet:

```php
<?php

namespace ApplicationTest\Controller;

use Zend\Test\PHPUnit\Controller\AbstractHttpControllerTestCase;

class Zf2Test extends AbstractHttpControllerTestCase
{
    public function setUp()
    {
        $this->setApplicationConfig(include
            '/path/to/application/config/test/
            application.config.php'          );
        parent::setUp();
    }

    public function testIndexActionCanBeAccessed()
    {
        $this->dispatch('/');
        $this->assertResponseStatusCode(200);

        $this->assertModuleName('application');
        $this->assertControllerClass('IndexController');
        $this->assertActionName('index');
        $this->assertQueryContentContains('h1','Hello World!');
    }
}
```

The test for Symphony 2 is shown in the following code snippet:

```php
<?php
namespace Application\Tests\Controller;

use Symfony\Bundle\FrameworkBundle\Test\WebTestCase;

class IndexControllerTest extends WebTestCase
{
    public function testIndex()
    {
        $client = static::createClient();

        $crawler = $client->request('GET', '/');

        $this->assertTrue($client->getResponse()->isSuccessful());

        $this->assertGreaterThan(0,
            $crawler->filter('html:contains
            ("Hello World!")')->count());
    }
}
```

Testing controllers can be very useful, for example, when writing an API. An API can be tested quite easily and should be tested. But to test controllers in this way can be very expensive, as for each test the whole framework and application have to be started again and again, which takes time and resources. You might be tempted to take this approach because when the full application is started, you have all available resources, including a connection to the database.

Summary

This chapter was a quick introduction to unit testing, but the best way to learn how to swim is jumping into the water. That's why we have looked at more than just a couple of PHPUnit tests.

The *Understanding unit testing* section was important to understand why tests are written, how to write good tests, and what the limitations are. The basic PHPUnit test structure was followed by an example of how to test functions and how to test classes and their methods.

But before you start to test anything, you have to think about your application structure and how the MVC design pattern helps with unit testing. As most PHP applications are web applications, we took a short visit to the world of MVC frameworks to see how testing controllers is supported and what you can expect.

In the next chapter, we are going to look at one of the biggest problems when writing tests: dependencies.

4
Testing Dependencies and Exceptions

In this chapter, you will see that one of the biggest problems faced when writing PHPUnit tests is dependencies. You might be wondering what we mean by dependencies. Obviously, code needs to interact with other code, and you need to know it works. Yes, this is true, but with unit testing, you are trying to verify that the smallest possible piece of code works as expected, and to be sure that nothing else is breaking the tested code, you need to isolate the code. Code isolation is one way to do it, and you should start with this.

But what really are dependencies? The following are the parts of the application and code that might be causing problems:

- **Global variables**: For example, you create a `$config` object when the application starts, and then you use this object almost anywhere in the application (in PHP stored, in `$_GLOBALS` array).

- **Session variables**: Similar to global variables, these are variables stored in the session (`$_SESSION`). This is a standard way to handle the application state with the stateless HTTP protocol.

- **Usage of registry**: This is a slightly different way of accessing global variables.

- **Other code**: This is used inside a tested function/method.

Detecting dependencies

Surprisingly, this is quite easy. Just remember one of the golden rules of unit testing: isolation. In a program, if another function is called or another class is used, then the code containing it is not isolated. This may result in test failure outside the tested method or function. Hence, it cannot be considered a unit test. The same goes with using resources such as a filesystem, database, and network. The result could be affected by these resources, thereby causing the code to be non-isolated, and hence it's not a unit test.

To demonstrate what dependency means in the real world, the following code snippet is a simple example of the User class. This class wraps code to create a user, stores it in the database, and sends an activation e-mail.

```php
<?php

namespace Application;

/**
 * Class User
 * @package Application
 */
class User
{
    public $userId;
    public $firstName;
    public $lastName;
    public $email;
    public $password;
    public $salt;

    /**
     * @param array $options
     */
    public function __construct(array $options)
    {
        foreach ($options as $key => $value) {
            if (property_exists($this, $key))
            {
                $this->{$key} = $value;
            }
        }
    }

    /**
     * validates properties
```

```php
     * @return bool
     */
    public function isInputValid()
    {
        if (empty($this->firstName) || empty($this->lastName) ||
          empty($this->email) || empty($this->password) ||
          !filter_var($this->email, FILTER_VALIDATE_EMAIL))
        {
            return false;
        }
        else
        {
            return true;
        }
    }


    /**
     * creates password hash
     */
    public function createPassword()
    {
        $this->salt =
          substr(str_shuffle("0123456789abcdefghijklmnopqrstuvwxyz
          ABCDEFGHIJKLMNOPQRSTUVWXYZ"), 0, 15);
        $this->password = sha1($this->password . $this->salt);
    }


    /**
     * verifies password
     * @param  string $password
     * @return bool
     */
    public function verifyPassword($password)
    {
        return ($this->password === sha1($password . $this->salt));
    }
```

As you can see, so far so good. No problems here. Code can be tested quite easily. Each method is straightforward; only code from the User class is used. However, the following code snippet is worse from the testing point of view:

```php
    /**
     * sends activation email
     */
```

```php
    private function sendActivationEmail()
    {
        global $config;

        $email = new \Util\Mail($config);
        $email->setEmailFrom($config->email);
        $email->setEmailTo($this->email);
        $email->setTitle('Your account has been activated');
        $email->setBody("Dear {$this->firstName}\n
                        Your account has been activated\n
                        Please visit {$config->site_url}\n
                        Thank you");
        $email->send();
    }


    /**
     * stores user to the database
     * @return bool
     */
    public function createUser()
    {
        global $config;

        if (!$this->isInputValid())
        {
            return false;
        }

        $this->createPassword();

        $db = $config->db;
        /* @var $db \PDO */
        $sql = "INSERT INTO users(firstname, lastname, email,
          password, salt) VALUES (:firstname, :lastname, :email,
          :password, :salt)";
        $statement = $db->prepare($sql);

        $statement->bindParam(':firstname', $this->firstName);
        $statement->bindParam(':lastname', $this->lastName);
        $statement->bindParam(':email', $this->email);
        $statement->bindParam(':password', $this->password);
        $statement->bindParam(':salt', $this->salt);
```

```
if ($statement->execute())
{
    $this->userId = $db->lastInsertId();
    $this->sendActivationEmail();

    return true;
}
else
{
    throw new \Exception('User wasn't saved:
        '.implode(':',$statement->errorInfo()));
}
}
}
```

This is a simple `User` class that contains more or less a normal PHP code that handles the creation of the user account and stores data in the database. You can say that it's simple, efficient code; there is nothing wrong with it, so why worry about it?

First, let's have a look at what the code does:

- The constructor accepts an array and assigns properties to the object
- The `isInputValid()` function does basic validation
- The `createPassword()` function creates the `salt` variable and then uses the `sha1()` function to create a password hash
- The `verifyPassword()` function verifies if the provided user password matches with the one stored in the `sha1()` hash
- The `sendActivationEmail()` function sends a notification e-mail about a newly created account
- The `createUser()` function stores the user account to the database

The following are the problems while testing this class:

- Usage of the global variable `$config`
- Usage of the `\Util\Mail` class, which is an external class, and as expected, will send an e-mail
- Usage of the `PDO` database connection (`$config->db`)

And why are these problems? Are they really problems?

By adding dependencies in your code, you are adding complexity. The more complex the code, the greater the chance of it containing bugs, and it is more difficult to refactor. For example, global variables can be passed to tests very easily by simply setting `$config` as the global variable. However, the problem is that what starts as a simple passed object usually ends up being more complex. To set up the application's configuration, you need to create a class loader, error handler, load configuration, and probably much more. Suddenly, you have to start your application and execute hundreds of lines of code; instead of testing one class, you are testing half of your application. A simple advice is to avoid global variables and session variables inside your classes.

Another problem in our example is the usage of the `Mail` class. When you want to run tests, you don't want to send e-mails.

Similarly, another problem is the connections to the database. PHP has become so popular as a scripting language that is used for quickly storing and retrieving data from MySQL databases. This sort of code that just pipes data to and from databases is very common. It works, but consider if you want to change behavior; for example, import users and not have their passwords? What can you do in such a scenario; use another method and perform code duplication?

To be fair, there are many ways to do it. Sometimes you might be happy with leaving the database interaction in your class, but this might become problematic later when you end up with all the code sitting in one huge class.

The following might be basic options of how to test this code:

- Refactor code and split logic into an entity and a manager
- Use integration testing and connect to the database
- Use mocks to create a dummy class that imitates the functionality of the dependent code

Handling dependencies

In our case, the cleanest method to solve the dependency problem would be to separate the `User` class from database access and the `Mail` class usage. The logic is that the `User` class is an entity, but then we will have a second `UserManager` class that will allow us to persist (store) the objects of the `User` class in the database. To test the `User` class, we will use unit tests, and to test `UserManager`, we will use integration testing. In our case, we will move `sendActivationEmail()` and `createUser()` to the `UserManager` class.

The User class then becomes a lightweight class, as shown in the following code snippet:

```php
<?php

namespace Application;

/**
 * Class User
 * @package Application
 */
class User
{
    public $userId;
    public $firstName;
    public $lastName;
    public $email;
    public $password;
    public $salt;

    /**
     * @param array $options
     */
    public function __construct(array $options)
    {
        foreach ($options as $key => $value) {
            if (property_exists($this, $key))
            {
                $this->{$key} = $value;
            }
        }
    }

    /**
     * validates properties
     * @return bool
     */
    public function isInputValid()
    {
        if (empty($this->firstName) || empty($this->lastName) ||
            empty($this->email) || empty($this->password) ||
            !filter_var($this->email, FILTER_VALIDATE_EMAIL))
        {
            return false;
```

```
        }
        else
        {
            return true;
        }
    }


    /**
     * creates password hash
     */
    public function createPassword()
    {
        $this->salt =
          substr(str_shuffle("0123456789abcdefghijklmnopqrstuvwxyz
          ABCDEFGHIJKLMNOPQRSTUVWXYZ"), 0, 15);
        $this->password = sha1($this->password . $this->salt);
    }


    /**
     * verifies password
     * @param  string $password
     * @return bool
     */
    public function verifyPassword($password)
    {
        return ($this->password === sha1($password .
          $this->salt));
    }
}
```

First, let's have a look at how to write tests for the User class, where we decided to do a bit of refactoring and moved sendActivationEmail() and createUser() to the UserManager class, as shown in the following code snippet:

```php
<?php

namespace ApplicationTest;

use Application\User;

require_once 'User.php';

class UserTest extends \PHPUnit_Framework_TestCase
{
```

```php
/**
 * @var \Application\User
 */
private $user;

public function setUp()
{
    $this->user = new User(array('firstName' => 'FirstName',
        'lastName' => 'LastName', 'email' => 'example@test.com',
        'password' => 'password123'));
}

public function testValidInput()
{
    $this->assertTrue($this->user->isInputValid());
    $this->user->email = null;
    $this->assertFalse($this->user->isInputValid());
}

public function testInValidInput()
{
    $this->user->email = null;
    $this->assertFalse($this->user->isInputValid());
}

public function testCreatedPassword()
{
    $this->user->createPassword();
    $this->assertEquals(sha1('password123' .
        $this->user->salt), $this->user->password);
    $this->assertNotEquals(sha1(null), $this->user->password);
}

public function testEmptyPassword()
{
    $this->user->createPassword();
    $this->assertNotEquals(sha1(null), $this->user->password);
}

public function testValidPassword()
{
    $this->user->createPassword();
    $this->assertTrue($this->user->verifyPassword('password123'));
}
```

```
public function testInvalidPassword()
{
    $this->user->createPassword();
    $this->assertFalse($this->user->verifyPassword(null));
}
}
```

When you execute tests in your IDE, you should see a similar output as shown in the following screenshot:

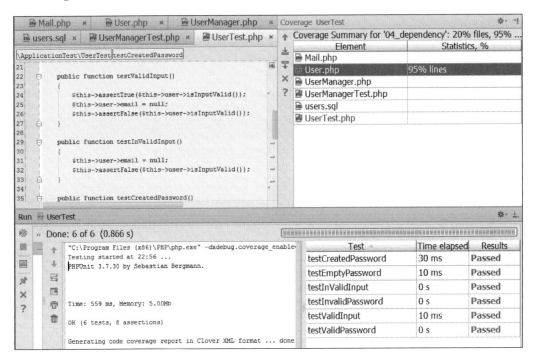

In this way, we are only writing and running unit tests, and the reported code coverage on this class is 95 percent. It is important to not only test the expected results such as assertTrue() but also pass invalid parameters and verify assertFalse() in order to ensure that the code handles all scenarios well.

In this case, we are testing User, and each test needs the user object. The setUp() method, which will be described in depth in *Chapter 6, Test Isolation and Tests Interaction*, is used to create the user object for each test, so code doesn't have to be duplicated. The UserManager class contains the sendActivationEmail() and createUser() methods, which connect to the database and send e-mails. The difference is that the required dependencies, email, db, and config objects, are passed in the constructor, as shown in the following code snippet:

```php
<?php

namespace Application;
class UserManager
{
    private $db;
    private $email;
    private $config;

    public function __construct(\Util\Mail $email, \PDO $db,
      $config)
    {
        $this->email = $email;
        $this->db = $db;
        $this->config = $config;
    }

    /**
     * sends activation email
     */
    private function sendActivationEmail(\Application\User $user)
    {
        $this->email->setEmailFrom($this->config->email);
        $this->email->setEmailTo($user->email);
        $this->email->setTitle('Your account has been activated');
        $this->email->setBody("Dear {$user->firstName}\n
                    Your account has been activated\n
                    Please visit {$this->config->site_url}\n
                    Thank you");
        $this->email->send();
    }

    /**
     * @param  User $user
     * @return bool
     */
    public function createUser(\Application\User $user)
    {
        if (!$user->isInputValid())
        {
            throw new \InvalidArgumentException('Invalid user
              data');
        }

        $user->createPassword();
```

```php
/* @var $this->db \PDO */
$sql = "INSERT INTO users(firstname, lastname, email,
    password, salt) VALUES (:firstname, :lastname, :email,
    :password, :salt)";
$statement = $this->db->prepare($sql);

$statement->bindParam(':firstname', $user->firstName);
$statement->bindParam(':lastname', $user->lastName);
$statement->bindParam(':email', $user->email);
$statement->bindParam(':password', $user->password);
$statement->bindParam(':salt', $user->salt);

if ($statement->execute())
{
    $user->userId = $this->db->lastInsertId();
    $this->sendActivationEmail($user);

    return true;
}
else
{
    throw new \Exception('User wasn\'t saved:
        '.implode(':',$statement->errorInfo()));
}

    return false;
    }
}
```

To test the code, we have the following two options:

- **Unit testing**: This verifies the core functionality and the exercise piece of code in isolation
- **Integration testing**: This verifies the interaction with other components

Both of them are important. If you go down the unit-test-only route, it might be difficult to verify if we can really store/retrieve data from the database. In this case, it would be a problem. For e-mails, let's say we are not worried about sending e-mails; we have tests for the Mail class and we don't want to test it here. To have a complete picture, the following code snippet shows the skeleton of the Mail class:

```php
<?php

namespace Util;
```

```
class Mail
{
    public function setEmailFrom($emailFrom) {}
    public function setEmailTo($emailTo) {}
    public function setTitle($title) {}
    public function setBody($body) {}
    public function send() {}

}
```

The following code snippet shows tests for the UserManager class:

```php
<?php

namespace ApplicationTest;

use Application\UserManager;
use Application\User;

require_once 'User.php';
require_once 'UserManager.php';
require_once 'Mail.php';

class UserManagerTest extends \PHPUnit_Framework_TestCase
{
    public function testCreateUser()
    {
        $db = new
          \PDO('mysql:host=localhost;port=3306;
          dbname=test','root','');
        $config = new \stdClass();
        $config->email = 'test@example.com';
        $config->site_url = 'http://example.com';

        $user = new User(array('firstName' => 'FirtsName',
          'lastName' => 'LastName', 'email' => 'user@example.com',
          'password' => 'password123'));

        $email = $this->getMock('\Util\Mail');

        $userManager = new UserManager($email, $db, $config);

        $this->assertTrue($userManager->createUser($user));
```

```
        $this->assertEquals(sha1('password123'.$user->salt),
          $user->password);
        $this->assertTrue($user->userId > 0);

    }

}
```

> To simplify things, we used `require_once` to load the required classes. In the real world, it would be better to use the class loader. If your classes match the PSR-0 standard, then it is very easy to use any PSR-0 compatible class loader without the need to use `require_once` (`https://github.com/php-fig/fig-standards/blob/master/accepted/PSR-0.md`).

This code illustrates how to handle dependencies in a better way. Instead of using global and session variables or having hardcoded classes in the code, we are going to pass the global variables (`$db`, `$email`, and `$config`) in a constructor, or you can set them using setters if you like. In your application, you can use techniques such as dependency injection to automatically pass the required dependency into your class. For tests, it is an advantage to be able to pass their customized versions of these objects. For example, we used PDO (MySQL), and we connected to a MySQL database, but with PDO, you can use a SQLite database PDO (using `'sqlite:/tmp/myDB.db'`) and just use a local database. We will see how to interact with databases in *Chapter 9, Database Testing*. For now, it is shown here just as an example of how to handle the required database connection.

For the `Mail` class, we used a different trick. As we are not interested in sending e-mails here, we created a dummy object e-mail using PHPUnit `getMock()`, as shown in the following line of code:

```
$email = $this->getMock('\Util\Mail')
```

This object has all the `Mail` class methods but with no implementation; this just returns NULL. For us, it is fine. The code works, and we don't want any e-mail to be sent here. More about these techniques will be discussed in *Chapter 8, Using Test Doubles*.

Exceptions are expected

Errors are common when executing code. Sometimes they are wanted, sometimes unwanted. A better way to handle unexpected or unwanted situations is to use exceptions. The reason is that you can recover from exceptions by wrapping code into a `try-catch` statement and then decide what to do, instead of letting it die. When writing tests, you want to test even these scenarios, and yes, it is possible.

Testing errors and exceptions

In PHPUnit, error handling works on the `set_error_handler()` and `set_exception_handler()` function levels. This means assigning a special function that is called when an error/exception occurs and is not caught in the exception handler.

This is also the limitation. If your code causes a fatal error, the script stops execution, and the error handler is not called. If this happens during the test execution, then the test is stopped and no test results are displayed. This happens, for example, when you are running out of memory, after which the code execution dies, and that's it.

If we look back at our code, around lines 39 and 40, you can see the following lines of code:

```
if (!$user->isInputValid())
        throw new \InvalidArgumentException('Invalid user data');
```

We are throwing an exception and we didn't test this scenario. Obviously, we should, but how can we test an exception? One of the options is as shown in the following code snippet:

```
public function testCreateUserException(){

    $db = new \PDO('mysql:host=localhost;port=3306;dbname=test',
     'root');
    $config = new \stdClass();
    $config->email = 'test@example.com';
    $config->site_url = 'http://example.com';
    $email = $this->getMock('\Util\Mail');

    $userManager = new UserManager($email, $db, $config);

    $user = new User(array('firstName' => 'FirtsName',
      'lastName' => 'LastName', 'email' => null,
      'password' => 'password123'));

    try{
        $userManager->createUser($user);
        $this->fail();
    }
    catch(\InvalidArgumentException $e){
        // correct behavior
    }
}
```

This way we tested that the exception is thrown.

However, PHPUnit offers a more elegant way to test an exception. You can use annotations to mark the test as the one throwing an exception, as shown in the following code snippet:

```
/**
 * @expectedException InvalidArgumentException
 */
public function testCreateUserException()
{
    $db = new \PDO('mysql:host=localhost;port=3306;dbname=test',
        'root','');
    $config = new \stdClass();
    $config->email = 'test@example.com';
    $config->site_url = 'http://example.com';

    $user = new User(array('firstName' => 'FirtsName',
        'lastName' => 'LastName', 'email' => null,
        'password' => 'password123'));

    $email = $this->getMock('\Util\Mail');

    $userManager = new UserManager($email, $db, $config);
    $userManager->createUser($user);
}
```

As you can see, there is no assert, but when you run the test, you will get the following result:

`OK (1 test, 1 assertion)`

In this case, an assertion is `@expectedException InvalidArgumentException`, and an exception is thrown. Another way to test an exception is to call the `$this->setExpectedException()` method.

To test errors, you can use the following lines of code:

```
/**
 * @expectedException PHPUnit_Framework_Error
 */
```

As all the PHP errors are converted to exceptions in PHPUnit, and `PHPUnit_Framework_Error` is the top-level exception for generic errors, it verifies that this exception was thrown. It's handy, but using exceptions is a better way to do it, because you can specify the exception type and you can verify that the right exception was thrown.

Summary

In this chapter, we looked at what could be called typical PHP code. In this code, we detected dependencies, which are difficult to test. There are a few different ways to handle this, but the best way is to write clean code, code that can be easily extended or refactored if necessary.

In our example, we went the refactoring way, splitting code into two classes. We tested User as an entity that holds the core functionality with unit tests. We then had a part of the code to access databases and send e-mails. We moved this code to the second class, UserManager, where we used integration testing and mocked the email object. In this way, we were able to handle dependencies and run tests for our classes. In later chapters, we will see what else you can do when running database integration tests or using test doubles to create dummy objects with the same API as the original object.

When you write code, you must try to write testable code. If it is a legacy code full of nested functionalities and dependencies, it might be very difficult or even impossible to test.

Finally, we looked at how to test errors and exceptions. PHPUnit offers really nice support for testing exceptions, so please throw and test exceptions.

In the next chapter, we will see what else you can do with tests, how to run them from the command line, what extra information you can obtain, and how to process results.

5
Running Tests from the Command Line

In the first chapter, we installed PHPUnit and then tried to run one simple test from the command line in order to test whether that PHPUnit works. In the second chapter, we saw how to configure and run tests in IDE. However, IDE is just a bridge between you and the command-line test runner, providing a nice and easy way to run and debug tests when you write code. But IDEs are not the best way to run and process the results of many tests. When you have tests written, there comes a time when you will need to look back at PHPUnit on the command line. The PHPUnit command-line test runner invoked through the `phpunit` command can do much more then just execute tests, as we will see in this chapter.

In this chapter, we are going to explore the following topics:

- Running tests
- Processing test results
- Configuring options
- Generating code coverage

Running tests

If you followed *Chapter 1, Installing PHPUnit*, you should have PHPUnit installed. You can test this by running the following command line:

```
phpunit --version
```

You should see an output similar to the following result:

```
PHPUnit 3.7.30 by Sebastian Bergmann.
```

If you see a command not found, or a similar error, please see *Chapter 1, Installing PHPUnit*, on how to install PHPUnit; this error means that PHPUnit has not been installed correctly.

```
developer@precise64: ~
developer@precise64:~$ phpunit
The program 'phpunit' is currently not installed.  To run 'phpunit' please ask your
administrator to install the package 'phpunit'
developer@precise64:~$ 
```

With PHPUnit, you can specify what exactly you want to run, a test case or all the tests, or what to include or exclude.

To run all tests in a test case (the `test` class), just provide the filename as the first parameter, as shown in the following command line:

```
phpunit UserTest.php
```

To run all tests from a directory, just provide the directory name as the first parameter, as shown in the following command line:

```
phpunit ./Tests
```

> If you see an error such as **PHP Fatal error: Cannot redeclare class...** when running all tests in a directory, please check the class name, as it looks like a class with the same name was already loaded.

In this case, PHPUnit, by default, loads all classes with the suffix `Test.php`.

Processing test results

Let's take the test from the previous chapter for the `User` class, `UserTest`. When you run the test, you should get a result similar to the following result:

```
PHPUnit 3.7.30 by Sebastian Bergmann.


...
```

```
Time: 60 ms, Memory: 3.75Mb

OK (3 tests, 6 assertions)
```

This is standard output, but it contains some very important information. The first line tells you what version of PHPUnit you have installed; in this case 3.7.30.

Three dots mean three tests passed; a dot is the mark for a success status.

The third line tells you how long the execution took (60 ms) and memory usage (3.75Mb). Memory usage is important because when you execute hundreds of tests, PHPUnit might need at least a few hundred MBs.

And the last line tells you if all tests were executed successfully (OK), and how many tests (3) and assertions (6) were executed.

Test statuses

You might say there is not much interesting here, but that's not exactly true. The test can end up with the following results:

- .: As you can see in our case, a dot means the test is successful
- F: You get this result when a test has failed, or an assertion didn't match
- E: You get this result when an error is triggered during test execution
- S: You get this result when the test is skipped
- I: You get this result when the test is incomplete or not implemented yet

To see exactly what each result means, let's create a simple test case, which will return all these results as shown in the following code snippet:

```php
<?php

class ResultTest extends PHPUnit_Framework_TestCase
{
    public function testSucceeds()
    {
        $this->assertEquals(2, 2/1);
    }

    public function testFails()
    {
        $this->assertEquals(1, 2/1);
    }
```

```
        public function testError()
        {
            $this->assertEquals(2, 2/0);
        }

        public function testSkipped()
        {
            $this->markTestSkipped('We don\'t want to test is now');
            $this->assertEquals(2, 2/1);
        }

        public function testIncomplete()
        {
            $this->markTestIncomplete('Needs to be implemented');
            $this->assertEquals(2, 2/1);
        }
    }
```

To get more information, you can run PHPUnit with switch --verbose, which tells you a bit more about how the tests were executed, as shown in the following command line:

```
>phpunit --verbose ResultTest.php
Test.php
PHPUnit 3.7.30 by Sebastian Bergmann.

.FESI

Time: 30 ms, Memory: 3.75Mb

There was 1 error:

1) ResultTest::testError
Division by zero

ResultTest.php:17

--



There was 1 failure:
```

```
1) ResultTest::testFails
Failed asserting that 2 matches expected 1.

ResultTest.php:12


--



There was 1 incomplete test:

1) ResultTest::testIncomplete
Needs to be implemented

ResultTest.php:28


--



There was 1 skipped test:

1) ResultTest::testSkipped
We don't want to test is now

ResultTest.php:22

FAILURES!
Tests: 5, Assertions: 2, Failures: 1, Errors: 1, Incomplete: 1, Skipped:
1.
```

We want our tests to succeed. The test fails (F) on line 12; this means the expected and actual results didn't match. On line 17, we caused a division by zero error (E). Then there is incomplete (I) and skipped (S); their usage might not be as obvious as the others so let's explain it.

Incomplete usually means you didn't write the test yet. The difference between leaving an empty test and marking it as incomplete is that the empty test would be marked as passed without any warning — @todo something needs to be done about this test.

`Skipped` means that the test wasn't executed. You can mark a test or even a test case as skipped, for example, when you have written an integration test calling API and you want to run it only manually, not as often as possible as with other unit tests. But there is also another possibility when the test can be skipped. You can use annotations and set required extensions or a version of PHP for tests:

```
/**
 * @requires extension pdo_sqlite
 */
```

If the extension is not loaded, the test is going to be skipped. Other requirements are also available, which you can specify as follows:

- **PHP**: This is the minimum required PHP version. For example, check out the following command line:

  `@requires PHP 5.4.6`

- **PHPUnit**: This is the minimum required PHPUnit version. For example, check out the following command line:

  `@requires PHPUnit 3.7`

- **function**: This requirement uses `function_exists` to detect whether a function is available in your code or in a loaded extension. For example, check out the following command line:

  `@requires function Imagick::readImage`

- **extension**: This indicates the required PHP extension that needs to be loaded using the following command line:

  `@requires extension pdo_sqlite`

Command-line switches

Switch is an extra parameter that will affect how tests are executed. The PHPUnit command-line tools offer many switches. To see all the available switches, just run the following command line:

`>phpunit --help`

You will now see help for the PHPUnit command-line tool, including all available switches. The list is pretty long, but let's explore some of the most important switch groups by their categories.

Logging results

When you run tests on the command line, you see results on the screen. But very often tests are run by automated tests or a continuous integration server. In this case, you need to log results into a file, and then process these files to display results or notify developers if tests fail. The following are the command-line switches:

- `--log-junit`: With this switch, results are stored in the Java JUnit format. Why is this handy for PHP? It's more or less a standard way to store test results and many tools can process these files. We will see later in *Chapter 13, Continuous Integration*, how to use it with a Jenkins server.

- `--log-json`: This might be another option, because JSON files are very easy to process. The disadvantage compared to the JUnit format is that JSON, by default, doesn't have a fixed structure or an easy way to validate data.

Code coverage

Code coverage is a process that detects usage of your code when you execute tests; simply put, how much code is executed when tests run. Later in this chapter, we try to generate code coverage for our tests, because it's very handy and also fun to see the results.

- `--coverage-clover`: This is similar to the JUnit logging format. Clover is a Java application that generates code coverage, and this format is XML-format compatible with Clover code coverage.

- `--coverage-html`: This generates code coverage for HTML files that you can publish and instantly have results.

- `--coverage-php`: This generates a serialized `PHP_CodeCoverage` object for a file. This might come in handy when you want to use it in your application.

- `--coverage-text`: This generates code coverage results in text files.

Including and excluding tests from the execution

Sometimes you don't want to run all of your tests. You might have a different set of tests and you might want to run just some of them, for example, unit tests after every commit as a post-commit hook and integration tests once an hour. If you want to include or exclude tests from execution, PHPUnit has a few switches that will help:

- `--filter`: Using this you can specify a pattern that selects tests to be executed. For example, check out the following command line:

```
>phpunit --debug --filter Validation UserTest.php
```

- `--testsuite`: This is similar to `--filter`. You can specify a filter that will include only test suites matching this pattern.

- `--group`: This can be used to set a group to which a test belongs by using annotations. Check out the following lines of code:

```
/**
 * @group math
 */
public function testOnePlusOne()
```

- `--exclude-group`: In the same way as `--group`, you can specify which group to exclude from execution.

- `--list-groups`: This lists all available groups.

- `--test-suffix`: Using this you can specify a test suffix. By default, it uses `Test.php`.

When to stop the test execution

Tests should be independent. But sometimes, just one error might be enough to decide if tests should stop or continue when a test doesn't pass. You can set when a test execution should be stopped by using the following switches:

- `--stop-on-error`: This stops execution if an error occurs (recoverable error not fatal error)

- `--stop-on-failure`: This stops PHPUnit execution when the first test fails

- `--stop-on-skipped`: This stops execution when any test is marked as skipped

- `--stop-on-incomplete`: This stops execution when any test is marked as incomplete

Configuration options

The following list is the last group of switches that are configuration options. You should definitely know these.

- `--strict`: This switches PHPUnit to the strict mode. Don't mix this with PHP `E_STRICT`.

- `--verbose`: PHPUnit returns more detailed information. For example, when a test fails, it gives the line number where it failed.

- `--debug`: This displays extra debugging information during test execution.

- `--process-isolation`: This is used to run each test in a separate process. It helps if you are having problems with memory usage, but it's much slower.

- `--no-globals-backup`: This switches to disable backup and restore $_GLOBAL variables before each test.

- `--static-backup`: This backs up and restores static class properties before each test.

- `--bootstrap`: This is a very useful switch to set the bootstrap file, very often containing the class loader.

- `--configuration`: This reads the XML configuration file (usually phpunit.xml) containing a test configuration.

- `--no-configuration`: This ignores the default configuration file (phpunit.xml).

- `--include-path`: This prepends your PHP files' path with another set of include paths.

- `-d key=value`: This changes the configuration to loaded php.ini. The key is the value from this file.

Code coverage analysis

Code coverage checks the lines that execute when you run PHPUnit tests. You can tell which code was executed and which wasn't. The aim is to have as much code coverage as possible, to have tested all possible scenarios, and execute the entire code to make sure there are no hidden bugs. In real life, it might be difficult to have 100 percent code coverage, but even 75 percent is considered decent code coverage.

To calculate code coverage, PHPUnit uses the Xdebug extension, which was mentioned as the recommended extension in *Chapter 1*, *Installing PHPUnit*, during PHPUnit installation.

Let's try to run code coverage for tests `UserManagerTest.php` and `UserTest` from the previous chapter. We get the following results:

```
>phpunit --coverage-text ./
PHPUnit 3.7.30 by Sebastian Bergmann.


........


Time: 536 ms, Memory: 5.25Mb


OK (8 tests, 12 assertions)
```

```
Code Coverage Report
   2014-04-05 23:25:29


  Summary:
   Classes: 0.00% (0/3)
   Methods: 41.67% (5/12)
   Lines:   87.04% (47/54)


\Application::User
   Methods: 100.00% ( 4/ 4)    Lines:   95.00% ( 19/ 20)
\Application::UserManager
   Methods: 100.00% ( 3/ 3)    Lines:   96.55% ( 28/ 29)
```

We get 96.55 percent code coverage for the `UserManager` class and 95.0 percent for the `User` class. It's not bad, but why not 100 percent?

There is a very easy way to find out. Previously, we generated code coverage results as text. But if you use HTML output, you get great detailed results where you can see exactly which part of the code wasn't executed. The only difference is that you need to add an extra parameter to export HTML files, as shown in the following command line:

```
>phpunit --coverage-html c:/temp/codeCoverage ./
PHPUnit 3.7.30 by Sebastian Bergmann.


........


Time: 439 ms, Memory: 5.25Mb


OK (8 tests, 12 assertions)


Generating code coverage report in HTML format ... done
```

PHPUnit creates a report in the HTML format. When you open `index.html` in the web browser, you will see a similar output as shown in the following screenshot:

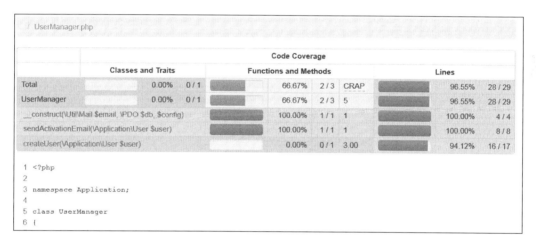

	Code Coverage					
	Lines		Functions and Methods		Classes and Traits	
Total	87.04%	47 / 54	41.67%	5 / 12	0.00%	0 / 3
Mail.php	0.00%	0 / 5	0.00%	0 / 5	0.00%	0 / 1
User.php	95.00%	19 / 20	75.00%	3 / 4	0.00%	0 / 1
UserManager.php	96.55%	28 / 29	66.67%	2 / 3	0.00%	0 / 1

Legend

Low: 0% to 35%   Medium: 35% to 70%   High: 70% to 100%

Generated by PHP_CodeCoverage 1.2.16 using PHP 5.3.28 and PHPUnit 3.7.30 at Sat Apr 5 23:30:40 BST 2014.

You see a list of tested classes and code coverage statics. You can click on the class name and see detailed statistics for each class. In the following screenshot, you can see details of the UserManager class:

/ UserManager.php

	Classes and Traits		Functions and Methods			Lines	
					Code Coverage		
Total	0.00%	0 / 1	66.67%	2 / 3	CRAP	96.55%	28 / 29
UserManager	0.00%	0 / 1	66.67%	2 / 3	5	96.55%	28 / 29
__construct(\Util\Mail $email, \PDO $db, $config)			100.00%	1 / 1	1	100.00%	4 / 4
sendActivationEmail(\Application\User $user)			100.00%	1 / 1	1	100.00%	8 / 8
createUser(\Application\User $user)			0.00%	0 / 1	3.00	94.12%	16 / 17

```php
1  <?php
2
3  namespace Application;
4
5  class UserManager
6  {
```

For this class, you will see similar statistics with one extra piece of information, which is CRAP.

The **Change Risk Anti-Patterns (CRAP)** index and the number tell you how complex the code is and how big a risk is it going to be to change this code. A lower number means better code, lower risk when changing this code.

Another helpful feature of the HTML code coverage is to visualize code execution. The green color lines indicate code that was executed, red color lines indicate code that wasn't executed, and yellow color lines indicate dead code that is never executed, as shown in the following screenshot:

```
55
56          if ($statement->execute())
57          {
58              $user->userId = $this->db->lastInsertId();
59              $this->sendActivationEmail($user);
60
61              return true;
62          }
63          else
64          {
65              throw new \Exception('User wasn\'t saved: '.implode(':',$statement->errorInfo()));
66          }
67
68          return false;
69      }
```

Legend

| Executed | Not Executed | Dead Code |

Generated by PHP_CodeCoverage 1.2.16 using PHP 5.3.28 and PHPUnit 3.7.30 at Sat Apr 5 23:30:40 BST 2014.

Summary

The PHPUnit command-line tool is a powerful tool, which can do much more than just execute tests. It's good to know the options it offers because many tools and applications depend on the PHPUnit command-line tool running in the background, and if you know what you can expect, it's much easier to configure and use it.

But of course, it's also a way to run tests directly and to see what else you can find out about your code. Code coverage is a brilliant way to visualize your efforts to have as much code tested as possible and to see where the gaps are.

Try an HTML code coverage report; it really helps you visualize what are the tests doing and how well your code is tested. It's important to see that all the efforts make sense and the progress you have made. It's important for you, as a developer, for your project manager, and of course, for the customers as well.

In the next chapter, you will see how to ensure that there is a well known and fixed environment in which tests are run so that the results are repeatable, also known as test fixture, and how PHPUnit helps with setting up a test environment.

Test Isolation and Interaction

6

So far, we've seen PHPUnit tests that have been designed as isolated tests, and this is how it should be. In the perfect world, each test should test just an isolated piece of code. Sometimes you face a situation that needs you to repeat the same code execution for each test, for example, to set up same objects for each test. This is called test fixtures. It creates a known state or fixed state for tests or also known as the test context.

PHPUnit offers various ways to share data between tests. Each of them is useful in different scenarios, but please keep in mind the golden rule of unit testing—isolation. If your test is not independent and repeatable, then the chance that you will have negative fails is much higher and your tests will become limited and possibly less reliable and useful.

In this chapter, we are going to explore the following topics:

- Test fixtures
- Global state
- Test dependencies
- Data providers

Even though these are different things for different situations, it is good to have them all in one place to see their purpose, usage, and limitations.

Test fixtures

When you are setting up a known state for tests, you have the following two options:

- Set it before each test case class, runs once before and/or after each test case
- Set it before each test method, runs before each test and/or after each test

Before and after each test method

The setUp() and tearDown() methods are the most common ones used to set a known state for tests and do clean up after the test is executed. By definition, it is called the fixture or test context — known state for tests.

The setUp() method is called before every test is executed. Each test method has set up know state and all required settings; you don't have to duplicate the same code for similar tests.

The tearDown() method is opposite to setUp(), and it is called when the test finishes. For example, when working with a file, it might be placed where fclose (closes an open file pointer) is required.

 There is one problem with the tearDown() method. If you have a bug in the code causing a fatal error, tearDown() will not be called. This is similar to normal PHP error handling. You can use set_error_handler and set_exception_handler to be your handlers, and handle errors efficiently in your application. However, when a fatal error happens, PHP stops execution and the script simply dies.

The setUp() method is very useful when you need to set up complex objects for tests. However, to see how it works, let's use one very simple example as follows:

```php
<?php
class CounterTest extends PHPUnit_Framework_TestCase
{
    private static $countFrom = 1;
    private $result = 0;

    public function setUp()
    {
        $this->result = self::$countFrom;
    }

    public function testAdd()
    {
        $this->result += 1;
        $this->assertEquals(2, $this->result);
    }

    public function testTakeAway()
    {
```

```php
        $this->result -= 1;
        $this->assertEquals(0, $this->result);
    }
}
```

As you can see, the `result` property has a default value of zero. Before each test is executed, the `setUp()` method is called and the `result` value is set to `$countFrom`, which in this case is one. This is a very simple example, but the `setUp()` method can do the complex setup necessary for each test case without the need to duplicate the code.

Before and after each test suite class

The `setUpBeforeClass()` and `tearDownAfterClass()` methods are the other two methods that can be used to set up a test context. The difference between `setUpBeforeClass()` and `tearDownAfterClass()` is that these methods are executed only when the `testCase` class is loaded and not before each test as `setUp()` or after test execution as `tearDown()`. This can be useful when you need to set up something such as a connection to the database. There is no point connecting to the database before each test when just one connection is needed for all tests.

Just to demonstrate how it works, let's extend the previous example as follows:

```php
<?php
class CounterTest extends PHPUnit_Framework_TestCase
{
    private static $countFrom = 1;
    private $result = 0;

    public static function setUpBeforeClass()
    {
        self::$countFrom = 2;
    }

    public function setUp()
    {
        $this->result = self::$countFrom;
    }

    public function testAdd()
    {
        $this->result += 1;
        $this->assertEquals(3, $this->result);
    }
}
```

```
public function testTakeAway()
{
    $this->result -= 1;
    $this->assertEquals(1, $this->result);
}
}
```

This example demonstrates how `setUpBeforeClass()` works. You can see that `self::$countFrom` value changes; it doesn't start with one but two, because `setUpBeforeClass()` was called only once, but `setUp()` was called twice before each test.

Global state

Global state is something that you know from PHP scripts very well. PHP contains a number of predefined variables that you use. Some of these can be backed up and restored before and after every test run. PHPUnit can store some of the global variables such as `$GLOBALS`, `$_ENV`, `$_POST`, `$_GET`, `$_COOKIE`, `$_SERVER`, `$_FILES`, and `$_REQUEST`. As you can see, one of the most important variables `$_SESSION` is missing there, which means PHPUnit will not store and restore your `$_SESSION` data.

Before relying on global state and sharing data between tests, you should know one thing, global state is EVIL! Again, the point of unit testing is isolation; tests should be fast, independent, and reliable. When you start sharing data quickly, these rules are broken and tests become unreliable and unhelpful. However, on the other hand, there are situations where testing legacy code and setting up global variables might be the only way to set up a known environment state.

From the testing point of view, some problems caused by relying on global state are as follows:

- **Unwanted side effects**: One piece of code changes global state, while another piece not expecting this change, behaves differently
- **Hidden dependencies**: It is difficult to spot required dependency, which is a high risk when changing the code
- **Not clearly defined responsibility**: It is difficult to figure out how to test when code might change behavior depending on change, which is difficult to predict and replicate

PHPUnit offers configuration options to switch global variables backup on or off. This could be done on the command-line switch, as mentioned in *Chapter 5, Running Tests from the Command Line*, in the test configuration file (`phpunit.xml`) or in the code. By overriding property, you can change it on test case level as shown in the following line of code:

```
protected $backupGlobals = true;
```

An alternative is to use annotations is as follows:

```
/**
 * @backupGlobals disabled
 */
```

This means anything stored in $GLOBALS[] will be accessible in the next test.

You can restrict what will be restored by adding it to `backupGlobalsBlacklist` as shown in the following line of code. Then it will be ignored.

```
protected $backupGlobalsBlacklist = array('variable');
```

All data that needs to be stored and restored needs to be serializable, so there should be resource variables such as a database connection or a file pointer.

Another way to share data is the usage of `backupStaticAttributes` as shown in the following line of code:

```
protected $backupStaticAttributes = true;
```

Alternatively, you can use annotations as shown in the following lines of code:

```
/**
 * @backupStaticAttributes disabled
 */
```

Similar to using `backupGlobalsBlacklist`, you can exclude static properties being backed up/restored, as shown in the following line of code:

```
protected $backupGlobalsBlacklist = array('propertyA');
```

 All of these configuration options need to override the parent PHPUnit_Framework_TestCase class; their usage in setUp() has no effect.

To demonstrate how you can modify and use global variables, the following code snippet is a small example:

```php
<?php
/**
 * @backupGlobals enabled
 */
class GlobalTest extends PHPUnit_Framework_TestCase
{
    public static function setUpBeforeClass()
    {
        $config = new stdClass();
        $config->date = new DateTime("today");

        $GLOBALS['config'] = $config;
    }

    public function testToday()
    {
        $today   = new DateTime("today");
        $this->assertTrue($today == $GLOBALS['config']->date);
        //not affecting global state, backupGlobals is enabled
        $GLOBALS['config']->date = new DateTime("tomorrow");
    }

    /**
     * @backupGlobals disabled
     */
    public function testTomorrow()
    {
        $tomorrow   = new DateTime("tomorrow");
        $this->assertTrue($tomorrow > $GLOBALS['config']->date);
        //will change global value
        $GLOBALS['config']->date = $tomorrow;
    }

    public function testTomorrowIsolated()
    {
        $tomorrow   = new DateTime("tomorrow");
        $this->assertEquals($tomorrow, $GLOBALS['config']->date);
    }
}
```

When `backupGlobals` is disabled, then the value in `$GLOBALS['config']` changes, in our case to `tomorrow`; otherwise, it is restored and stays at today's date.

Test dependencies

Another way to share data between tests is to use the `@depends` annotation to specify when one test is depending on another. Also, one test can return a value that will be passed as an input parameter to the depending test. Sometimes, this is also called producer test and consumer test. The following code snippet is a simple example:

```php
<?php

class DependsTest extends PHPUnit_Framework_TestCase
{
    public function testArrayFill()
    {
        $testedArray = array_fill(0,11,1);
        $this->assertInternalType('array', $testedArray);

        return $testedArray;
    }

    /**
     * @param  array $inputArray
     * @return array
     * @depends testArrayFill
     */
    public function testPop(array $inputArray)
    {
        array_pop($inputArray);
        $this->assertEquals(10,count($inputArray));

        return $inputArray;
    }

    /**
     * @param  array $inputArray
     * @return array
     * @depends testPop
     */
    public function testSum(array $inputArray)
    {
        $this->assertEquals(10,array_sum($inputArray));
    }
}
```

In PHPUnit, you can't be sure in which order tests are going to be executed. But in this case, `testPop` is depending on `testArrayFill` and `testSum` is depending on `testPop`. So, `testArrayFill` will be called first and then the created array will be passed to `testPop`. One element will be removed from the array, and then the array will be passed to `testSum`. This way, you can set in which order the test will run and also pass parameters between tests.

Data providers

Data providers are very handy features. Each test can have an input parameter or multiple input parameters, and data provider is a magical method that will populate data for tests. This can be hardcoded or dynamic. To specify what a data provider for a test is, you must use the following annotation:

```
@dataProvider providerXY
```

Here, `providerXY` is the method name. The provider then must return an array of arrays or object implementing the `Iterator` interface, where each element is passed as an input to test using data provider. If you want to pass multiple parameters, then the array needs to have as many elements as the number of parameters you want to pass. If it sounds complicated, check out the following example:

```php
<?php

class DataProvidersTest extends PHPUnit_Framework_TestCase
{
    /**
     * @return array
     */
    public function providerArray()
    {
        $inputOne = array(1,2,3,4,5);
        $inputTwo = array(10,20,30,40,50);
        $inputThree = array(100,200,300,400,500);

        return array(array('inputArray' => $inputOne),
            array('inputArray' => $inputTwo),
            array('inputArray' => $inputThree));

    }

    /**
     * @param   array $inputArray
     * @dataProvider providerArray
```

```php
 */
public function testPop(array $inputArray)
{

    $expectedResult = count($inputArray)-1;
    array_pop($inputArray);
    $this->assertEquals($expectedResult,count($inputArray));

}

/**
 * @param  array $inputArray
 * @dataProvider providerArray
 */
public function testSum(array $inputArray)
{
  $expectedResult = 0;

  for ($i = 0; $i < count($inputArray); $i++) {
      $expectedResult += $inputArray[$i];
  }

  $this->assertEquals($expectedResult,array_sum($inputArray));
}
}
```

This is a previous example slightly modified to use a data provider. Data provider is a method `providerArray()` that generates array with random data.

What is interesting is that tests are actually going to be executed three times, because data provider returns an array with three elements. You can imagine that PHPUnit is iterating over the returned array and executes tests with each element of this array as input parameter.

When you run the test with the `--debug` switch, you will see something similar to the following command line:

```
>phpunit --debug DataProvidersTest.php
PHPUnit 3.7.30 by Sebastian Bergmann.


Starting test 'DataProvidersTest::testPop with data set #0 (array(1,
  2, 3, 4, 5))'.


....
```

Summary

PHPUnit offers several different ways to set up test fixtures and share data. Each of them is handy in different scenarios.

The `setUp()` and `tearDown()` methods are two methods that are often used, necessary for test fixtures. The `setUpBeforeClass()` and `tearDownAfterClass()` methods are similar and can be very handy when setting up shared resources for a test case.

Backing up and restoring global state could be crucial when you test legacy code. Test dependencies can be very useful, for example, when you want to split a very complex test into several tests.

And data provider is a very efficient way to create and pass data to the tests. Data could be dynamic, even loaded from a database when you do integration testing.

All of these PHPUnit features are in one chapter so that you see them together and understand the differences between them.

In the next chapter, we look closer at how to organize tests and how to use the `phpunit.xml` configuration file, which is a very powerful and efficient way to organize tests and configure how tests are executed.

7
Organizing Tests

So far we have been writing tests but were not worried how to organize them, because each test should be independent and repeatable. So, it didn't matter when and how you ran it, you should always get the same result. But when you have more tests, the need to organize them presents itself. They might be all unit tests that you run with the same configuration, but sooner or later, you will have more than one set of tests, which you need to run differently with different configurations. Unit tests are going to run very often, because they are fast and it is good to be notified about problems as soon as possible. However, you will have integration tests and functional tests, which are going to be much slower and you will want to run them, for example, every four hours. Then you will need to split the tests.

PHPUnit offers a way to configure tests and how they are going to be executed with the help of an XML configuration file, usually called `phpunit.xml`. In this chapter, we are going to explore how to use this powerful tool and how it can help to organize tests.

When you run multiple sets of tests, then you need to prepare the environment for the tests. An easy and efficient way is to use a bootstrap file. We are going to see how to use bootstrap files to set up the environment and use a class loader.

The PHPUnit XML configuration file

The `phpunit.xml` file is the default name for the PHPUnit XML configuration file. When you run PHPUnit from the command line, it checks if the file is available, and then tries to use it to execute the tests. The `phpunit.xml` file is the default and recommended filename, but you can use any file name you like. In the command line, you need to use the switch `-c` or `--configuration XX`, where XX is the name of your configuration file, as shown in the following command line:

```
>phpunit --configuration config.xml
```

In *Chapter 5, Running Tests from the Command Line*, we saw many switches that you can use when running tests. Most of these switches you can use as an attribute in the configuration file instead of passing them as a switch on the command line. Of course, it's up to you if you prefer to write a simple script that will hold all the switches you use, but a better place for them is the XML configuration file, because you have all things in one place and by storing it under the version control system, you can track changes and create a history.

The following code snippet is a simple example of what the XML configuration file looks like:

```
<?xml version="1.0" encoding="UTF-8" ?>
<phpunit backupGlobals="true" backupStaticAttributes="false"
strict="false" verbose="true">
  <php>
    <includePath>./Pear</includePath>
    <ini name="memory_limit" value="128M"/>
    <env name="ENVIRONMENT" value="test"/>
    <post name="is_test" value="1"/>
  </php>
</phpunit>
```

In the `<phpunit>` element, you can use attributes that are matching or are very similar to the command-line switches. The following are the attributes and their command-line alternatives:

- `backupGlobals` and `--no-globals-backup`
- `backupStaticAttributes` and `--static-backup`
- `strict` and `--strict`
- `verbose` and `--verbose`

The following `<php>` elements allow you to set up test environments for tests:

- The `<includePath>` element is used to call the `set_include_path()` function
- The `<ini>` element is used for `ini_set` and setting up PHP configuration values
- The `<env>` element is for setting up environment variables
- The `<post>` element sets, in our case, `$_POST['is_test'] = 1`

In the same way as setting up post values, you can set values in `$_GET`, `$_COOKIES` and all global variables except `$_SESSION`.

Test listeners

PHPUnit listeners allow you to hook into test execution process. You can create your test listener and, for example, monitor tests execution by writing results to the database.

Your listener class needs to implement the PHPUnit_Framework_TestListener interface, as shown in the following code snippet:

```
interface PHPUnit_Framework_TestListener
{
  public function addError(PHPUnit_Framework_Test $test,
    Exception $e, $time);
  public function addFailure(PHPUnit_Framework_Test $test,
   PHPUnit_Framework_AssertionFailedError $e, $time);
  public function addIncompleteTest(PHPUnit_Framework_Test $test,
    Exception $e, $time);
  public function addSkippedTest(PHPUnit_Framework_Test $test,
    Exception $e, $time);
  public function startTestSuite(PHPUnit_Framework_TestSuite
    $suite);
  public function endTestSuite(PHPUnit_Framework_TestSuite
    $suite),
  public function startTest(PHPUnit_Framework_Test $test);
  public function endTest(PHPUnit_Framework_Test $test, $time);
}
```

Each of these methods is called when specific event is triggered such as startTest or startTestSuite.

In phpunit.xml, you can use the listeners tag to attach your listeners as shown in the following code snippet:

```
<listeners>
  <listener class="SomeListener">
    <arguments>
    <string>For listener constructor</string>
    </arguments>
  </listener>
</listeners>
```

In this case, the SomeListener class is attached, and the string parameter is passed to constructor.

Configuring the code coverage

In *Chapter 5, Running Tests from the Command Line*, we saw how to generate code coverage. However, very often, you would want to specify what exactly should be or shouldn't be included in the code coverage. Usually, you are interested only in code coverage for your classes, and you would want to exclude third-party libraries from the code coverage to have a clear picture about your code.

In `phpunit.xml`, you can use the `filter` tag to specify what is included or excluded from code coverage by using `blacklist` to exclude files and `whitelist` to include files, as shown in the following code snippet:

```
<filter>
  <blacklist>
    <directory suffix=".php">vendor/zendframework</directory>
    <directory suffix=".php">vendor/symfony</directory>
  </blacklist>
  <whitelist>
    directory suffix=".php">src</directory>       </whitelist>
</filter>
```

Where to store tests

In *Chapter 3, Tests And What They're All About*, it was briefly mentioned that every class should be mirrored by a test class with the same name but with `Test` added to the name. For example, `Util.php` and `UtilTest.php` are stored in the same file structure but at different locations for both classes and tests, which is similar to the following structure:

```
.
|-- src
|    '-- library
|         '-- DB
|              '-- User.php
|              '-- Group.php
|         '-- Permission
|              '-- User.php
|              '-- Group.php
|              '-- Manager.php
|         '-- Util
|              '-- File.php
|              '-- Password.php
'-- tests
     '-- library
```

```
'-- DB
      '-- UserTest.php
      '-- GroupTest.php
'-- Permission
      '-- UserTest.php
      '-- GroupTest.php
      '-- ManagerTest.php
'-- Util
      '-- FileTest.php
      '-- PasswordTest.php
```

This is a great starting point, and it is good to stick to this structure.

The place where `phpunit.xml` really shines is when you need to organize tests more granularly and decide what is included or excluded from test execution.

There are two basic ways to organize tests using the configuration file as follows:

- Test suites
- Groups included or excluded from execution

One of the reasons why tests are split into multiple sets is to separate unit tests and integration tests. Integration tests are usually much slower to execute, and you might need to set up the environment for them, such as database structures or the like. Because of this, you might want to run them differently than unit tests, which are fast, and it is a good habit to execute them as a post-commit or post-receive hook in the version control system to verify committed code to the repository and immediately notify the developer who is pushing the bad code.

Obviously, you can do it by storing them in different locations, but then it might be tricky to mirror class and package structures and keep everything organized. This is the moment when group and test suites help.

Test suites

A test suite is a way to organize tests into batches. You can have multiple test suites in your configuration file. You can specify what is included in each test suite (file or directory) or what is excluded. Check out the following example:

```xml
<?xml version="1.0" encoding="UTF-8" ?>
<phpunit>
  <testsuites>
    <testsuite name="Permissions">
      <directory>./library/Permissions</directory>
```

```
        <exclude>./library/Permissions/ManagerTest.php</exclude>
      </testsuite>
      <testsuite name="Util">
        <file>./library/Util/PasswordTest.php</file>
      </testsuite>
    </testsuites>
  </phpunit>
```

This example uses the file structure, which we used previously, and demonstrates how to include or exclude tests in test suites.

The test suite `Permissions` contains all tests in the `./library/Permissions` directory, except `ManagerTest.php`. The `Util` test suite runs only tests in the `PasswordTest.php` suite. For the rest of the tests (package `DB` and `FileTest.php`), we will create another configuration file similar to the following example:

```
<?xml version="1.0" encoding="UTF-8" ?>
<phpunit>
  <testsuites>
    <testsuite name="DB">
      <directory>./library/DB</directory>
    </testsuite>
    <testsuite name="Util">
      <file>./library/Util/FileTest.php</file>
    </testsuite>
  </testsuites>
</phpunit>
```

Groups

We have seen how to group tests in *Chapter 5, Running Tests from the Command Line*. Simply, each test can be marked to which group or groups it belongs by using annotations, as shown in the following code snippet:

```
/**
 * @group security
 */
public function testCheckPassword(){}

/**
 * @group security
 * @group user
 */
public function testUpdatePassword(){}
```

You can get a list of all groups by running PHPUnit from the command line with the switch `--list-groups`.

In the configuration file, you then can specify which groups should be included or excluded from execution:

```xml
<?xml version="1.0" encoding="UTF-8" ?>
<phpunit>
  <groups>
    <include>
      <group>security</group>
    </include>
    <exclude>
      <group>user</group>
    </exclude>
  </groups>
</phpunit>
```

Using the bootstrap file

Bootstrap is a file that is executed before the tests. A bootstrap file (usually `bootstrap.php`) contains a test-specific configuration such as setting up the include path, environment variables, class loader, and anything else that you need. You've seen that by using the `phpunit.xml` configuration file, you can even set PHP configuration options, but it is cleaner to do it in PHP code, which is going to be just as possible as your application configuration.

The following code snippet is a simple example of how this bootstrap file can look:

```php
<?php
ini_set('memory_limit', '512M');
error_reporting( E_ALL | E_STRICT );

// Define application environment
defined('APPLICATION_ENV') || define('APPLICATION_ENV',
  (getenv('APPLICATION_ENV') ? getenv('APPLICATION_ENV') :
  'development'));

spl_autoload_register('loadClass');

function loadClass($className)
{
    $base_dir = __DIR__ . '/src/';
    $test_dir = __DIR__ . '/tests/';
```

```
        set_include_path($base_dir . PATH_SEPARATOR . $test_dir);

        $file = str_replace('\\', '/', $className) . '.php';

        if(file_exists($file))
        {
            require_once $file;
        }
    }
```

The function `loadClass($className)` is a class loader function used to load any used class by registering it and then calling `spl_autoload_register('loadClass')`. The only difference between bootstrap for tests and application is `/tests/` is added to the include path for tests.

Summary

When storing tests, it's important to have clear rules about where and how to store tests. File structure, mirroring packages, and classes' structures are the recommended ways to do it. However, when you want to execute tests, you might need to split them into multiple batches, which you are going to execute differently. Here the XML configuration file really helps to configure how tests are going to be executed and how to organize them by using test suites or groups. However, when configuring tests, don't forget about the bootstrap file, which is a really simple and powerful tool that can be used to set up the test environment.

In the next chapter, we will see the dark art. Test doubles is the method we should use to replace code with code used only for tests. Why would you do that? You will see and will agree that it's one of the coolest PHPUnit features in the next chapter.

8
Using Test Doubles

PHPUnit offers ways to modify the code on the fly and create test doubles. This means that you can create a double of your code (class), which might look and behave the same way, but it's going to be a simplified version that will reduce the complexity and solve dependencies. After reading how to write good tests, this doesn't sound right. You want to be sure that the executed code works as expected, but when you replace a part of the code, how can you be sure that it will work?

The reason for replacing a part of the code is to eliminate dependencies on other code, databases, and third-party APIs. When you have to use them, it's not a unit test but a functional or an integration test. However, you should always start with unit tests. Take each unit step as a cornerstone on which your application stands; these cornerstones must be solid blocks on which you can build the code. The code needs to be tested in isolation to verify its functionality.

By using test doubles, you can replace the complex code and simply focus on testing the isolated code, without worrying about how to set up a test environment or complex structures required by the tested code.

With test doubles, there are a few different types that you can use, and each of them is handy in different situations. When talking about theory and distinguishing between types of test doubles, this could be confusing—especially for developers who haven't used them before. Sometimes there is a very thin, even blurred line between them, and it may be tricky to say which exact type is used. Once you understand how it works, you will know when to use it, without worrying too much about what it is exactly.

The following are the most common types of test doubles:

- **Dummy**: This is just an empty shell which is not called or used; however, it is used only when you need to pass things such as required arguments.
- **Fake**: This imitates the real object functionality, but is written and used only for tests.

- **Stub**: This returns predefined values for the method that is called or null for other methods. Sometimes, they are also called indirect input to the tests.
- **Spy**: This is similar to the stub. It just remembers returned values that can be verified later.
- **Mock**: The simplest definition of this double is a stub with expectations. An expectation is the specification of the method on when and how it should be called during a test execution.

As you can see, this may well be a bit confusing if you haven't used test doubles before. You will see that it's much easier than it sounds once you read the examples.

To make things easier and to get rid of the annoying `require_once` statement, let's use, for these examples, the `bootstrap.php` file with a very simple class loader, as shown in the following code snippet:

```php
<?php
spl_autoload_register('loadClass');

function loadClass($className)
{
    $file = dirname(__FILE__) . DIRECTORY_SEPARATOR . $className .
'.php';

    if(file_exists($file))
        require_once $file;
}
```

All that it does is loads the class from the same directory, nothing sophisticated.

Creating test doubles

PHPUnit offers two basic ways of creating test doubles, which are as follows:

- $double = $this->getMock('MyClass');
- $double = $this->getMockBuilder('MyClass')->getMock();

Both of them do the same thing—create a test double—just in slightly different ways. The `getMock()` method accepts eight different (10 in Version 4) parameters, which affects how the double will be created. They are described as follows:

- `string $originalClassName`: This is a class name from which the double will be created.
- `array $methods`: This will replace all methods by default and will return `Null`. If the name of the methods are passed in an array, then only these methods will be replaced and the original methods stay untouched.

- array $arguments: These arguments are used for the original constructor.
- string $mockClassName: This indicates the class name for the created test double.
- boolean $callOriginalConstructor: This is used when you want to enable/disable the original constructor call.
- boolean $callOriginalClone: This is used when you want to enable/disable the original clone method usage.
- boolean $callAutoload: This is used when you want to disable __autoload() for loading classes.
- boolean $cloneArguments: This allows to enable/disable cloning of all object parameters.

PHPUnit Version 4 added two more arguments for test proxies, which are as follows:

- boolean $callOriginalMethods: This argument allows to call the original methods, when test double is used
- Object $proxyTarget: This calls the original object for the test proxy

The getMockBuilder() method does the exact same thing as the getMock() method, except instead of passing 10 arguments, you can use method chaining to set them up, as shown in the following code snippet:

```
$double = $this->getMockBuilder('MyClass')->enableOriginalClone()
    ->enableArgumentCloning()->getMock();
```

While creating a test double, it is good to know what will happen. PHPUnit uses reflection to create a modified version of your class, which will probably look similar but will behave as though it's configured to the original class.

Reflection is defined as the ability of the code to inspect, modify, and call other code at runtime. You can find more information about reflection in PHP at the following link:

http://www.php.net/manual/en/book.reflection.php

Let's use a very simple class (MockTester) to demonstrate what PHPUnit does when you use the getMock() or getMockBuilder() methods, as shown in the following code snippet:

```
<?php

class MockTester
{
```

```
        public function getOne()
        {
            return 1;
        }

        public function getTwo()
        {
            return 2;
        }
    }
```

Now, create a set of tests to demonstrate how mocking works in PHPUnit. As a first step, let's create a simple test double, as shown in the following code snippet:

```
        public function testOne()
        {
            $mockTester = $this->getMock('MockTester');
            $this->assertEquals(1, $mockTester->getOne());
            $this->assertEquals(2, $mockTester->getTwo());
        }
```

When you run this, it fails as shown in the following command-line output:

1) MockTesterTest::testOne

Failed asserting that null matches expected 1.

MockTesterTest.php:8

So, what happened? When you create a mock without the second parameter, $methods = array(), all the class methods are replaced simply with the NULL return.

However, let's see another slightly different example:

```
        public function testTwo()
        {
            $mockTester = $this->getMock('MockTester',
              array('getTwo'));
            $this->assertEquals(1, $mockTester->getOne());
            $this->assertEquals(2, $mockTester->getTwo());
        }
```

When you pass the method name, only the methods with these names are replaced; otherwise, the original methods are used, and sometimes this is called partial mock. The point is that in this case, you want to replace the method with a stub, where the replacement is executed for tests that imitate the original functionality.

When you run the test, you will get the following output:

```
2) MockTesterTest::testTwo
Failed asserting that null matches expected 2.
```

```
MockTesterTest.php:16
```

The following is an example where we replace the getOne() method, and when this method is called, it now returns three, not one, as shown in the following code snippet:

```
public function testThree()
{
    $mockTester = $this
        ->getMock('MockTester',array('getOne'));

    $mockTester->expects($this->any())->method('getOne')
        ->will($this->returnValue(3));

    $this->assertEquals(3, $mockTester->getOne());
    $this->assertEquals(2, $mockTester->getTwo());
}
```

In this case, we replaced the getOne() method with the implementation that is used only when the test is executed.

Test doubles in action

Enough of theory, let's have a look at a simple example that will show us where test doubles can be very useful.

Let's create an example that will demonstrate a simple Transaction class. It will take the passed data, create an XML request, send it to the third-party API, and log the request. This is quite a common situation. Let's keep this example simple, and see how you can use test doubles to write tests, as shown in the following code snippet:

```
<?php

class Transaction
{
    private $logger;
    private $client;
    private $data;
    private $response;
```

```php
    public function __construct(ILogger $logger, HttpClient $client,
array $data)
    {
        $this->logger = $logger;
        $this->client = $client;
        $this->data = $data;
    }

    public function prepareXMLRequest()
    {
        if(!isset($this->data['userId']))
        {
            throw new InvalidArgumentException('Missing userId');
        }

        if(!isset($this->data['items']) ||
          !is_array($this->data['items']))
        {
            throw new InvalidArgumentException('Missing items');
        }

        $requestXML = new SimpleXMLElement("<request></request>");
        $requestXML->addAttribute('userId', $this->data['userId']);
        $itemsXML = $requestXML->addChild('items');

        foreach ($this->data['items'] as $item)
        {
            $itemXML = $itemsXML->addChild('item');
            $itemXML->addAttribute('id', $item['id']);
            $itemXML->addAttribute('quantity', $item['quantity']);
        }

        return $requestXML->asXML();
    }

    public function sendRequest()
    {
        $xmlRequest = $this->prepareXMLRequest();
        $this->client->setRequest($xmlRequest);
        $this->logger->log($xmlRequest, ILogger::PRIORITY_INFO);
        $this->response = $this->client->send();
        return $this->response;
    }
```

```php
    public function wasSent()
    {
        return !empty($this->response);
    }
}
```

Now, let's go through the code.

```php
public function __construct(ILogger $logger, HttpClient $client,
    array $data)
```

The constructor requires three parameters. This way you can inject an external dependency into the class, and we have free hands while writing tests to decide about their implementation. Now, we are going to see different test doubles for these parameters.

The first argument, `ILogger $logger`, is a logger that will record requests. Usually, while sending a request to the third party, it is a good idea to record every request and response, especially while sending payments for example. In this case, just to keep things simple, we will log just the request. As the name suggests, the parameter specifies that `$logger` is of the type `ILogger`; usually, interface names start with the capital letter I. The following interface is very simple:

```php
<?php

Interface ILogger
{
    public function log($request, $priority);

    const PRIORITY_ERROR = 1;
    const PRIORITY_INFO = 2;
    const PRIORITY_WARNING = 3;
}
```

There is just one method to log the event, and it's up to the implementation to decide whether it's going to be a database, filesystem, or anything else. A simple database implementation could look like the following code snippet:

```php
<?php

class DBLogger implements ILogger
{
    private $db;

    public function __construct(\PDO $db)
```

```
    {
        $this->db = $db;
    }

    public function log($request, $priority)
    {
        $sql = "insert into transaction_log(priority, timestamp,
          data)
                values (:priority, :timestamp, :data)";

        $statement = $this->db->prepare($sql);

        $statement->bindParam(':priority', $priority);
        $statement->bindParam(':timestamp', time());
        $statement->bindParam(':data', $request);

        return $statement->execute();
    }
}
```

Using fake

This is something that would be immediately problematic for tests—connecting to the database. However, you are writing a unit test, and you don't want to connect anywhere! That's where an interface can be an advantage. You can create an implementation to be used only for tests, and in the test doubles' terminology, it's going to be fake. You can write the following code snippet; you don't need any PHPUnit support for it. It's just a very simple PHP code that basically does nothing, it only helps to create fake object for input parameters:

```
<?php

class FakeLogger implements ILogger
{
    public function log($request, $priority)
    {
        return true;
    }
}
```

Using stubs

The second constructor argument is HttpClient $client. This is going to be a very simple implementation using curl—a PHP extension to send a HTTP request. A very simple implementation could look like the following code snippet:

```php
<?php

class HttpClient
{
    private $url;
    private $request;

    public function __construct($url)
    {
        $this->url = $url;
    }

    public function setRequest($request)
    {
        $this->request = $request;
    }

    public function send()
    {
        if(!$this->request)
        {
            throw new InvalidArgumentException('Missing request
                body');
        }

        $curl = curl_init($this->url);
        curl_setopt($curl, CURLOPT_HEADER, 0);
        curl_setopt($curl, CURLOPT_RETURNTRANSFER, 1);
        curl_setopt($curl, CURLOPT_POSTFIELDS, array('xml' =>
          $this->request));

        $response = curl_exec($curl);
        curl_close($curl);

        if($response === false)
        {
            return false;
        }
```

```
        else{
            return true;
        }
    }
}
```

You can create a test double by using the PHPUnit `getMock()` method, as shown in the following line of code:

```
$client = $this->getMock('HttpClient');
```

As was mentioned earlier, PHPUnit provides the `getMock()` and `getMockBuilder()` methods to create test doubles. When you look at the code, you will see the following code snippet:

```
$this->client->setRequest($xmlRequest);
....
$this->response = $this->client->send();
return $this->response;
```

This is where the `client` object is involved. Obviously, you don't want to send the HTTP request; you merely want to focus on testing the `Transaction` class.

When you call the `getMock()` method with just one parameter and class name, you get only a fake class, and any called method returns just NULL.

However, looking back at the code, the following methods are called on the client object:

- `setRequest($xmlRequest)`
- `send()`

The `setRequest()` method is fine because you can use the original class code, but the `send()` method is problematic because it uses curl and sends an HTTP request. For tests, you have to replace this method with a stub to make the code easier and to allow you to test the `Transaction` class, as shown in the following code snippet:

```
$client = $this->getMock('HttpClient', array('send'),
    array('http://localhost'));

        $client->expects($this->any())->method('send')
            ->will($this->returnValue(true));
```

In this way, we created a `client` object; the second parameter was method name, and the third parameter was the parameter for a client constructor.

We then created a stub for the `send()` method to replace the original code with an HTTP call, which will return `true`.

So, the whole test for the `Transaction` class would look like the following code snippet:

```php
<?php

class TestTransaction extends PHPUnit_Framework_TestCase
{
    private $data;

    public function setUp()
    {
        $this->data = array('userId' => 1,'items' =>
            array('item'=> array('id' => 1, 'quantity' => 99)));
    }

    public function testPrepareXMLRequest()
    {
        $logger = new FakeLogger();
        $client = $this->getMock('HttpClient', array(),
            array('http://localhost'));
        $transaction = new Transaction($logger, $client, $this->data);

        $request = new SimpleXMLElement(
            $transaction->prepareXMLRequest());
        $item = $request->items->item[0];

        $this->assertEquals("1", $request['userId']);
        $this->assertEquals("1", $item['id']);
        $this->assertEquals("99", $item['quantity']);
    }

    /**
     * @expectedException InvalidArgumentException
     */
    public function testPrepareXMLRequestFail()
    {
        $logger = new FakeLogger();
        $client = $this->getMock('HttpClient', array(),
            array('http://localhost'));
```

```
        $dataMissingUserId = $this->data;
        unset($dataMissingUserId['userId']);

        $transaction = new Transaction($logger, $client,
          $dataMissingUserId);

        $xmlRequest = $transaction->prepareXMLRequest();
    }

    public function testSendRequest()
    {
        $logger = new FakeLogger();
        $client = $this->getMock('HttpClient', array('send'),
          array('http://localhost'));

        $client->expects($this->any())->method('send')
          ->will($this->returnValue(true));

        $transaction = new Transaction($logger, $client,
          $this->data);

        $this->assertFalse($transaction->wasSent());
        $this->assertTrue($transaction->sendRequest());
        $this->assertTrue($transaction->wasSent());


    }
}
```

The following three methods are the tests:

- `testPrepareXMLRequestFail()`: This test checks if an exception was thrown.
- `testSendRequest()`: This uses stubs, as we've just seen.
- `testPrepareXMLRequest()`: This is the second test to verify the creation of an XML request. It verifies whether the XML created is valid in the `SimpleXMLElement` class, where an XML string is passed to a constructor and then the element attributes are verified.

Using mocks and expectations

PHPUnit doesn't have any special built-in functionality for mocks, or at least it doesn't look like it at first glance. Mocks look very similar to stubs.

Both stubs and mocks are created using the following lines of code:

```
$double = $this->getMock('MyClass', array('someMethod'));
$double = $this->getMockBuilder('MyClass')
  ->setMethods(array('someMethod'))->getMock();
```

An obvious question at this point is, what's the difference? From the code point of view, there is no difference; they will look very similar. The difference lies in when and how they are used.

A stub is just returning a known value, as you have seen in previous examples, to make tested code happy.

The quick definition for a mock is that it's a stub with an expectation. A mock looks similar to a stub, but verifies whether the method was called, how many times it was called, and/or if input parameters match our expectations. You can imagine it like the injected code that keeps an eye on what's going on, and lets us know if there is any problem.

Let's go back to our previous example where we used the stub:

```
$client = $this->getMock('HttpClient', array('send'),
  array('http://localhost'));

        $client->expects($this->any())->method('send')
           ->will($this->returnValue(true));
```

In this case, we just returned the dummy data, without worrying about how and when it was called.

When you look closely, you will see three basic methods are used that create any stub or expectation. Expectation, as the name suggests, has a functionality that asserts when and how a method is called. Its basic structure has the following elements:

- `expects`: This shows how many times a method is called
- `method`: This calls a method name
- `with`: This shows what needs to be passed to the method
- `will`: This shows what the method will return

You can simply translate it to a method will be called N times with the given argument and will return `this`.

When we look closely, `expects` can use the following methods and an input parameter:

- `any()`: This can be called as many times as you want or not even once.
- `never()`: This is never called.
- `atLeastOnce()`: This is similar to the `any()` method but needs to be called.
- `once()`: This is called just once.
- `exactly($count)`: You can specify how many times this method must be called.
- `at($index)`: This calls a method when an index matches the number of times it was called. For example, `at(0)` will be called first, and `at(1)` will be called second.

The `method()` method is, as you would expect, the name of the method called, and that's all that you can do with it. However, the `will()` method tells us what will happen. The method `will()` can have the following values:

- `returnValue($value)`: This returns the passed value
- `returnValueMap(array $valueMap)`: This returns different values depending on the passed argument to the called method and their result in passed `$valueMap`

Let's see the following lines of code:

```
$valueMap = array(array(1,2),array(2,3));
$mock->expects($this->any())->method('someMethod')
  ->will($this->returnValueMap($valueMap));
```

In this case, when `someMethod` is called with the argument one, it will return two, and when it is called with two, it will return three.

- `returnArgument($argumentIndex)`: This returns an unchanged passed argument
- `returnCallback($callback)`: This returns a callback

To demonstrate how `returnCallback()` works, we can take the `returnValueMap()` method example, and use callback to replicate the same behavior:

```
$mock->expects($this->any())->method('someMethod')
  ->will($this
  ->returnCallback(array($this, 'myCallback')));

public function myCallback()
```

```
    {
        $arguments = func_get_args();
        return $arguments[0] + 1;
    }
```

In this case, `myCallback()` is a method that returns as a result input argument plus one.

- `returnSelf()`: This returns itself, that is, the called object
- `throwException(Exception $exception)`: This simply throws an exception
- `onConsecutiveCalls()`: This returns different predefined values after each call:

```
$mock->expects($this->any())->method('someMethod')
    ->will($this->onConsecutiveCalls(2,3));
```

When `someMethod` is called for the first time, it returns two, and the second time, it returns three.

The `with()` method is assertion for the passed parameters. You can verify whether the passed parameter is what you expect.

When you look back at our example, you can promote logger and client to mocks by setting expectations. This means that they will monitor how and where they are called, and if they match, we expect an expectation. The following code snippet demonstrates how to use mocks in `sendRequest()` example:

```
public function testPrepareXMLRequest()
{
    $logger = new FakeLogger();
    $client = $this->getMock('HttpClient', array(),
      array('http://localhost'));
    $transaction = new Transaction($logger, $client, $this->data);

    $xmlRequest = $transaction->prepareXMLRequest();
    $request = new SimpleXMLElement($xmlRequest);
    $item = $request->items->item[0];

    $this->assertEquals("1", $request['userId']);
    $this->assertEquals("1", $item['id']);
    $this->assertEquals("99", $item['quantity']);

    return $xmlRequest;
}
```

```
/**
 * @depends testPrepareXMLRequest
 */
public function testSendRequest($xmlRequest)
{
    $logger = $this->getMock('ILogger');
    $logger->expects($this->once())->method('log')
        ->with($this->equalTo($xmlRequest),$this
        ->isType('integer'))->will($this->returnValue(true));

    $client = $this->getMock('HttpClient',
        array('send','setRequest'), array('http://localhost'));

    $client->expects($this->once())->method('send')
        ->will($this->returnValue(true));

    $client->expects($this->once())->method('setRequest')
        ->with($this->equalTo($xmlRequest));

    $transaction = new Transaction($logger, $client, $this->data);

    $this->assertFalse($transaction->wasSent());
    $this->assertTrue($transaction->sendRequest());
    $this->assertTrue($transaction->wasSent());
}
```

This is a modified test using mocks, or to be precise, the `testSendRequest` test. We used the test dependency to pass an XML string request so that we can verify this string. Another difference is that we create mocks for loggers based on the interface, not on the implementation. The interface tells us how an implementation should look, and the stub replaces it with what you need for the test. On top of this, there is an added expectation that the `log()` method that will be called only once with the parameter matching our XML string and integer as a log priority.

Similarly, for the client, we added expectations for the `send()` method to be called only once and the `setRequest()` method to be called once with the parameter matching the XML string.

When you run tests, you get similar outputs:

```
OK (3 tests, 7 assertions)
```

In the test case, there are four asserts but seven assertions. Each expectation (`expects`) is also an assertion, and PHPUnit verifies whether the expectation was fulfilled.

Test proxies

PHPUnit 4 introduced a new feature called test proxies. The syntax is very similar to creating mocks or stubs but the behavior is slightly different. Test proxies are useful for integration testing because they behave in the exact same way as the original class, except that you can set expectations on any method. The advantage is that you are not modifying any code, but you can verify how and when a method was called.

The best explanation is to see the following example. You can see the stub usage in the `TestTransaction` class and the `testSendrequest()` method:

```
    public function testSendRequest()
    {
        $logger = new FakeLogger();
        $client = $this->getMock('HttpClient', array('send'),
array('http://localhost'));

        $client->expects($this->any())
          ->method('send')
          ->will($this->returnValue(true));

        $transaction = new Transaction($logger, $client, $this->data);

        $this->assertFalse($transaction->wasSent());
        $this->assertTrue($transaction->sendRequest());
        $this->assertTrue($transaction->wasSent());
    }
```

Here, the `HttpClient::send()` method was replaced with a stub. However, if you need to call the API (integration testing) and use the original class but still have an expectation in place, then a proxy helps. To see how we can use test proxies, we can retrieve `HttpClient`, call the API, but monitor that the `send()` method was called and called only once:

```
    /**
     *  @requires PHPUnit 4
     */
    public function testSendRequestProxy()
    {
        $logger = new FakeLogger();
        $client = $this->getMockBuilder('HttpClient')
          ->setConstructorArgs(array('http://localhost'))
          ->enableProxyingToOriginalMethods()->getMock();

        $client->expects($this->once())->method('send');

        $transaction = new Transaction($logger, $client, $this->data);
```

```
        $this->assertFalse($transaction->wasSent());
        $this->assertTrue($transaction->sendRequest());
        $this->assertTrue($transaction->wasSent());
    }
```

In this case, the `send()` method is called, and it also verifies whether that method was called and called only once. To make the code simpler, `getMockBuilder()` is used instead of `getMock()`, and you can take advantage of the fluent interface without the need to pass all eight arguments to the `getMock()` method.

Understanding Mockery

So far we have seen how to use test doubles using the default PHPUnit functionality. It is a very handy functionality, but it could be a bit tricky to understand and get used to. However, when you learn how to use it, it could be of real help while testing the complex code.

So what is Mockery, and how is it related to PHPUnit and test doubles? Mockery is a simple yet flexible PHP mock object framework for use in unit testing with PHPUnit, PHPSpec, or any other testing framework.

Mockery is a third-party library that you can use together with PHPUnit, but instead of using the PHPUnit functionality to create mocks, you can use the functionality provided by Mockery.

Why would we use that? For simple projects, whatever PHPUnit offers is enough. However, for bigger projects and complex code, Mockery might offer a few tricks which really help. I also really like Mockery's syntax, which is a bit easier to read than the PHPUnit syntax.

Installation methods

There are multiple installation methods available; the best idea is to use the one that you used for the PHPUnit installation. It would be advantageous to use a package manager because Mockery uses Hamcrest, which is a library of matcher objects.

To install Mockery using Composer, add the following lines to `composer.json`:

```
"require-dev": {
    "mockery/mockery": "dev-master@dev"
}
```

To install this, run the following command line:

```
>composer.phar install –dev
```

To install PEAR, you need to add new channels, as shown in the following command lines:

```
>pear channel-discover pear.survivethedeepend.com
>pear channel-discover hamcrest.googlecode.com/svn/pear
```

To install Mockery using PEAR, run the following command line:

```
>pear install --alldeps deepend/Mockery
```

For other installation methods, see the Mockery documentation on GitHub at `https://github.com/padraic/mockery`.

Comparing Mockery to PHPUnit

The basic functionality and logic of Mockery is the same or very similar to PHPUnit; only the syntax is slightly different.

In PHPUnit, we used the following lines of code:

```
$client = $this->getMock('HttpClient', array('send','setRequest'),
    array('http://localhost'));

$client->expects($this->once())->method('send')
    ->will($this->returnValue(true));
```

With Mockery, you use the following lines of code:

```
$client = \Mockery::mock('HttpClient[send,setRequest]',
    array('http://localhost'));

$client->shouldReceive('send')->once()->andReturn(true);
```

As you can see, the functionality is almost identical, but the Mockery API seems to be more intuitive and straightforward. With PHPUnit, you have to understand how it works to be able to use it.

If you want to call a method more than once and return different results, you can use the at() matcher and specify the index in PHPUnit. When you need to call it 10 times, it can be quite a few lines of code like the following code snippet:

```
$object = $this->getMock('MyClass',array('method'));
        $object->expects($this->at(0))->method('method')
            ->will($this->returnValue(1));
```

```
$object->expects($this->at(1))->method('method')
  ->will($this->returnValue(2));

$this->assertEquals(1,$object->method());
$this->assertEquals(2,$object->method());
```

With Mockery, it's much easier as shown in the following lines of code:

```
$object = \Mockery::mock('MyClass');
$object->shouldReceive('method')->andReturn(1,2);

$this->assertEquals(1,$object->method());
$this->assertEquals(2,$object->method());
```

Another interesting option is to create a proxy mock. This is a mock created from the object, not the class name, as shown in the following line of code:

```
$object = \Mockery::mock(new MyClass());
```

This allows you to bypass some PHPUnit limitations with mocking final classes and methods.

Check out the Mockery documentation; it has many more tricks up its sleeves. Let's see just one more example which might help.

You might have heard about the fluent interface. It is something that allows you to use method chaining. For example, see the following line of code:

```
$user->setEmail('user@sowmehere')->resetPassword()
  ->sendActivationEmail();
```

This is done in a very simple way; each method returns $this, so you can access any other method on the called object.

```
public function setEmail($email){
  $this->email = $email;
  return $this;
}
```

This really helps to make your code more readable, but imagine setting up mocks for all methods to be able to check on the end of the chain.

With Mockery, it's easy:

```
$mock = \Mockery::mock('User');
$mock->shouldReceive('setEmail->resetPassword
  ->sendActivationEmail')->with('user@sowmehere')
  ->andReturn(true);
```

How to use Mockery

As you have already seen, Mockery's usage and logic is very similar to PHPUnit. The syntax is easier to understand, and it might be an advantage when you start with test doubles, or if you want to get junior members of the team involved in testing as any good developer should be.

If you installed Mockery through Composer, then you use the Composer class loader. If you used another installation method, then you need to use the Mockery class loader. In our case, we update using `bootstrap.php`:

```php
<?php
spl_autoload_register('loadClass');

require_once 'Mockery/Loader.php';
require_once 'Hamcrest/Hamcrest.php';
$loader = new \Mockery\Loader;
$loader->register();

function loadClass($className)
{
    $file = dirname(__FILE__) . DIRECTORY_SEPARATOR . $className .
      '.php';
    if(file_exists($file))
        require_once $file;
}
```

Another requirement is to use the `tearDown()` method to call `\Mockery::close()`, as shown in the following lines of code:

```php
public function tearDown()
    {
        \Mockery::close();
    }
```

This is the moment when Mockery cleans up the environment and verifies expectations.

The best example of how to use it would be to go to our `TransactionMockTest` class and the `testSendRequest()` method, which we used earlier:

```php
/**
 * @depends testPrepareXMLRequest
 */
public function testSendRequest($xmlRequest)
```

```
    {
        $logger = $this->getMock('ILogger');
        $logger->expects($this->once())->method('log')
          ->with($this->equalTo($xmlRequest),
          $this->isType('integer'))->will($this->returnValue(true));

        $client = $this->getMock('HttpClient',
          array('send','setRequest'), array('http://localhost'));

        $client->expects($this->once())->method('send')
          ->will($this->returnValue(true));

        $client->expects($this->once())->method('setRequest')
          ->with($this->equalTo($xmlRequest));

        $transaction = new Transaction($logger, $client, $this->data);

        $this->assertFalse($transaction->wasSent());
        $this->assertTrue($transaction->sendRequest());
        $this->assertTrue($transaction->wasSent());
    }
```

Now, do the same thing with Mockery:

```
    /**
     * @depends testPrepareXMLRequest
     */
    public function testSendRequest($xmlRequest)
    {
        $logger = \Mockery::mock('ILogger');
        $logger->shouldReceive('log')->once()
          ->with(\Mockery::mustBe($xmlRequest),
          \Mockery::type('integer'))->andReturn(true);

        $client = \Mockery::mock('HttpClient[send,setRequest]',
          array('http://localhost'));
        $client->shouldReceive('send')->once()->andReturn(true);

        $client->shouldReceive('setRequest')->once()
          ->with(\Mockery::mustBe($xmlRequest));

        $transaction = new Transaction($logger, $client, $this->data);
```

```
        $this->assertFalse($transaction->wasSent());
        $this->assertTrue($transaction->sendRequest());
        $this->assertTrue($transaction->wasSent());
    }
```

As you can see, it does the same job but there are slight differences.

PHPUnit uses the following line of code:

```
        ->with($this->equalTo($xmlRequest),
            $this->isType('integer'))
```

Whereas, Mockery uses the following line of code:

```
        ->with(\Mockery::mustBe($xmlRequest),
        \Mockery::type('integer'))
```

PHPUnit uses the following line of code:

```
$client = $this->getMock('HttpClient', array('send','setRequest'),
    array('http://localhost'));
```

Whereas, Mockery uses the following line of code:

```
$client = \Mockery::mock('HttpClient[send,setRequest]',
    array('http://localhost'));
```

Summary

Using test doubles is a specific approach that you don't use very often when you write code, except while writing tests. However, in that instance, it can be a real lifesaver. However, it can be a double-edged sword: it really helps to isolate the tested code, but of course, the replaced code is not real code, and you can miss potential problems. The solution is to have several levels of testing (unit, functional, and integration), and each of them is important.

It's good to mention different types of test doubles, but it is more important to know how to use them.

PHPUnit has good support for mocks and stubs, and it is easy to use them. So, once you have learnt this technique, you will use it quite often. When using mocks to verify how and when each method is called, it is interesting that you can tests code internally, where you can imagine a mock as a submarine that reports what's going on under the "code surface".

Even though PHPUnit has good support for mocks and stubs, we discovered a good alternative available called Mockery, which makes mocking even easier, and some developers might find it easier to use. Another advantage is that the same library can be used for other testing frameworks, so that you can reuse the skills learned.

In the next chapter, we are going to explore how to test the code connecting to the database, and test doubles is something that can definitely help.

9
Database Testing

So far, we have been trying to write unit tests and isolate the tested code. The unit tests are the best approach, and you should always start with unit testing, but when you are testing code, sooner or later you will come across code that needs to read or write to a database. Database testing is tricky, and there are several options to test it. You have to decide on which level you need to test code. The problem comes with database complexity. Database and data in the database are as important as working code, and you need to be sure that everything works together.

The following different approaches can be tried to test a database:

- Use mocking to replace code that connects to the database
- Use a specific database driver only for tests
- Set up a database for integration tests and run tests against this database
- Use a complete development environment and run functional tests against this database

Mocking could be really handy when you need to verify an internal functionality without storing and reading data from a database. A specific database driver could be the solution for some projects that use a custom database abstraction layer, for example, applications that use the MySQLi extension, but for tests, you want to use the SQLite database. The reason to use SQLite is to have a lightweight, fast solution for test execution. Therefore, you might need a specific implementation that allows you to switch to a different database engine.

PHPUnit has a DBUnit extension that allows you to set a database in a known state (clear the database and import data before running tests). This is really handy for database integration tests; you know what is in the database and you can verify changes done by the tests.

The final option is to run tests against the full development database. These tests would then be called functional tests because the database is not in a known state. Testing is focused on code, very often forgetting how a database could be a complex and important part of an application.

Which database to use

Which database to use is a simple yet very important question. As mentioned earlier, a database can be a very complex thing, and the environment for tests must mirror the production environment settings as closely as possible. You should never ever run tests against the production database. Accidentally dropping all tables might not be what you want.

For integration testing, you need a clean database structure, including mandatory data. Surprisingly, this crucial information is often missing. When talking about database structures, a database should be an independent, rock-solid block. Don't look at the compatibility with other database systems, don't look at the limitations that your database persistent layer has, but design a database well. Use database features such as referential integrity definitions (foreign keys) and unique indexes, normalize a database, and when it's convenient, use views and database triggers. Very often, you will see code doing everything, and the database is just a hole to dump data in. A good database is not just a hole. Often, you can do things more easily at the database level. For example, instead of having a super complex SQL query, you can use a stored procedure.

In this chapter, as in the previous chapters, we will use a simplified example that will demonstrate a situation that you might face, and see what we can do.

Going back to the question of which database to use, the answer depends on what your production system is and the way in which you access the database. If your production database is MySQL and you use the PDO_MySQL extension, then PDO allows you to use a lightweight database such as SQLite to run tests against a different database engine. The advantage is that in this way, you can verify that the system will work with different database engines. The disadvantage is that you might miss the MySQL behavior that is going to be based on database-specific features such as stored procedures, triggers, and views. Another aspect that many developers just ignore is database permissions, thinking that the GRANT ALL statement or root user fixes everything. It does, until you realize that the code you wrote is dependent on the DROP permission (enable databases, tables, and views to be dropped), which a user doesn't have on the production system.

The conclusion is that when you write tests, try to make your development environment as close as possible to the production system. Virtualization is a great way to achieve it, and you have to keep the database structure up to date. It depends on which system you use in order to track and deploy database changes, but if the database structure is not kept up to date, then it could be very frustrating to chase and fix bugs that don't exist. When talking about data, the PHPUnit extension, DBUnit, can really help with setting up and cleaning data for tests, but even these datasets need to be kept up to date.

Yes, this can be time-consuming, and in addition to the development environment, you need to keep the test environment, staging environments, and of course production environments up to date. Then, you need to decide which parts are critical and necessary to invest in writing and keeping integration tests running.

Tests for a database

A better way to test a database is to look at one real-life example where we need to sort out a task: a customer buys N products and we need to raise and store an invoice in a database. This is quite a common situation if you create an e-shop or anything similar.

As money is involved, we need to be very careful. We need to test the calculations to ensure that not only are all numbers correct, but also operations that involve storing and obtaining data from a database perform as expected and data is not modified. This is going to be a core functionality that should be covered by tests as much as possible. Every mistake there could be a very expensive mistake.

With similar tasks, it might be a good idea to start with database design if the database is not already available. This usually answers the question about what data is available and how to store it. As mentioned earlier, it is a good idea to set very tight rules about how data is stored. There is nothing more annoying than spending half a day debugging your code and trying to figure out where the problem is, and then realizing that there is nothing wrong with the code but the problem is caused by inconsistent data in the database.

In our case, we used the MySQL Workbench tool (`http://www.mysql.com/products/workbench`) to create the following EER diagram of the database structure:

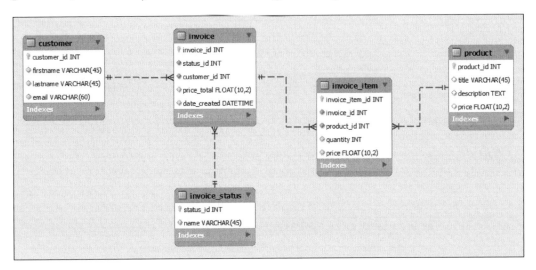

The advantage of this approach is that you can visualize how your data will be stored, and then export SQL scripts to create tables with all the required indexes and foreign keys.

As you can see, the main table for us is the `invoice` table. Each item in the `invoice` table is linked to the `customer` table, has a status (issued, paid, and canceled), and can have multiple invoice items. The `invoice_item` table is linked to the `product` table. Then, we can export (synchronize) the diagram to SQL. It depends on which database you use, but PHP is most commonly used together with MySQL or MariaDB. The following example is for MySQL and MariaDB, but this can be easily converted to any similar RDBMS database:

```
CREATE TABLE 'customer' (
  'customer_id' int(11) NOT NULL AUTO_INCREMENT,
  'firstname' varchar(45) NOT NULL,
  'lastname' varchar(45) NOT NULL,
  'email' varchar(60) NOT NULL,
  PRIMARY KEY ('customer_id'),
  UNIQUE KEY 'email_UNIQUE' ('email')
  ) ENGINE=InnoDB DEFAULT CHARSET=utf8;
```

```
CREATE TABLE 'invoice' (
  'invoice_id' int(11) NOT NULL AUTO_INCREMENT,
  'status_id' int(11) NOT NULL,
  'customer_id' int(11) NOT NULL,
  'total_gross' float(10,2) NOT NULL,
  'total_net' float(10,2) NOT NULL,
  'total_vat' float(10,2) NOT NULL,
  'date_created' datetime NOT NULL,
  PRIMARY KEY ('invoice_id'),
  KEY 'fk_invoice_customer_idx' ('customer_id'),
  KEY 'fk_invoice_invoice_status1_idx' ('status_id'),
  CONSTRAINT 'fk_invoice_customer' FOREIGN KEY ('customer_id')
  REFERENCES 'customer' ('customer_id') ON DELETE NO ACTION ON
  UPDATE NO ACTION, CONSTRAINT 'fk_invoice_invoice_status1'
  FOREIGN KEY ('status_id') REFERENCES 'invoice_status'
  ('status_id') ON DELETE NO ACTION ON UPDATE NO ACTION
  ) ENGINE=InnoDB DEFAULT CHARSET=utf8;

CREATE TABLE 'invoice_status' (...........);

CREATE TABLE 'product' (...........);

CREATE TABLE 'invoice_item' (...........);
```

This SQL code creates the required database structure. As you can see, foreign keys are in place because they are part of any decent database structure.

When we have the database structure in place, we can start thinking of how to fill this structure with the required data. While working with databases, it is handy to turn data into objects and work with objects in PHP. It is then clear as to when and how to store/load data from a database, but the data structure can still be used in a PHP code without too much hassle. For this example, we just use PDO, but later, we will see how to use Doctrine ORM, which works as a bridge between PHP code and a database.

To make the code cleaner, every table is represented as a class, as shown in the following code snippet. We are going to use these classes while fetching data by the fetch mode PDO::FETCH_CLASS and when the returned data is going to be bound to these classes.

```
class Customer {

    public $customer_id;
    public $firstname;
    public $lastname;
    public $email;

}
```

```
class Product {

    public $product_id;
    public $title;
    public $description;
    public $price;

}

class Invoice {

    const STATUS_ISSUED = 1;
    const STATUS_PAID = 2;
    const STATUS_CANCELLED = 3;

    public $invoice_id;
    public $status_id;
    public $customer_id;
    public $price_total = 0;

    public $date_created;
    /**
     * @var InvoiceItem[]
     */
    public $invoiceItems = array();
}

class InvoiceItem {

    public $invoice_item_id;
    public $invoice_id;
    public $product_id;
    public $quantity;
    public $price;

}
```

Now, the task is to create an invoice, store the invoice in the database, and then verify that the data is stored correctly. For this, we will create a class, `InvoiceManager`, which will provide the required functionality.

As our code will mainly communicate with the database, in this case, we jump directly into writing the code. This is possible, but please do remember that you have to write tests, if not before writing the code, at least on the same day when you write the code. It is very easy to slip back to the habit that code somehow works: now I have something more urgent, I will write the test later — and later almost equals never.

In our example, we created the `InvoiceManager` class that will store and load invoices from the database. A simple `InvoiceManager` class that uses the PDO driver could look like the following code snippet:

```
class InvoiceManager{
    public function __construct(PDO $db){}
    public function loadInvoice($invoiceId){}
    public function raiseInvoice(Invoice $invoice, Customer
        $customer, array $productsArray){}
    protected function storeInvoice(Invoice $invoice){}
}
```

It is now important to think about what the class will do. We pass the database connection to the constructor. The `raiseInvoice` method creates the `invoice` and `invoiceItem` objects based on the passed arguments: `invoice`, `customer`, and `productsArray`. You can imagine `productsArray` as an array of products and quantities, as shown in the following line of code:

```
array('product' => $product1, 'quantity' => 1),
    array('product' => $product2, 'quantity' => 2)
```

Here, `product` is an instance of the `Product` class, and `quantity` indicates how many of these products were ordered. Each of these products then needs to be turned into `InvoiceItem`. When the total values for the invoices are set, we can store the invoices in the database.

The complete, simple implementation of the `InvoiceManager` class could look like the following code snippet:

```
<?php

class InvoiceManager
{
    private $db;

    public function __construct(PDO $db)
    {
        $this->db = $db;
    }
```

The PDO object is passed to the constructor. For testing, a dependency is important. If you have a dependency inside your class, then it might be very difficult to replace it with something else. The `loadInvoice()` method uses the passed PDO object to the constructor and performs database calls:

```
    public function loadInvoice($invoiceId)
    {
```

```
    $sql = 'SELECT * FROM invoice where invoice_id =
      :invoice_id';
    $stm = $this->db->prepare($sql);
    $stm->execute(array(':invoice_id' => $invoiceId));
    $stm->setFetchMode(PDO::FETCH_CLASS, 'Invoice');
    $invoice = $stm->fetch();

    $sql = "SELECT * FROM invoice_item where invoice_id =
      :invoice_id";
    $stm = $this->db->prepare($sql);
    $stm->execute(array(':invoice_id' => $invoiceId));
    $stm->setFetchMode(PDO::FETCH_CLASS, 'InvoiceItem');

    while ($invoiceItem = $stm->fetch())
    {
        $invoice->addInvoiceItem($invoiceItem);
    }

    return $invoice;
}
```

The `loadInvoice()` method is a simple method to load an invoice from the database and binding results to objects. To keep examples short, there is no added error handling mechanism, for example, when an invoice or invoice item is not found. The `raiseInvoice()` method creates an invoice from passed parameters:

```
public function raiseInvoice(Invoice $invoice, Customer
  $customer, array $productsArray)
{
    $invoice->customer_id = $customer->customer_id;
    $invoice->status_id = Invoice::STATUS_ISSUED;
    $invoice->date_created = new DateTime();

    foreach ($productsArray as $productItem)
    {
        $product = $productItem['product'];
        $quantity = $productItem['quantity'];

        $invoiceItem = new InvoiceItem();
        $invoiceItem->product_id = $product->product_id;
        $invoiceItem->quantity = $quantity;
        $invoiceItem->price = $product->price;

        $invoice->addInvoiceItem($invoiceItem);
    }
```

```
            $invoice->setTotals();
            return $this->storeInvoice($invoice);
        }
```

The `raiseInvoice()` method translates the ordered products into an invoice, calculates the total value of the invoice, and then calls the `storeInvoice()` method to store data into the database, as shown in the following code snippet:

```
        protected function storeInvoice(Invoice $invoice)
        {
            $sql = "INSERT INTO invoice (status_id, customer_id,
              price_total, date_created) VALUES (:status_id,
              :customer_id, :price_total, :date_created)";
            $stm = $this->db->prepare($sql);

            $stm->execute(array(':status_id' => $invoice->status_id,
              ':customer_id' => $invoice->customer_id, ':price_total'
              => $invoice->price_total, ':date_created' =>
              $invoice->date_created->format("Y-m-d H:i:s")));

            $invoiceId = $this->db->lastInsertId();
            if (!$invoiceId) throw new Exception('Invoice not saved');
            $invoice->invoice_id = $invoiceId;

            foreach ($invoice->invoiceItems as $invoiceItem)
            {
                $invoiceItem->invoice_id = $invoiceId;

                $sql = "INSERT INTO invoice_item (invoice_id,
                  product_id, quantity, price) VALUES (:invoice_id,
                  :product_id, :quantity, :price)";
                $stm = $this->db->prepare($sql);

                $stm->execute(array(':invoice_id' =>
                  $invoiceItem->invoice_id,
                  ':product_id' => $invoiceItem->product_id,
                  ':quantity' => $invoiceItem->quantity, ':price'
                  => $invoiceItem->price));
            }

            return $invoice;
        }
    }
```

To have a complete example that we are going to use for testing and see different testing methods, let's take a look at the `Invoice` class to see all its methods properly, as shown in the following code snippet:

```
public function addInvoiceItem(InvoiceItem $item)
    {
        $this->invoiceItems[$item->product_id] = $item;
    }


    public function removeInvoiceItem(InvoiceItem $item)
    {
        unset($this->invoiceItems[$item->invoice_id]);
    }


    public function setTotals()
    {
        $this->price_total = 0;

        foreach ($this->invoiceItems as $invoiceItem)
        {
            $this->price_total += $invoiceItem->price *
            $invoiceItem->quantity;
        }
    }
```

To test the `InvoiceManager` class, you have two options: unit tests by using mocking techniques, which we learned in *Chapter 8*, *Using Test Doubles*, or integration tests where you call a database and you also verify interactions with the database. This data is stored/retrieved from the database.

Now, let's take a look at how to write tests using mocks. As you can see, a database interacts with the constructor through the passed PDO object, so for testing purposes, you need to replace the PDO object with mock. With mocking PDO, there is one known problem. When you run it, you will get the following error:

PDOException: You cannot serialize or unserialize PDO instances.

It doesn't help even to disable the constructor, but there is a simple solution; for the test, you need to extend the PDO class and replace its constructor in the child class, as shown in the following lines of code:

```
<?php

class PDOMock extends PDO
{
```

```php
    public function __construct() {}
}
```

This does the trick. Now, we can use the mock object to replace the PDO class object as shown in the following code snippet:

```php
<?php

class InvoiceManagerTest extends PHPUnit_Framework_TestCase
{
    private $pdoMock;
    private $stmMock;

    public function setUp()
    {
        $this->stmMock = $this->getMock('PDOStatement',
          array('execute','fetch'));
        $this->stmMock->expects($this->any())->method('execute')
          ->will($this->returnValue(true));

        $this->pdoMock = $this->getMock('PDOMock',
          array('prepare','lastInsertId'));
        $this->pdoMock->expects($this->any())->method('prepare')
          ->will($this->returnValue($this->stmMock));
    }
```

In the `setUp()` method, we created the mock object for the PDO class, or, to be precise, for our extended class PDOMock. As the PDO `prepare()` method returns the PDOStatement object, we also need to replace this object to imitate database calls. Instead of calling the database using the PDO object, we use our mock object passed to the `InvoiceManager` constructor:

```php
    public function testRaiseInvoice()
    {
        $this->pdoMock->expects($this->once())
          ->method('lastInsertId')->will($this->returnValue(1));

        $invoiceManager = new InvoiceManager($this->pdoMock);

        $product1 = new Product();
        $product1->price = 10;
        $product1->product_id = 1;

        $customer = new Customer();
        $customer->customer_id = 1;
```

```
        $invoice = new Invoice();
        $productsArray = array(array('product' => $product1,
          'quantity' => 2));
        $invoiceManager->raiseInvoice($invoice, $customer,
          $productsArray);

        $this->assertEquals(20, $invoice->price_total);
    }
```

This test calls the `raiseInvoice()` method, which stores data into the database. So for us, it is enough to just use `stmMock`, which is the mock of `PDOStatement`, and replace the `execute()` method with the one returning `true`, and `lastInsertId()` method with the one returning 1. This way we can exercise the code and test for the `loadInvoice()` method, which could look like the following code snippet:

```
        public function testLoadInvoice()
        {
            $invoice = new Invoice();
            $invoice->invoice_id = 1;
            $invoice->price_total = 100;

            $invoiceItem = new InvoiceItem();
            $invoiceItem->invoice_item_id = 1;
            $invoiceItem->invoice_id = 1;
            $invoiceItem->price = 100;
            $invoiceItem->product_id = 1;

            $this->stmMock->expects($this->at(1))->method('fetch')
              ->will($this->returnValue($invoice));

            $this->stmMock->expects($this->at(3))->method('fetch')
              ->will($this->returnValue($invoiceItem));

            $invoiceManager = new InvoiceManager($this->pdoMock);
            $invoice = $invoiceManager->loadInvoice(1);

            $this->assertEquals(100, $invoice->price_total);
            $this->assertEquals(100, $invoice->invoiceItems[1]
              ->price);
        }
    }
```

The test `testLoadInvoice()` might look a bit tricky. When you look at the `InvoiceManager` class code, it is calling the method `fetch()` twice while loading data from the database. We need to replace these methods, but both should return different results, first `invoice` and second `invoiceItem`. To be sure that different results are returned, we used `expects($this->at())` and the index number. The reason why the index is one and three, and not zero and one, as you might expect, is that PHPUnit is counting calls on mocked methods for `execute` and `fetch` on the mocked `PDOStatement` object. First, `execute` is called and then `fetch`, followed by the second `execute` and `fetch` methods.

To ensure that different results are returned, another option would be to use `returnValueMap` or `returnCallback`.

When we run the unit test, everything looks good, and we get the following result:

```
PHPUnit 3.7.30 by Sebastian Bergmann.

Time: 87 ms, Memory: 4.75Mb

OK (2 tests, 7 assertions)
```

At this stage, testing really helps. When you write code that has more than 10 lines, then there is a really good chance of you making at least one mistake. When you write code like this, which has 160 lines, then there are going to be a few mistakes. At this stage, tests allow you to immediately verify and fix the written code, and the initial investment in writing tests pays off. If you allow buggy code to be used, then you are going to spend ages testing applications in the browser, going back, fixing one problem, pushing a new release to the testing environment, and then having another reported bug. In the worst case, the customer can be used as the tester, and the initial impression is not going to be good.

When we look back at our code, we have unit tests, but the problem is the database. The `storeInvoice()` and `loadInvoice()` methods are also crucial parts of the code. If the invoice is not going to be stored in the database as we expect, numbers will be changed. Then, it's as serious a problem as doing the wrong calculations. This is finally the moment when we move to integration testing.

The point of integration testing is to verify how our code will interact with the database. We need to be sure that all the insert, select, and update statements are executed. We are not going to receive any database errors, and the data will be stored/loaded correctly.

DBUnit

DBUnit is a PHPUnit extension that makes our integration testing easier. DBUnit allows you to clear the database and import a prepared dataset to set the database to a known state. This is important for database testing. If you set up a test database and allow data to be stored there without cleaning it, sooner or later you will have negative fails, and your test will be less reliable.

To make it clear, DBUnit helps with database testing, but it's not a magical tool that will solve all problems. You need to create and maintain your database's structure. In addition, you need to maintain datasets used for tests. I don't remember the last time I worked on a project that didn't use a database abstraction layer. When you use a database abstraction layer, it is better to rely on your implementation rather than on DBUnit's assert features, but DBUnit is still a good starting point and a big help.

Installing DBUnit

You should follow the installation method used for your PHPUnit's installation.

For PEAR installation, run the following command line:

```
>pear install phpunit/DbUnit
```

For the Composer installation, modify `composer.json` as shown in the following code snippet:

```
{
    "require": {
        "phpunit/phpunit": "3.7.*",
     "phpunit/dbunit": "1.2.*"
    }
}
```

Database test cases

When we wish to use DBUnit, we have to make one change. When writing the unit test, our test case extends `PHPUnit_Framework_TestCase`. When using DBUnit, our test case has to extend `PHPUnit_Extensions_Database_TestCase`. This class has the following two abstract methods, which we have to implement:

- `getConnection()`: This method must return `PHPUnit_Extensions_Database_DB_IDatabaseConnection`

- `getDataSet()`: This method must return `PHPUnit_Extensions_Database_DataSet_IDataSet`

The first method returns a database connection but not directly a PDO or MySQLi connection; it is a connection wrapped in the PHPUnit class. However, don't worry; usually it's easy; just specify the database server, username, password, and database name, as shown in the following line of code:

```
return $this->createDefaultDBConnection
    (new PDO('mysql:host=localhost;dbname=book','root','password'));
```

Otherwise, the database's test case is the same test case as the normal test case with a few extra assertions.

Datasets

Datasets are probably the most useful DBUnit feature. You can define a set of data to be included in the database. Data from tables that are to be populated by a dataset are truncated. This is called through the setUp() method before every test is executed. This is great for restoring a database to a known state, but as you can guess, it's not going to be the fastest thing in the world.

DBUnit supports datasets in several different formats, which are as follows:

- **A flat XML dataset**: This is an XML format where each row is a record in the table, and the columns are attributes

- **An XML dataset**: This is a structured XML format and is more complex than a flat XML dataset

- **A MySQL XML dataset**: This is created with the mysqldump utility using the --xml switch

- **A CSV dataset**: This is a dataset in the CSV format

- **A YAML dataset**: This is a dataset in the YAML format

All datasets are very similar. They are just in a different format. NULL values may be problematic as they are not handled very well by the flat XML format and are better handled, for example, by the YAML format.

The content of these basic datasets can be modified by other datasets, which use them as inputs and then perform some operations before returning a modified dataset, as follows:

- **Replacement dataset**: This applies rules to modify the dataset's content and helps to overcome the XML problems with NULL values

- **Composite dataset**: This merges multiple datasets

- **Dataset filter**: This filters the content of a dataset

These are static datasets created with prepared data, but DBUnit also offers dynamic datasets. These datasets are created on the fly, for example, as the result of a query, and they are handy when you want to compare data.

Using DBUnit

A good way to understand how DBUnit works is by going back to our invoice example and seeing what we can do. So far, we have created a unit test that verified the calculations. What remains to be done is testing the `loadInvoice()` and `storeInvoice()` methods to verify that they are stored and loaded from the database correctly.

If you look back at the database's structure, you will see that the invoice status is required and sits in the `invoice_status` table, so this is definitely a table that needs to be populated. To store an invoice, we need the customer ID, and for invoice items we need products, and we need more two tables, `customers` and `products`, which need to be populated. It would then be good to insert some dummy invoice data there to ensure that the invoice is inserted correctly.

Probably one of the easiest ways to use datasets is to use a flat XML dataset. So let's have a look at what this dataset could look like:

```xml
<?xml version="1.0"?>
<dataset>
    <customer customer_id="1" firstname="John" lastname="Smith"
      email="john.smith@localhost"/>
    <customer customer_id="2" firstname="Jenny" lastname="Smith"
      email="jenny.smith@localhost"/>
    <product product_id="1" title="test product 1"
      description="some description" price="10.00"/>
    <product product_id="2" title="test product 2"
      description="some description" price="20.00"/>
    <invoice_status status_id="1" name="issued"/>
    <invoice_status status_id="2" name="paid"/>
    <invoice_status status_id="3" name="canceled"/>
    <invoice invoice_id="1" status_id="1" customer_id="1"
      price_total="100.00" date_created="2013-01-20 08:00:00"/>
    <invoice_item invoice_item_id="1" invoice_id="1"
      product_id="1" quantity="1" price="100.00"/>
</dataset>
```

As you can see, each dataset element is a table name, and the attributes match the column names. In this way, we define all data that needs to be inserted into the database. Each table mentioned in the dataset will be truncated.

To see how a dataset works and what you can do with it, let's use a simple test as shown in the following code snippet:

```php
<?php
class DatasetTest extends PHPUnit_Extensions_Database_TestCase
{
    protected $connection = null;

    public function getDataSet()
    {
        return $this->createFlatXmlDataSet('dataset.xml');
    }
```

The getDataset() method loads an XML dataset from our flat XML file that contains data to be injected into the database:

```php
    protected function setUp()
    {
        $conn=$this->getConnection();
        $conn->getConnection()->query("set foreign_key_checks=0");
        parent::setUp();
        $conn->getConnection()->query("set foreign_key_checks=1");
    }
```

The setUp() method disables foreign key checks and then injects the data from the dataset into the database. The reason why the foreign keys are disabled is that MySQL would refuse to store the data. Another solution to avoid referential integrity problems might be to order data in the XML dataset that will be inserted in order to avoid referential integrity problems:

```php
    protected function getConnection()
    {
        if ($this->connection === null)
        {
            $connectionString =
                $GLOBALS['DB_DRIVER'].':host='.$GLOBALS['DB_HOST'].
                ';dbname='.$GLOBALS['DB_DATABASE'];
            $this->connection =
                $this->createDefaultDBConnection(
                new PDO($connectionString,
                $GLOBALS['DB_USER'],$GLOBALS['DB_PASSWORD']));
        }

        return $this->connection;
    }
```

The getConnection() method creates the PDO database connection for tests. It uses the $GLOBALS variable and stores GLOBALS configuration, such as $GLOBALS['DB_HOST'], which is taken from the configuration file:

```
public function testConsumer()
{
    $stm = $this->getConnection()->getConnection()
      ->prepare("select * from customer where customer_id =
      :customer_id");

    $stm->execute(array('customer_id' => 2));
    $result = $stm->fetch();

    $this->assertEquals("jenny.smith@localhost",
      $result['email']);

    $dbTable = $this->getConnection()->createQueryTable(
      'customer', 'SELECT * FROM customer');

    $datasetTable = $this->getDataSet()
      ->getTable("customer");

    $this->assertTablesEqual($dbTable, $datasetTable);
}
```

The testConsumer() method uses the createQueryTable() method to load the data from the database and assertTablesEqual to verify that the data is the same as the data in the dataset:

```
public function testInvoice()
{
    $dataSet = new
     PHPUnit_Extensions_Database_DataSet_QueryDataSet
     ($this->getConnection());
    $dataSet->addTable('customer');
    $dataSet->addTable('product');
    $dataSet->addTable('invoice');
    $dataSet->addTable('invoice_item');
    $dataSet->addTable('invoice_status');
    $expectedDataSet = $this->getDataSet();

    $this->assertDataSetsEqual($expectedDataSet, $dataSet);
}
}
```

The `testInvoice()` method is similar, except that it compares not just one table but all tables with the dataset.

The `assertDataSetsEqual()` and `assertTablesEqual()` methods are handy when you need to verify data, and you can use sets of predefined datasets.

When you look at this code, you will see a few differences compared to the usual unit test, and these are as follows:

- It extends `PHPUnit_Extensions_Database_TestCase`
- It implements `getDataSet()` and `getConnection()`
- The `setUp()` method contains DB queries
- It does not use mocks

When the test is executed, the `setUp()` method is called. We need to use the SQL query to disable foreign key checks on a MySQL level. DBUnit is just trying to truncate tables, and when you have foreign keys in place, MySQL would refuse to truncate them without disabling foreign key check. For a connection, we use the `getConnection()` method that creates a database connection, and the `getDataSet()` method is called.

The `getDataSet()` method returns a flat XML dataset from our XML configuration file. DBUnit processes this file, truncates tables, and inserts data into the database, and then the test is executed.

For the connection details, we used the `$GLOBALS` variable. You might wonder where the data came from. Instead of hardcoding it in tests, you can store it in a configuration file, usually `phpunit.xml`:

```
<?xml version="1.0" encoding="UTF-8" ?>
<phpunit bootstrap="bootstrap.php">
    <php>
        <var name="DB_DRIVER" value="mysql" />
        <var name="DB_USER" value="root" />
        <var name="DB_PASSWORD" value="password" />
        <var name="DB_HOST" value="localhost" />
        <var name="DB_DATABASE" value="book" />
    </php>
</phpunit>
```

We can use the `DatasetTest` class because it has everything that we need to test the database, extend it, and create integration tests for the `InvoiceManager` class, as shown in the following code snippet:

```php
<?php

class InvoiceManagerDBTest extends DatasetTest
{
    public function testRaiseInvoice()
    {
        $invoiceManager = new InvoiceManager(
            $this->getConnection()->getConnection());

        $product1 = new Product();
        $product1->price = 10;
        $product1->product_id = 1;

        $customer = new Customer();
        $customer->customer_id = 1;

        $invoice = new Invoice();
        $productsArray = array(array('product' => $product1,
            'quantity' => 2));
        $invoiceManager->raiseInvoice($invoice, $customer,
            $productsArray);

        $invoiceFromDB = $invoiceManager
            ->loadInvoice($invoice->invoice_id);

        $this->assertEquals($invoice->price_total,
            $invoiceFromDB->price_total);
        $this->assertEquals(count($invoice->invoiceItems),
            count($invoiceFromDB->invoiceItems));
    }
}
```

We are not using mocks because in this case we want to test the entire functionality. The `raiseInvoice()` method inserts a new record into the database and then uses `loadInvoice()` to load the newly created invoice. When you execute the test case, you should see an output similar to the following command line:

```
PHPUnit 3.7.30 by Sebastian Bergmann.

Time: 444 ms, Memory: 5.00Mb

OK (3 tests, 5 assertions)
```

Doctrine 2 ORM and database testing

When you are working on a modern application, you almost use a database abstraction layer. As an example of how to use DBUnit with a third-party library, let's have a look at how to use Doctrine 2 ORM, which is a heavyweight but very powerful object-relational mapper using our own **Database Abstraction Layer (DAL)**. Doctrine is quite complex, and the aim is not to explain how it works, but to show you how to use database integration testing with other database abstraction layers.

To be able to run code, you have to install the required libraries. In this case, it is strongly suggested that you use the Composer installation and a class loader to install Doctrine by setting the required dependency in the composer.json file. Along with Doctrine ORM, there is also added beberlei/DoctrineExtensions for the OrmTestCase class, which makes testing easier:

```
{
"require": {
  "doctrine/orm": "2.4.*",
  "beberlei/DoctrineExtensions": "dev-master"
},
"autoload": {
  "psr-0": {"": "src/"}
},
"minimum-stability" : "dev"
}
```

This sets the required dependency in the composer.json file, and also loads the OrmTestCase class, which makes testing easier.

When you work with Doctrine, instead of accessing database tables, you work with entities that are mapped to the database tables. When required, EntityManager persists these entities and stores them in the database. You are not touching the database, and all the database interaction is done through these entities. As an example, you can see the Invoice entity's properties and mapping declarations, which are done through annotations. All other entities can be found on https://github.com/machek/PHPUnit_Essentials.

```php
<?php

namespace MyEntity;

use Doctrine\ORM\Mapping as ORM;
```

```php
/**
 * Invoice
 *
 * @ORM\Table(name="invoice")
 * @ORM\Entity
 */
class Invoice
{
    /**
     * @var integer
     *
     * @ORM\Column(name="invoice_id", type="integer", nullable=false)
     * @ORM\Id
     * @ORM\GeneratedValue(strategy="IDENTITY")
     */
    private $invoiceId;


    /**
     * @var \DateTime
     *
     * @ORM\Column(name="date_created", type="datetime",
nullable=false)
     */
    private $dateCreated;

    /**
     * @var \MyEntity\Customer
     *
     * @ORM\ManyToOne(targetEntity="MyEntity\Customer")
     * @ORM\JoinColumns({
     *    @ORM\JoinColumn(name="customer_id",
     *        referencedColumnName="customer_id")
     * })
     */
    private $customer;
```

....

As you can see, this is similar to the `Invoice` class that we used for PDO, but it also describes how it's mapped.

When we look at the `InvoiceManager` class that we used for storing an invoice to the database by using the `PDO` class with Doctrine, it looks slightly different, but not too much, as shown in the following code snippet:

```php
<?php

use Doctrine\ORM\EntityManager;

class InvoiceManagerDoctrine
{

    /**
     * @var \Doctrine\ORM\EntityManager
     */
    private $em;

    public function __construct(EntityManager $em)
    {
        $this->em = $em;
    }

    /**
     * @param  Customer $customer
     * @param  array      $productsArray
     * @return mixed
     */
    public function raiseInvoice(MyEntity\Invoice $invoice,
      MyEntity\Customer $customer, array $productsArray,
      MyEntity\InvoiceStatus $invoiceStatus)
    {
        $invoice->setCustomer($customer);
        $invoice->setStatus($invoiceStatus);
        $invoice->setDateCreated(new DateTime());

        foreach ($productsArray as $productItem)
        {
            $product = $productItem['product'];
            $quantity = $productItem['quantity'];

            $invoiceItem = new MyEntity\InvoiceItem();
            $invoiceItem->setProduct($product);
            $invoiceItem->setQuantity($quantity);
            $invoiceItem->setPrice($product->getPrice());
            $invoice->addInvoiceItem($invoiceItem);
        }
```

```php
        $invoice->setTotals();
        return $this->storeInvoice($invoice);
    }


    /**
     * @param $invoiceId
     * @return \MyEntity\Invoice
     */
    public function loadInvoice($invoiceId)
    {
        return $this->em->find('\MyEntity\Invoice',$invoiceId);
    }


    /**
     * @return bool
     * @throws Exception
     */
    protected function storeInvoice(MyEntity\Invoice $invoice)
    {
            foreach($invoice->getInvoiceItem() as $item)
            {
                $this->em->persist($item);
            }

            $this->em->persist($invoice);
            $this->em->flush();
    }
}
```

As you can see, it's quite similar. The only difference is that instead of assigning the IDs, such as customer_id, you set the Customer entity, and Doctrine handles how it's stored.

Why do you need to see all of this? If you remember, DBUnit is not taking care of your database's structure, it's just importing data from datasets. This is where a different approach could be really useful, but keeping a database structure up to date can be a real pain.

With Doctrine, it's easier. You use entities. Each entity describes how it is mapped to the database. When you want to make any change in the database's structure, you have to update the entity. This way, you know that you always have an up-to-date description of what a database looks like, and then you can recreate the database. It sounds like magic, but it works.

Let's have a look at an example of how to test our `InvoiceManager` class using Doctrine ORM, as shown in the following code snippet:

```php
<?php

require_once '../vendor/autoload.php';

use DoctrineExtensions\PHPUnit\OrmTestCase,
    Doctrine\ORM\Tools\Setup,
    Doctrine\ORM\EntityManager,
    Doctrine\ORM\Tools\SchemaTool;

class InvoiceManagerDoctrineTest extends OrmTestCase
{
    /**
     * @var Doctrine\ORM\EntityManager
     */
    protected static $em = null;

    public static function setUpBeforeClass()
    {
      $config =
       Setup::createAnnotationMetadataConfiguration(array
        (__DIR__ . "/../src"), true, null, null, false);

        $connectionOptions = array('driver' => 'pdo_sqlite',
          'memory' => true);

        // obtaining the entity manager
        self::$em = EntityManager::create($connectionOptions,
          $config);

        $schemaTool = new SchemaTool(self::$em);

        $cmf = self::$em->getMetadataFactory();
        $classes = $cmf->getAllMetadata();

        $schemaTool->dropDatabase();
        $schemaTool->createSchema($classes);

    }

    protected function tearDown()
```

```
{
    self::$em->clear();
    parent::tearDown();
}

protected function createEntityManager()
{
    return self::$em;
}

protected function getDataSet()
{
    return $this->createFlatXmlDataSet(__DIR__ .
      "/../../dataset.xml");
}

public function testLoadInvoice()
{
    $invoiceManager = new \InvoiceManagerDoctrine(self::$em);
    $invoice = $invoiceManager->loadInvoice(1);

    $this->assertEquals(1, $invoice->getInvoiceId());
    $this->assertEquals(1, $invoice->getCustomer()
      ->getCustomerId());
    $this->assertEquals(100, $invoice->getPriceTotal());

    $invoiceItems = $invoice->getInvoiceItem();

    $this->assertEquals(100, $invoiceItems[0]->getPrice());
    $this->assertEquals(1, $invoiceItems[0]->getProduct()
      ->getProductId());
}

public function testRaiseInvoice()
{
    $invoiceManager = new \InvoiceManagerDoctrine(self::$em);

    $product = self::$em->find('\MyEntity\Product', 1);

    $customer = self::$em->find('\MyEntity\Customer', 1);
    $status = self::$em->find('\MyEntity\InvoiceStatus', 1);

    $invoice = new \MyEntity\Invoice();
    $invoiceManager->raiseInvoice($invoice, $customer,
```

```
            array(array('product' => $product, 'quantity'
                => 2)), $status);

        $this->assertEquals(20, $invoice->getPriceTotal());

        $invoiceFromDB = $invoiceManager->loadInvoice($invoice
            ->getInvoiceId());

        $this->assertEquals($invoice, $invoiceFromDB);
    }
}
```

This test case is slightly different, but not much. When we open a connection to the database, we can share it between tests, because the database content is going to be wiped out anyway. For this, we used the setUpBeforeClass() method and the protected static $em property to share EntityManager between tests.

The following code snippet is the most interesting part:

```
        $connectionOptions = array('driver' => 'pdo_sqlite',
            'memory' => true);

        // obtaining the entity manager
        self::$em = EntityManager::create($connectionOptions,
            $config);

        $schemaTool = new SchemaTool(self::$em);

        $cmf = self::$em->getMetadataFactory();
        $classes = $cmf->getAllMetadata();

        $schemaTool->dropDatabase();
        $schemaTool->createSchema($classes);
```

As Doctrine can use different database engines without any code change, we used pdo_lite in the memory database. The code then loads metadata from all entities and creates all tables on the fly. Even though Doctrine is a heavyweight champion, because it runs just through the PHP and is kept in memory, its performance is not bad. The following is the result we get:

```
PHPUnit 3.7.30 by Sebastian Bergmann.
Time: 120 ms, Memory: 13.25Mb
OK (2 tests, 9 assertions)
```

Summary

Database integration tests are very important. When data is not stored correctly in the database or if we can't load data correctly, then even the best code is not good. When you start thinking about integration testing, it sounds really tricky. How do you isolate it? How do you write reliable tests? Mocking helps to isolate the code as a starting point, but when we need to test database interactions, then DBUnit really helps with setting up the database into a known state.

Database integration tests could be as important as unit tests, but they can be slower and sometimes less reliable. Because of these reasons, it is suggested that you keep them separate from unit tests. There are several options of how to do this, which we have seen in *Chapter 7, Organizing Tests*.

In the next chapter, we will see a similar topic, the testing API, which could be even worse than testing the database. The database is yours, you can trust it, but not the third-party API. You need tests to help you develop and verify code.

10
Testing APIs

According to Wikipedia, an API is defined as an "application programming interface". Well, it is a nice definition but it would be good to be more precise. In the context of web development, an API usually refers to a server-side API. The described interface is called over an HTTP protocol with a set of defined request/response messages that are usually in the XML or JSON format.

From the programming point of view, it doesn't matter which technology is behind the web service; communication is based on a set of standards.

Not so long ago, there existed very popular services based on **Service Oriented Architecture (SOA)** that used **Simple Object Access Protocol (SOAP)** messages together with **Web Services Description Language (WSDL)** and **XML Schema Definition (XSD)**. You can already imagine from all of these abbreviations that it was a very complex solution. These days, there is more progress towards solutions based on **Representational State Transfer (REST)**. Again, this sounds complicated but it is much more straightforward. REST is a resource-oriented service that uses the HTTP protocol and the GET, POST, PUT, and DELETE methods to access and manipulate resources.

Testing an API is even more problematic than testing a database. Usually, we have complete control over the database and are able to set up a database just for integration testing, with the same structure as a production system but with a known set of data; only then are we able to verify our code's functionality.

Server-side API testing is trickier. If it's an API that you have under control, then for tests, we can bring it to a known state in a way similar to a database. If it's a third-party API, then it's more problematic. Similar to database testing, you have to decide the level you want to test on. Mocking is definitely a good starting point. One option is to call the test API or sandbox if you wish, or you can mock the web service and create a dummy web service. This chapter will show you a few examples of how to test code using some of the most popular services such as Facebook, Twitter, or PayPal.

An example of integration testing

It is more useful to see a real-life example so that you can imagine everything that is involved. As a developer, you must know of a brilliant site named Stack Overflow — http://stackoverflow.com. This site is a very good source of information about PHPUnit. It is definitely not only about PHPUnit; it also comprises many developers who have faced similar problems as you, and you can find many answers there. So, if you haven't used it before, you should definitely give it a try.

This site also has an interface that allows you to access its functionality and data through the API and get responses in the JSON format. This is not only very well-documented, but you can also try and see exactly what each method does. Documentation for this is available at https://api.stackexchange.com/docs.

For our example, let's use the search method to find something about PHPUnit.

At https://api.stackexchange.com/docs/search, you can find not only the method description but also the form with all the input parameters, and when you send a request, you can see the corresponding JSON response:

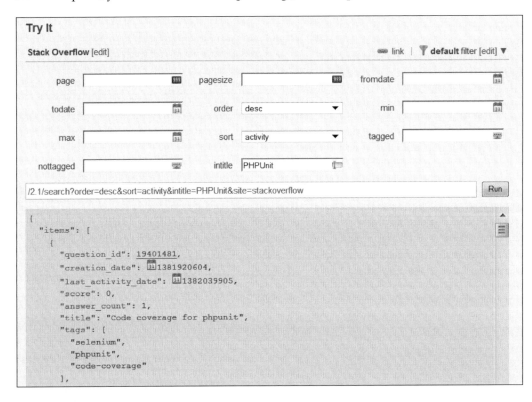

This console is very useful indeed. It shows you what the request should look like and also allows you to capture and save responses.

Now, let's build foundations that can be used by any other project, and see what the project structure looks like. In the previous chapters, we used a simple class loader, but an easier way is to use a Composer class loader. This way, you can add any additional required library later, and Composer adds the required dependencies for you, including installation, updates, and class loading.

If we follow the PSR-0 standard for where and how to store classes, then the Composer class loader can load these classes for us. The code for this is as follows:

```
{
  "autoload": {
    "psr-0": {"": "src/"}
  }
}
```

 PSR-0 is an autoloading standard that was created by PHP Framework Interop Group (http://www.php-fig.org/) and is used by most modern PHP frameworks and libraries.

This is our `composer.json` file that tells the autoload classes to follow the PSR-0 standard stored in the `src` folder:

```
>php composer.phar install
Loading composer repositories with package information
Installing dependencies (including require-dev)
Nothing to install or update
Generating autoload files
```

This command creates the class loader and, if required, also installs additional libraries.

Now, let's go back to our Stack Overflow example and look at the simple client library that will perform the search for the PHPUnit questions.

To do tests, we need two things. Use the Composer class loader and store the configuration in the `config.php` file.

To use the Composer class loader, we can just add `require_once` to the bootstrap file:

```
<?php

require_once __DIR__ ."/../vendor/autoload.php";
require_once "config.php";
```

In the preceding code, the second line loads the configuration. This is quite important because for tests, you can have a configuration that is different from the configuration for staging or production sites. You shouldn't store configuration files under version control systems such as GIT or SVN. Instead, provide a sample config file such as `config.php.dist` and during deployment or manually change it to `config.php`, which is loaded by tests or application.

In our case, `config.php` will be very simple:

```php
<?php

const STACK_END_POINT_URL = "http://api.stackexchange.com";
const STACK_API_VERSION = "2.1";
```

It just contains the web service's URL and the API version used.

If you remember, in *Chapter 8, Using Test Doubles*, we had a simple `Transaction` class using HttpClient, which was passed into the class constructor. This was very handy for testing because we could easily replace HttpClient with mock. We are going to use the same technique for this `StackOverflow` example. A very simple Client class should look like this:

```php
<?php

class CurlClient
{

    public function sendRequest($url)
    {
        $curl = curl_init($url);
        // Include header in result? (0 = yes, 1 = no)
        curl_setopt($curl, CURLOPT_HEADER, 0);
        // Should cURL return or print out the data? (true =
           return, false = print)
        curl_setopt($curl, CURLOPT_RETURNTRANSFER, true);
        curl_setopt($curl, CURLOPT_TIMEOUT, 10);
        curl_setopt($curl, CURLOPT_ENCODING, "gzip");

        $response = curl_exec($curl);
        curl_close($curl);

        if (!$response || !$jsonResponse = json_decode($response))
        {
            throw new \Exception('Invalid response');
        } else
```

```
        {
            return $jsonResponse;
        }
    }
}
```

This is a very simple class with just one method, sendRequest, which uses the curl extension to send a request. You might be tempted to change the method to public static. Do not do this. Static methods are a problem for tests because the static method calls inside the class can't be replaced with a mock.

Our client for calling StackOverflow will be a very simple class; the following is the code:

```php
<?php

namespace StackOverflow;

/**
 * Class Client
 * client for Stack Exchange API v2.0
 * @see https://api.stackexchange.com/docs
 * @package StackOverflow
 */
class Client
{
    /**
     * @var \CurlClient
     */
    private $curlClient;

    public function __construct(\CurlClient $curlClient)
    {
        $this->curlClient = $curlClient;
    }

    /**
     * @param $action
     * @param array $parameters
     * @return string
     */
    private function buildUrl($action, array $parameters)
    {
        $url = STACK_END_POINT_URL;
```

```
        $url .= '/' . STACK_API_VERSION;
        $url .= '/' . $action . '?';
        $url .= http_build_query($parameters);

        return $url;
    }

    public function search($term)
    {
        $url = $this->buildUrl('search',
            array('site' => 'stackoverflow', 'order' => 'desc',
            'sort' => 'activity', 'intitle' => $term,
            'filter' => 'default'));
        return $this->curlClient->sendRequest($url);
    }
}
```

This class has three methods:

- __constructor: This method is where CurlClient is passed
- buildUrl: This method builds the URL where the request needs to be sent based on the parameters that are passed in
- search: This is our search method implementation that uses the buildURL method

By creating and passing CurlClient to the constructor, we are on the right track to have code that calls the API but can also easily be tested. The question is how do we test the API in this case? We have the following two options:

- Call the API directly
- Use mocks to replace the CurlClient::send method

Both of the preceding options could be useful. If we call the API directly, we can verify whether our code works with the web service as expected, but it is going to be slower, and it will require us to create connections to the web service. Another problem is if we start to overload the web service with too many requests, it might be problematic because very often we are limited by the number of requests, or each request could even be a paid request. One of the biggest problems with mocking a web service is authentication. Complex solutions such as OAuth are very difficult to mock, and you really need to call a web service in order to test them.

Mocking can be handy, especially if we have saved the responses returned by the web service. This way, we are confident that our code works as expected when developed, but we might have problems when the web service changes. On the other hand, tests don't have to make a connection to the web service, and there might be fewer problems with negative fails. Both of these are useful. You can run mock tests as often as you like. You can also run integration tests by calling the web service directly within a certain period to be sure that nothing was changed on the web service, and you will still get the same responses as before.

Now, let's have a look at what a test suite could look like:

```php
<?php
namespace StackOverflowTest;

use StackOverflow\Client;

class ClientTest extends \PHPUnit_Framework_TestCase
{
    /**
     * @group apiCall
     */
    public function testLiveSearch()
    {
        $curlClient = new \CurlClient();
        $client = new Client($curlClient);
        $response = $client->search('phpunit');
        $this->assertNotNull($response);
        $this->assertObjectNotHasAttribute('error_id', $response);
    }

    /**
     * @group apiCall
     */
    public function testLiveSearchError()
    {
        $curlClient = new \CurlClient();
        $client = new Client($curlClient);
        $response = $client->search(NULL);
        $this->assertNotNull($response);
        $this->assertObjectHasAttribute('error_id', $response);
    }
}
```

Two tests are calling the API directly and just verifying that the JSON response was received and whether the response is an error. It is good that you get the response directly from the service. The bad thing is that you have to depend on the network connection and speed, and the test is going to be slower than just the unit test. Another problem with the data returned from the web service is that you can't be sure of what comes back; it means the tests are not running in a known context and are not repeatable. A different way of testing the code is by using test doubles, where we can inject recorded messages as shown in the following two tests:

```php
/**
 * @group mock
 */
public function testMockSearch()
{
    $curlClient = $this->getMockBuilder('\CurlClient')
        ->setMethods(array('sendRequest'))
        ->getMock();

    $curlClient->expects($this->once())->method('sendRequest')
        ->will($this->returnValue(
        json_decode(file_get_contents(dirname(__FILE__) .
        '/../messages/search.json'))));

    $client = new Client($curlClient);
    $response = $client->search('phpunit');
    $this->assertNotNull($response);
    $this->assertObjectNotHasAttribute('error_id',$response);
}

/**
 * @group mock
 */
public function testMockSearchError()
{
    $curlClient = $this->getMockBuilder('\CurlClient')
        ->setMethods(array('sendRequest'))->getMock();

    $curlClient->expects($this->once())->method('sendRequest')
        ->will($this->returnValue(
        json_decode(file_get_contents(dirname(__FILE__) .
        '/../messages/error.json'))));
```

```
        $client = new Client($curlClient);
        $response = $client->search(NULL);
        $this->assertNotNull($response);
        $this->assertObjectHasAttribute('error_id',$response);
    }
```

The other two test methods use good old mocks and load the recorded response
from the file.

The file, `search.json`, has a recorded response that looks like the following block
of code:

```
{"items": [
    {
        "question_id": 19398643,
        "creation_date": 1381912460,
        "last_activity_date": 1381938534,
        "score": 0,
        "answer_count": 1,
        "title": "Script for running PHPUnit with custom config and
data",
        "tags": ["php", "phpunit"],
        "view count": 8,
        "owner": {
            "user_id": 1851450,
            "display_name": "mfaerevaag",
            "reputation": 360,
            "user_type": "registered",
            "profile_image": "https://www.gravatar.com/avatar/36824284
f11a1960cbc7c64b5edfebc0?s=128&d=identicon&r=PG",
            "link": "http://stackoverflow.com/users/1851450/
mfaerevaag",
            "accept_rate": 83
        },
        "link": "http://stackoverflow.com/questions/19398643/script-
for-running-phpunit-with-custom-config-and-data",
        "is_answered": false
    }, ..........
```

The second file that we used was the recorded error response, `error.json`:

```
{
    "error_id": 404,
    "error_name": "no_method",
    "error_message": "no method found with this name"
}
```

Even that search method doesn't do much at the moment; it shows an approach using recorded messages that replace the direct API call. An advantage is that it's going to be fast and we know what the response will be; the disadvantage is that it will not highlight any change done on the web service.

As you can see for tests, the annotation `@group` is used, which allows us to include/exclude certain groups from execution; this has been described as a technique for organizing tests in *Chapter 7, Organizing Tests*:

```
>phpunit --bootstrap=bootstrap.php --exclude-group=apiCall ./StackOv
erflowTest/ClientTest.php
PHPUnit 3.7.30 by Sebastian Bergmann.


...


Time: 162 ms, Memory: 4.25Mb

OK (2 tests, 6 assertions)


>phpunit --bootstrap=bootstrap.php --group=apiCall ./StackOverflowTe
st/ClientTest.php

..


Time: 1 second, Memory: 3.50Mb


OK (2 tests, 4 assertions)
```

This way, you can run both tests separately, but as you can see, the `apiCall` group that directly calls the API is indeed slower.

Testing the PayPal API

If you ever worked with the PayPal API in the past, you might agree that it wasn't always easy. You had to decide whether you wanted to use the PayPal Name-Value Pair API (NVP), the PayPal SOAP API (SOAP), or Adaptive Payments, and then realized that the API you chose doesn't contain the method you need, such as currency conversion. I have to say that the documentation wasn't very helpful either. For developers, it was quite confusing and easy to get lost.

Fortunately, PayPal decided to offer another option—the new fresh REST API. It's much more straightforward and easier to implement. There is even a nice fresh library for PHP Version 5.3 and greater at `https://github.com/paypal/rest-api-sdk-php`.

When you check any library or project, it always is a good sign if it contains tests, and if you follow the link to GitHub, there are several tests.

As a package manager, Composer is slowly but surely becoming a standard in the PHP world. For the previous example, we used the Composer autoloader. To use the PayPal PHP SDK, we just need to add and install the required dependency. The updated `composer.json` file then looks like this:

```
{
    "require": {
        "php": ">=5.3.0",
        "ext-curl": "*",
        "ext-json": "*",
        "paypal/rest-api-sdk-php": "0.5.*"
    },
    "autoload": {
        "psr-0": {
            "": "src/"
        }
    }
}
```

Then, on the command line, run `composer update` to install the required libraries:

```
>php composer.phar update
Loading composer repositories with package information
Updating dependencies (including require-dev)
  - Installing paypal/sdk-core-php (V1.2.0)
    Downloading: 100%
```

```
- Installing paypal/rest-api-sdk-php (V0.5.0)
  Downloading: 100%
```

Writing lock file

Generating autoload files

You can see that it installed around 160 files in the vendor/PayPal directory. This is where integration testing helps to understand how to use these libraries and what the process should look like. It is very time-consuming to go through the payment process and debug it there, repeating payments again and again.

Since we are using a third-party library to use mocks, it might be a bit more difficult. However, PayPal has a very good sandbox environment for testing.

To use it, you need to register at `https://developer.paypal.com`, and the registration and usage is free.

When you have a developer account, you need to create an application. Look at the following screenshot for reference:

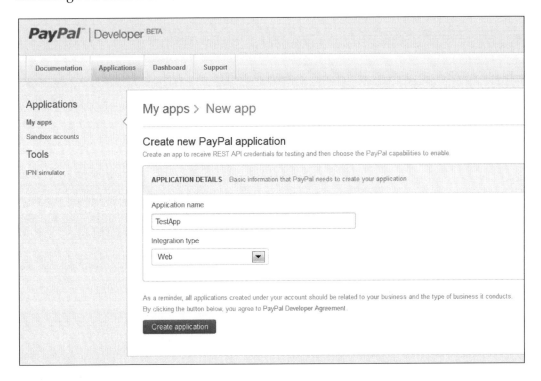

The reason for creating an application is to obtain your REST API credentials, which we are going to use for tests.

For our testing, we are going to use a simple example to make the payment and verify whether the payment was successful. In the real world, code needs to be robust, and expecting the unexpected, log everything that is suspicious, but for our test, we are going to keep it simple just to demonstrate how to use the API.

For authentication, the PayPal REST API uses OAuth 2, which can be very tricky to mock and test because it's based on a set of messages sent between the consumer — your app, and the service provider — in this case, PayPal.

For tests, we can assume that we want to test the following three scenarios:

- Authenticating and obtaining an access token
- Making the payment and getting back the transaction ID
- Verifying the transaction with the obtained transaction ID

In installed PayPal libraries, you can find some examples on how to use the API and the tests. What we need is the sdk_config.ini file that you need to copy to the project's root. Then, update acct1.ClientId and acct1.ClientSecret with the values that you find under the REST API credentials in your test application section on the PayPal website.

Then, just add the following line to the bootstrap or config.php file:

```
const PP_CONFIG_PATH = __DIR__;
```

This tells the PPConfigManager class where the config file is stored.

Now, let's have a look at what the PayPal test suite could look like:

```php
<?php
namespace PayPalIntegrationTest;

use PayPal\Api\CreditCard;
Use PayPalIntegration\Client;

class ClientTest extends \PHPUnit_Framework_TestCase
{
    /**
     * @var \PayPalIntegration\Client
     */
    private $client;
    const PAYMENT_TOTAL = 99;
```

```php
    public function setUp()
    {
        $this->client = new Client();
    }


    public function testGetAuthentication()
    {
        $token = $this->client->getAccessToken();
        $this->assertNotNull($token);
    }


    public function testMakePayment()
    {
        $card = new CreditCard();
        $card->setType("visa");
        $card->setNumber("4417119669820331");
        $card->setExpire_month("01");
        $card->setExpire_year("2016");
        $card->setCvv2("012");
        $card->setFirst_name("Peter");
        $card->setLast_name("Smith");

        $transactionId = $this->client->makePayment($card,
self::PAYMENT_TOTAL);
        $this->assertNotNull($transactionId);

        return $transactionId;
    }


    /**
     * @depends testMakePayment
     */
    public function testGetTransaction($transactionId)
    {
        $payment = $this->client->getTransaction($transactionId);
        $this->assertNotNull($payment);

        $transactions = $payment->getTransactions();
        $this->assertCount(1, $transactions);
        $this->assertEquals(self::PAYMENT_TOTAL,
          $transactions[0]->getAmount()->getTotal());
    }
}
```

The first test verifies the authentication by receiving the access token, the second test makes the payment with the test credit card, and the third test verifies this payment.

Now, let's see what a simple implementation using the PayPal PHP SDK libraries looks like:

```php
<?php
namespace PayPalIntegration;

use PayPal\Auth\OAuthTokenCredential;
use PayPal\Api\Amount;
use PayPal\Api\CreditCard;
use PayPal\Api\Payer;
use PayPal\Api\Payment;
use PayPal\Api\FundingInstrument;
use PayPal\Api\Transaction;
use PayPal\Rest\ApiContext;

class Client
{
    /**
     * @var \PayPal\Auth\OAuthTokenCredential
     */
    private $auth;

    public function __construct()
    {
        $this->setAuth();
    }

    private function setAuth()
    {
        if (!$this->auth) {
            $configManager = \PPConfigManager::getInstance();

            $this->auth =  new OAuthTokenCredential(
              $configManager->get('acct1.ClientId'),
              $configManager->get('acct1.ClientSecret'));
        }
    }

    public function getAccessToken()
    {
        return $this->auth->getAccessToken();
    }
```

To be able to make any API call as a first step, we need to authenticate and obtain the authentication token. Since the PayPal REST API uses OAuth 2.0, this is quite a complex process that consists of a few messages exchanged between the client and server before the access token can be issued:

```
/**
 * @param   CreditCard              $card
 * @param   float                   $value
 * @return string
 * @throws \PPConnectionException
 */
public function makePayment(\PayPal\Api\CreditCard $card,
  $value)
{
    $fi = new FundingInstrument();
    $fi->setCredit_card($card);

    $payer = new Payer();
    $payer->setPayment_method("credit_card");
    $payer->setFunding_instruments(array($fi));

    $amount = new Amount();
    $amount->setCurrency("USD");
    $amount->setTotal($value);

    $transaction = new Transaction();
    $transaction->setAmount($amount);
    $transaction->setDescription("This is the payment
      description.");

    $payment = new Payment();
    $payment->setIntent("sale");
    $payment->setPayer($payer);
    $payment->setTransactions(array($transaction));

    $apiContext = new ApiContext($this->auth, 'Request' .
      time());

    $payment->create($apiContext);

    return $payment->getId();
}
```

The `makePayment` method creates the transaction (payment) with the test credit card:

```
/**
 * @param   string                  $transactionId
 * @return \PayPal\Api\Payment
```

```
    */
    public function getTransaction($transactionId)
    {
        Payment::setCredential($this->auth);

        return Payment::get($transactionId);
    }
```

The `getTransaction` method retrieves the transaction using the provided `transactionId` variable.

As you can see, the class `\PayPalIntegration\Client.php` is more or less just a wrapper for the PayPal SDK, and it's a moment where tests are very useful. There will be moments when there is a library update or you decide to upgrade to the newer version. However, you need to be sure that the code still works as expected. Then, running tests could be a good way to quickly check whether updating the SDK library version is not breaking your code and everything works.

When we have code and implementation, then let's run tests to see what happens:

```
PHPUnit 3.7.30 by Sebastian Bergmann.


Time: 14.35 seconds, Memory: 4.50Mb
OK (3 tests, 5 assertions)
```

All the tests were successfully executed, but you can see that it's slow. On the other hand, you can go to your test application on the PayPal Developer site (`https://developer.paypal.com`) and see all the transactions there.

Testing the Facebook API

Facebook is another service that you might need to use. Let's take a look at how to access the Facebook API and what we can do about testing. For PHP, the official PHP SDK is available at `https://github.com/facebook/facebook-php-sdk`. The easiest installation method is to use Composer; just add the following code to `composer.json`:

```
{
    "require": {
    "facebook/php-sdk": "@stable"
    },
    "autoload": {
        "psr-0": {
            "": "src/"
        }
    }
}
```

To add the Facebook PHP SDK, just run the following command:

```
php composer.phar update
```

When you get used to Composer, then there's no going back. To update the library later, `composer update` does the job.

To call the Facebook web service, you need `FACEBOOK_APP_ID` and `FACEBOOK_APP_SECRET`. The process is similar to PayPal; you need to register at `https://developers.facebook.com` and create the test application there, as shown in the following screenshot:

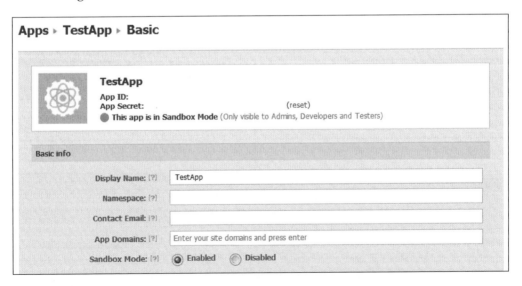

The application has an attribute, **Sandbox Mode**. This is the switch between making it accessible to everybody or only developers and testers. It means there are no different URLs for sandbox and live service as PayPal has; there is just one URL.

The Facebook library works in a way that is similar to our first `StackOverflow` example; it just sends a request to the API and returns a response. The authentication is based on OAuth 2.0, so it is the same process that PayPal is using.

Now, let's create a very simple client to use the Facebook class:

```php
<?php
namespace FacebookIntegration;

use Facebook;

class Client
{
    const TYPE_POST = 'post';
    const TYPE_PAGE = 'page';

    /**
     * @var \Facebook
     */
    private $facebook;

    public function __construct(\Facebook $facebook)
    {
        $this->facebook = $facebook;
    }

    /**
     * @return string
     */
    public function getAccessToken()
    {
        return $this->facebook->getAccessToken();
    }

    /**
     * @param string $term
     * @param string $type
     * @return mixed
     */
```

```
public function search($term, $type, $limit = 10)
{
    $params = array('q'=> $term, 'type'=>$type, 'limit'=>$limit);
    return $this->facebook->api('/search?'.http_build_
        query($params));
}
}
```

`Client` just has the following two methods:

- `getAccessToken`: This method is just a wrapper for the OAuth authentication process
- `search`: This method uses the Facebook Graph API (the Graph API is the primary way in which data is retrieved from or posted to Facebook)

As you can see, this is a really simple example, but for our testing example, it will suffice.

Now, we can write tests to verify that the web service returns what we expect:

```
<?php
namespace FacebookIntegrationTest;

use Facebook;
use FacebookIntegration\Client;

class ClientTest extends \PHPUnit_Framework_TestCase
{
    /**
     * @var \FacebookIntegration\Client
     */
    private $client;

    public function setUp()
    {
        $facebook =  new Facebook(array(
            'appId'  => FACEBOOK_APP_ID,
            'secret' => FACEBOOK_APP_SECRET,));
        $this->client = new Client($facebook);
    }

    public function testGetAccessToken()
    {
        $token = $this->client->getAccessToken();
        $this->assertNotNull($token);
    }
```

```
/**
 * @dataProvider searchProvider
 */
public function testSearch($type)
{
    $response = $this->client->search('phpunit', $type);
    $this->assertNotNull($response);
}

public function searchProvider()
{
    return array(
        array(Client::TYPE_POST),array(Client::TYPE_PAGE),);
}

}
```

As you can see, two constants are used: FACEBOOK_APP_ID and FACEBOOK_APP_SECRET. We stick to the same way as before with the config.php file.

Tests are just simple calls to the API that verify whether a response was received. It is really simple; you can see how it works and easily tweak it to add more tests. For testing and using the Facebook PHP SDK, you need to start the session because the SDK is using the session, and if you don't do it, you will see the error: **session_start(): Cannot send session cookie - headers already sent**.

To avoid this problem, add the following line at the beginning of bootstrap.php:

```
session_start();
```

When you run the tests, you should get the following output:

```
PHPUnit 3.7.30 by Sebastian Bergmann.


Time: 5.58 seconds, Memory: 4.75Mb


OK (4 tests, 5 assertions)
```

Tests have been passed, but the speed is not great. This is the way forward. If you dig into Facebook class to see how it works and then drill down into a parent class BaseFacebook, you will discover the method makeRequest. This method sends an HTTP request in a way that is very similar to our StackOverflow client. If it works similarly, then we can use the same technique to stub this method and return what we want without calling the API.

Capturing responses helps the Graph API Explorer tool (`https://developers.facebook.com/tools/explorer`), which allows you to test requests and see the returned responses.

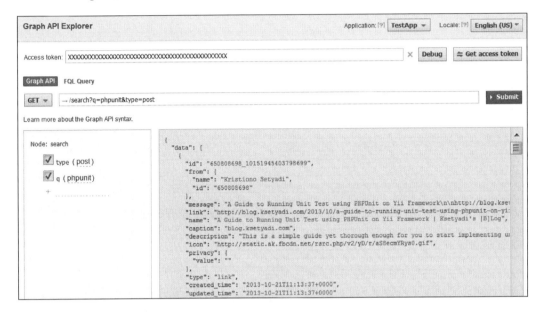

This tool allows you to play with the API and capture responses that you can store in files and use for tests. As you can see in the preceding screenshot, we send a search request for the keyword `phpunit` and `TYPE_POST` (for posted messages).

The `test` method will then look like the following block of code:

```php
public function testSearchPageMock()
{
    $facebook  = $this->getMockBuilder('\Facebook')
        ->setConstructorArgs(array(array(
        'appId'  => FACEBOOK_APP_ID,
        'secret' => FACEBOOK_APP_SECRET,)))
        ->setMethods(array('makeRequest'))->getMock();

    $facebook->expects($this->once())
        ->method('makeRequest')
        ->will($this->returnValue(
        file_get_contents(dirname(__FILE__) .
        '/../messages/facebook_search.json')));
```

```
$client = new Client($facebook);
$response = $client->search('phpunit', Client::TYPE_POST);
$this->assertNotNull($response);
}
```

We replace the `makeRequest` method with our stub even though it's not our library.

Testing the Twitter API

There is always another way to do things. Before you start writing code, it is always good to check that somebody else hasn't done the job already. There are many great libraries that you can use in your project, and there is no need to study and implement a third-party API.

When working with the Twitter API, let's take a slightly different approach and look at what we can use. One of the options is to use the Twitter library, which is a part of Zend Framework 2, but this allows us to use only this library and not the whole MVC framework.

The reason is that there is no official PHP SDK from Twitter, and even the official SDK does not always guarantee quality.

ZendService_Twitter can be found on GitHub at `https://github.com/zendframework/ZendService_Twitter` and is quite nice as a ready-to-use solution for accessing Twitter.

When we get a third-party library, it is good to know how it works, and of course, this is the moment when we have to write tests.

Again, by using Composer, it's easy to install this library and all the required dependencies. Also, this time, we include Mockery, which was mentioned in *Chapter 8, Test Doubles*:

```
{
    "require": {
        "php": ">=5.3.0",
        "ext-curl": "*",
        "ext-json": "*",
        "zendframework/zend-http": "2.2.3",
        "zendframework/zendservice-twitter": "2.x",
        "mockery/mockery": "0.8.x"
    }
}
```

Because of an unfixed bug in the ZendHttp library, this library needs to be set manually to the older version (2.2.3).

Similar to the testing of other web services, you need to create a developer account at `https://dev.twitter.com`. With the created account, you will need to create a test application to receive the access credentials.

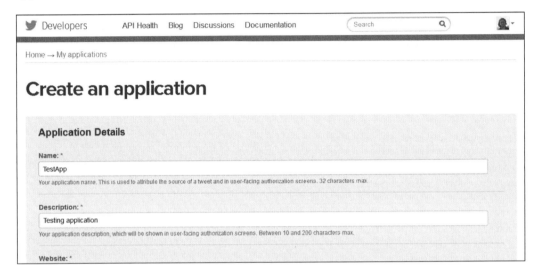

After running `composer update`, check the class `TwitterTest` under `ZendTest\Twitter`; it is a test case for `ZendService\Twitter`.

It is always good to check the code that somebody else wrote and learn from it. What is interesting in the mentioned class is how a mock was created to avoid calling the API directly; instead, it loads the responses saved in files in the same way as we did previously.

Now, you might think, so let's extend this class and write our own tests on top of the existing tests. However, there are two problems with this class. It's not compliant with PSR-0, which means it can't be loaded with a Composer loader. This can be sorted by hardcoding the class name and path in the `autoload_classmap.php` file. However, another problem is that the saved messages' location is using the `__DIR__` constant, which means its path is relative to this class and not very useful for us when we want to use our messages.

Never mind. Let's take it as an inspiration on how to create a mock. This is because for complex mocks, it's easier to use Mockery. Let's give it a try and take a look at what a test could look like:

```php
<?php

namespace TwitterTest;

use Mockery;
use Zend\Http;
use ZendService\Twitter;

class ClientTest  extends \PHPUnit_Framework_TestCase
{
    public function tearDown()
    {
        Mockery::close();
    }

    protected function stubTwitter($path, $method,
      $responseFile = null, array $params = null)
    {
        $client = Mockery::mock('ZendOAuth\Client')
          ->shouldIgnoreMissing();

        $client->shouldReceive('resetParameters')
          ->andReturn($client);

        $client->shouldReceive('setUri')->once()
          ->with('https://api.twitter.com/1.1/' . $path);

        if (!is_null($params)) {
            $setter = 'setParameter' . ucfirst(strtolower($method));
            $client->shouldReceive($setter)->once()->with($params);
        }

        $response = Mockery::mock('Zend\Http\Response');

        $response->shouldReceive('getBody')
          ->andReturn(isset($responseFile) ? file_get_contents
          (__DIR__ . '/../messages/' . $responseFile) : '');

        $client->shouldReceive('send')->once()->andReturn($response);

        return $client;
    }
```

The method `stubTwitter` is a helper method that allows us to create a mock of the `Client` class under `ZendOAuth` to inject its prerecorded response. This might look complicated, but with Mockery, it's much easier to read than the perform mocking that is done with PHPUnit:

```
/**
 * @group mock
 */
public function testSearch()
{
    $twitter = new Twitter\Twitter;
    $twitter->setHttpClient($this->stubTwitter(
      'search/tweets.json', Http\Request::METHOD_GET,
      'twitter_search.json'), array('q' => '#phpunit'));
    $response = $twitter->search->tweets('#phpunit');
    $this->assertInstanceOf('\ZendService\Twitter\
      Response', $response);
}
```

In the preceding code, the `testSearch` method is testing the API `search` method. We are using the response stored in `twitter_search.json`. You can test the API and record messages easily using the Twitter console at `https://dev.twitter.com/console`.

When we have written tests using mocks, it will be good to try live API calls just to ensure that it really works and the API wasn't upgraded to the newer version or something similar:

```
/**
 * @group apiCall
 */
public function testSearchLive()
{
    $twitter = new Twitter\Twitter(array(
        'access_token' => array(
            'token'  => TWITTER_ACCESS_TOKEN,
            'secret' => TWITTER_ACCESS_SECRET,
        ),
        'oauth_options' => array(
            'consumerKey' => TWITTER_CONSUMER_KEY,
            'consumerSecret' => TWITTER_CONSUMER_SECRET,
        ),
        'http_client_options' => array(
            'adapter' => 'Zend\Http\Client\Adapter\Curl',
            'curloptions' => array(
              CURLOPT_SSL_VERIFYHOST => false,
              CURLOPT_SSL_VERIFYPEER => false,
            ),
        ),
    )
    );

    $response = $twitter->search->tweets('#phpunit');
    $this->assertInstanceOf('\ZendService\Twitter\
      Response',$response);
        $this->assertTrue($response->isSuccess());
}
}
```

For a live API call, you will need credentials from the test application that you created and store them in the configuration file.

Testing the service-oriented architecture

The **Remote Procedure Call (RPC)** architecture, such as XML-RPC and SOAP, is a very powerful solution, but sometimes, it seems to be almost too powerful. Due to the progress towards REST-oriented architecture and its popularity in the recent years, all the examples in this chapter use REST.

However, the biggest advantage of RPC solutions is that they are self-documenting. The **Web Services Description Language (WSDL)** is an XML document that works as an interface that describes all the service functions. This is handy for testing, and PHPUnit has the `getMockFromWsdl` method, which works exactly like `getMock` but uses a WSDL file instead of a class to obtain a method's description.

Another option is to mock service. There are many handy tools available, such as SoapUI (`http://www.soapui.org`), which allow you to build a mocked service by using a WSDL file. Then, you can start this service as a server for testing. There are many other interesting things that you can do, but they are beyond the scope of this book; just to mention, one of them is to use SoapUI as a proxy to capture requests and responses between the client and server.

Summary

As you saw, testing an API is nothing difficult and could be very useful when you are exploring what you can do with an API, how to call it, and what comes back. Tests can be a very useful way to learn and see what an API offers and how to integrate it with your application. Since API calls are sent as HTTP requests, a network connection is required; we don't want to run them very often. Capturing responses and using them for our tests is a good way of writing integration tests. Almost every web service offers a console that allows you to explore the API and capture these messages.

However, it's good to have two sets of tests. One set of tests uses mocks to avoid calling the API directly, and the second set of tests actually calls the API to make sure that nothing was changed there.

When you use the integration test approach, then working with the API can be real fun, and you can also write reliable code using almost any decent web service very quickly. Using tests in this case can significantly reduce the time required for third-party API integration, and the quality of produced code will also be much higher than "wild integration" by using the try and see methods.

In this chapter, we saw something that is cool and fun to work with. However, we don't live in a perfect world; what if we need to test untestable legacy code?

We will see what techniques and solutions you can use for testing legacy code in the next chapter.

11
Testing Legacy Code

So far, we have looked at how to write better and more testable code. It is important to get into the habit of writing tests, and it doesn't matter if you take the "test first" approach or you write code and immediately write tests for it (if not immediately, then at least on the same day). The worst thing is to slip back into the habit of believing that somehow it will work and wondering why you should waste the time writing tests. Hopefully, you've seen the advantages of writing tests, and for you, it's not a problem. However, the problem occurs when you have a project based on legacy code, and you need to keep this code running, or even extend it. Of course, it's expected that there are not going to be any bugs, and the project will be delivered on time and on budget. Honestly, working with legacy code can be depressing. If you are facing a project in which you have to build it on top of legacy code, then you need to be brave. It's not necessary to sacrifice everything you have learned, all the good habits, but it's definitely more difficult than working with new, shiny, well-structured code. The question is—what is legacy code? There are many definitions, but from our point of view, it's code without any tests, or even worse, it is untestable. Something that might look unimportant to somebody becomes very important when you need to maintain, extend, or refactor this code.

As a developer, sometimes you have no choice and you have to work with legacy code. It's part of your job and you have to do it. However, even legacy code can be tested and made testable. In this chapter, we will look at how to test legacy code and the different techniques and tools we can use that we haven't used so far.

 Did you know that in PHP 5.3.0, the `goto` operator was introduced—yes, `goto`, which you might remember from BASIC. Another feature is the `eval()` function, which can be useful in specific circumstances. However, both `eval()` and `goto` are considered evil since they are features that help to create unreadable, unpredictable, and untestable code.

What exactly does legacy or untestable code mean?

Look at the following example. Many people start with PHP by writing similar code, and they are happy because it works:

```php
<?
    $dbhost = 'localhost';
    $dbuser = 'root';
    $dbpass = '';
    $conn = mysql_connect($dbhost, $dbuser, $dbpass);
    mysql_select_db('mydb');
?>
<html>
<head>
    <title>Super Page</title>
</head>
<body>
<form action="" method="post">
    <input name="column1" type="text">
    <input type="submit" value="Submit">
</form>
<?
    if($_POST['column1']){
        $sql = "INSERT INTO table1 (column1) VALUES
            ('".$_POST['column1']."')";
        mysql_query( $sql);
    }
?>
<table>
    <tr>
        <th>Id</th>
        <th>Column1</th>
    </tr>
    <?
    $query=mysql_query("SELECT * FROM table1");
    while($r = mysql_fetch_assoc($query)) {
      echo "<tr><td>".$r['id'].'</td><td>'.$r['column1'].
        "</td></tr>";
    }
    ?>
</table>
</body>
</html>
<?
mysql_close($conn);
?>
```

Now, what can you do with code like this? Nothing. Start again. If you can't, at least move the database operation to functions, and add validation and sanitization on all the inputs. Try to break the code in the MVC design pattern. For functions, you can write unit or integration tests, and a whole page can be tested with Selenium.

Testing spaghetti code

Spaghetti code sounds really funny, but it's not funny at all. This expression describes code that looks like a bowl of spaghetti. It's twisted and tangled, and when you call it, you see where it starts, but who knows where it comes back and how it looks inside. However, there's nothing wrong with this code. The application has worked fine for many years now and there is no need to change it; we just need to tweak it a little.

Now, when you work with this code, you have to modify it, but also, more than ever, you need a technique that will ensure that the whole thing is not falling apart. You might at least need to do some refactoring to put in place some meatballs (the code that you need to write in order to understand how it works and looks), then you can upgrade to spaghetti with meatballs. However, the situation is still far from perfect.

What you can do about testing and code like this is to use black box testing. Black box testing means we will have known inputs and we can check the outputs without worrying too much about what is happening inside. These tests are definitely not going to be unit tests but more integration tests or even functional tests.

Black box testing

The following are some basic approaches for black box testing:

- **Selenium tests**: We are going to look at selenium tests closely in the next chapter. But for now, we will just give you a quick introduction. Selenium tests are tests that send commands through the web browser and allow you to check the results and work with them. It is a completely different category, but a brilliant way to test any web-based application including JavaScript and Ajax calls, without any need to know how it works.

- **Integration tests**: In this case, it is good to cover the core functionality with integration tests, simply passing input and validating output without worrying too much what is happening under the hood.

- **Database-focused integration tests**: These tests focus not on validating the output but checking if an operation has affected the database records.

- **Isolation**: You isolate only the tested code by using mock or redefining functions or methods to stop propagation.

Using Reflection

Reflection is defined as the ability to inspect and modify code at runtime. It's very handy when you need to inspect an unknown object or an object of which you are not sure of the exact type. However, it can also be useful for tests because you can change the methods' visibility.

The problems for tests are final, private, and static methods. The main problem is that they can't be stubbed or mocked, and PHPUnit is ignoring them, leaving their original code.

Another problem is a bit philosophical — should I write unit tests for private and protected methods? Previously, it was said that you should just test public methods, but there are situations when it is also good to have tests for private or protected methods, for example, when you work with legacy code. Just changing these methods to public is bad.

Fortunately, PHP provides a way to handle it. It's called the Reflection API and was introduced in PHP5.

The following code snippet shows a very simple class with two methods that we shouldn't be able to test:

```php
<?php

class MathClass
{
    private function addition($a, $b)
    {
        return $a + $b;
    }

    protected static function subtraction($a, $b)
    {
        return $a - $b;
    }
}
```

To make these methods visible, we use the `ReflectionMethod` class and `setAccessible(TRUE)`. Then, we will be able to call these methods directly from outside this class. To make our life easier, we can create methods to change visibility on the fly and use it during test execution. The following code depicts a simple method that allows us to call private methods:

```
/**
 * @param $object
 * @param string $methodName
 * @return mixed
 * @throws Exception
 */
protected function callPrivate($object, $methodName /*, $arg1,
   $arg2, ... */)
{
    if (!is_object($object))
    {
        throw new Exception("{$object} is not an object");
    }

    if (!method_exists($object, $methodName))
    {
        throw new Exception(get_class($object)." has no method
           ".$methodName);
    }

    $args = array_slice(func_get_args(), 2);
    $method = ncw ReflectionMethod($object, $methodName);
    $method->setAccessible(TRUE);

    return $method->invokeArgs($object, $args);
}
```

This method accepts the object and method name as input parameters in places where we want to change visibility, followed by as many method parameters as you need. This is because PHP allows you to pass extra parameters, even though they are not declared in method declaration, and access them through the func_get_args() function. Then, the ReflectionMethod class allows us to change the method's visibility. Similar to callPrivate(), we can have another method that allows us to call private or protected static methods:

```
/**
 * @param string $className
 * @param string $methodName
 * @return mixed
 * @throws Exception
 */
```

```php
protected function callPrivateStatic($className, $methodName
    /*, $arg1, ... */)
{
    if (!class_exists($className))
    {
        throw new Exception("Class {$className} does not
            exist");
    }

    if (!method_exists($className, $methodName))
    {
        throw new Exception($className." has no static method
            ".$methodName);
    }

    $args = array_slice(func_get_args(), 2);
    $method = new ReflectionMethod($className, $methodName);
    $method->setAccessible(TRUE);

    return $method->invokeArgs(NULL, $args);
}
```

This is similar to the previous method, but it works for private and protected static methods.

Now, we can use it in tests for our simple `MathClass` to be able to test private method addition and protected static method subtraction:

```php
public function testAddition()
{
    $mathObject = new MathClass();
    $result = $this->callPrivate($mathObject,'addition', 1, 1);
    $this->assertEquals(2,$result);
}

public function testSubtraction()
{
    $result = $this->callPrivateStatic('MathClass','subtraction',
1, 1);
    $this->assertEquals(0,$result);
}
```

Handling dependencies

When you really need to test legacy code, you might very quickly discover that it's impossible. Even a simple function calls another function, which calls yet another function, and this one even stores results in the database before returning the result. When you test object-oriented code, it might not be too bad; you can stub and mock objects to replace unwanted dependencies and be able to focus on the tested piece of code.

But of course, there is a way to test the untestable, and we will see some libraries and extensions that might help us. But please, always try to keep things simple. Even test doubles can be a double-edged sword — when replacing actual code, you might miss real bugs.

The mentioned libraries and extensions might allow you to perform magic tricks, but I strongly suggest that you use them only as a last resort. Definitely don't use them on the production environment and possibly not even on staging. These tools are designed to be used for development and testing, and they are marked as beta or experimental versions. Nevertheless, they might be very useful in specific scenarios. For all of the following libraries, it is a good idea to disable opcode caching such as the usage of APC, Zend OPcache, and similar extensions.

As a real-life example, we can take one very popular system. WordPress is what I call legacy code (`https://github.com/WordPress/WordPress`). As legacy code, it's perfect. It is a nested procedural code that is almost exclusive, some classes of which look like survivors from PHP4 days, with global variables everywhere. So this is going to be a perfect example of how to write tests for legacy code.

The Patchwork library

Patchwork is a library that allows you to redefine user-defined functions at runtime. Installation and usage is very easy; just add the required dependency to `composer.json`, as shown in the following code snippet:

```
"require-dev": {
    "antecedent/patchwork": "*"
}
```

More information about the library can be found at `http://antecedent.github.io/patchwork/`. Let's see what we can do with this library.

The following line of code is the most important for us:

```
Patchwork\replace(callable $original, callable $redefinition);
```

This allows us to replace, on the fly, any user-defined function with our new function; the result is going to be similar to a method stub.

A good example of how to use it against legacy code is a file that can be found at the following link:

```
https://github.com/WordPress/WordPress/blob/master/wp-includes/
pluggable.php
```

We can try to write a test for the is_user_logged_in() function, and when we look at the function, we will immediately be able to see what the problem is for testing:

```
function is_user_logged_in() {
  $user = wp_get_current_user();
  if ( ! $user->exists() )
    return false;
  return true;
}
```

This is a simple straightforward function, but it is calling another function wp_get_current_user():

```
function wp_get_current_user() {
  global $current_user;

  get_currentuserinfo();

  return $current_user;
}
```

As you can see, there is a global user object and another function get_currentuserinfo(), which is called by wp_set_current_user(). If current_user is not set, then it's creating an instance of WP_User, which is also calling the database. For testing, it is just "brilliant". I mean it is bad, as it is very difficult to isolate each function and the global variables' usage deep inside the code database calls.

Now, let's try to write some tests and see how Patchwork will help us. WordPress can't be added directly with Composer; you need to download WordPress or clone a GitHub repository as shown:

```
>git clone https://github.com/WordPress/WordPress
```

In this case, I suggest that you keep it outside our project and add it to the bootstrap file's location where WordPress is stored. Also, when using Patchwork, you need to add an extra line, and then bootstrap would look like the following code snippet:

```php
<?php
const WORDPRESS_LOCATION = 'C:/projects/wordpress';
require_once __DIR__ ."/../vendor/autoload.php";
require_once __DIR__ ."/../vendor/antecedent/patchwork/Patchwork.php";
```

Now, we can write tests for the is_user_logged_in() and wp_get_current_user() functions. The WordPressTest class is an example where we used the Patchwok library:

```php
<?php
require_once WORDPRESS_LOCATION. DIRECTORY_SEPARATOR . 'wp-
    includes' . DIRECTORY_SEPARATOR . 'capabilities.php' ;
require_once WORDPRESS_LOCATION. DIRECTORY_SEPARATOR . 'wp-
    includes' . DIRECTORY_SEPARATOR . 'pluggable.php' ;
```

The constant WORDPRESS_LOCATION is the location where the WordPress code is stored. For the test, we need to include the original WordPress code. The test suite is quite simple, but it allows us to test the is_user_logged_in() function:

```php
class WordPressTest extends PHPUnit_Framework_TestCase
{
    public function testIs_user_logged_in()
    {
        $user = $this->getMockBuilder('WP_User')
          ->setMethods(array('exists'))
          ->disableOriginalConstructor()->getMock();

        $user->expects($this->any())->method('exists')
          ->will($this->returnValue(true));

        Patchwork\replace('wp_get_current_user', function () use
($user) {
                return $user;
            });

        $this->assertTrue(is_user_logged_in());
    }
}
```

This test combines the WP_User mock (the PHPUnit mocking feature) and the Patchwork replacement for the wp_get_current_user() function. Instead of calling the original function, it will just return a $user mock with a stub for the existing method and return true.

Then, when we replace the original function `wp_get_current_user()` to stop propagation and isolate `is_user_logged_in()`, we can call `is_user_logged_in()` and verify its functionality. By replacing the `get_currentuserinfo()` function to stop propagation, we can test the `wp_get_current_user()` function:

```
public function testWp_get_current_user()
{
    $user = $this->getMockBuilder('WP_User')
        ->setMethods(array('exists'))
        ->disableOriginalConstructor()->getMock();

    Patchwork\replace('get_currentuserinfo', function () {});

    $GLOBALS['current_user'] = $user;
    $this->assertEquals($user, wp_get_current_user());
}

public function tearDown()
{
    unset($GLOBALS['current_user']);
}
}
```

As we've modified `$GLOBALS`, it's a good habit to use the `tearDown()` method to restore the global state.

In a similar way, we created a stub for the `get_currentuserinfo()` function, where replacement is just an empty shell; then, we can directly call the `wp_get_current_user()` function.

The vfsStream library

vfsStream is a wrapper for a virtual filesystem and allows you to create mocks to access the filesystem. You can use it whenever access to the filesystem is required — when you need to check for the existence of a certain file or write output to the file.

Why would this be useful? For tests where you need to read/write files on the filesystem, you don't want to create and leave files in the filesystem. If the test execution is interrupted before you delete the file, the next test might fail because the file already exists. Another reason might be that the code is creating a file with a dynamic path and name, but you can't be sure about what it might be exactly (depending on the date/time), but you need to be sure that the environment is going to be clear and a file is stored where you need, not where it's hardcoded.

To install this library, just add the required dependency to `composer.json`, as shown in the following line of code:

```
"mikey179/vfsStream": "*"
```

Here is one common scenario where we need to export data to a CSV file:

```php
<?php

class UtilCsv
{
    /**
     * @param  array $data
     * @param string $path
     * @param $filename
     * @return bool
     */
    public static function createCsv(array $data, $path, $filename)
    {
        if(!file_exists($path))
            mkdir($path, 0770, true);

        $fp = fopen($path . DIRECTORY_SEPARATOR . $filename , 'w');

        if(!$fp)
        {
            return false;
        }

        foreach ($data as $row)
        {
            fputcsv($fp, $row);
        }

        fclose($fp);

        return true;
    }
}
```

For the static method, we pass an array of data and a second parameter that specifies where the CSV file is to be exported. Now, let's see how we can test this method with the traditional approach and with vfsStream usage:

```php
<?php

use org\bovigo\vfs\vfsStream;

class UtilCsvTest extends PHPUnit_Framework_TestCase
{
    /**
     * @var org\bovigo\vfs\vfsStreamDirectory
     */
    private $vfsDir;

    /**
     * @var string system temp directory
     */
    private $dir;

    public function setUp()
    {
        $this->vfsDir = vfsStream::setup('dataDir');
        $this->dir = sys_get_temp_dir();
    }

    public function tearDown()
    {
        if(file_exists($this->dir . DIRECTORY_SEPARATOR .
          'export.csv'))
        {
            unlink($this->dir . DIRECTORY_SEPARATOR .
              'export.csv');
        }
    }

    public function testCreateCsv()
    {
        $data = array(array('Column 1','Column 2',
          'Column 3'),array(1,2,3),array(5,6,7));

        $this->assertTrue(UtilCsv::createCsv($data,$this
          ->dir,'export.csv'));
        $this->assertFileExists($this->dir .DIRECTORY_SEPARATOR .
          'export.csv');
    }
```

This is a classic approach where we use the system's temporary directory (`sys_get_temp_dir`) as a location in which we store the created file, and in the `tearDown()` method, we delete the created file.

This is not difficult, but we are depending on the filesystem's access, and there are possible problems if the file already exists or is not writable and so on. Also, we know that our test should be independent and repeatable.

Now, let's see how we can simplify it by using vfsStream:

```
public function testCreateCsvVfs()
{
    $data = array(array('Column 1','Column 2',
        'Column 3'),array(1,2,3),array(5,6,7));

    $this->assertTrue(UtilCsv::createCsv
        ($data,vfsStream::url('dataDir'),'export.csv'));
    $this->assertFileExists($this->vfsDir
        ->getChild('export.csv')->url());
    }
}
```

Instead of the real file location, we use a virtual location:

```
$this->vfsDir = vfsStream::setup('dataDir');
```

The test is executed in exactly the same way, but instead of storing the file to the filesystem, we store it to a virtual filesystem.

The runkit PHP extension

The runkit extension is probably the most advanced but also the most dangerous weapon. It allows you to modify almost everything on the fly—user-defined functions and classes, and even the internal PHP functions when necessary. However, as mentioned earlier, this is heavyweight, and you should use it only when you know what you are doing and definitely only in a development or testing environment.

In comparison to the previous libraries, this is an extension. Here, Composer is not enough. So far, we have only used one extension, Xdebug, which we installed after installing PHPUnit.

Unfortunately, with runkit, it's even more difficult because it's not an extension as widely used as Xdebug. One option is to compile it from source files; it's not difficult, but to explain how to compile an extension is beyond the scope of this book.

Another option is to use PECL, which is a repository for PHP extensions. The PECL tool is also installed together with PEAR. It effortlessly compiles an extension for you. More information can be found at `http://www.php.net/manual/en/install.pecl.phpize.php`. In this case, it is safer to use virtual machines—one of the best is the Vagrant tool with VirtualBox VM (`http://www.vagrantup.com/`).

To install runkit, run the following command line:

```
>sudo pecl install runkit
```

You might see an error as shown in the following screenshot:

To fix it, you need to use the beta version; simply change the command to the following command line:

```
>sudo pecl install runkit-beta
```

Now, the extension is installed. If not, you will get an error similar to the one shown in the following command line:

```
/usr/include/php5/Zend/zend_hash.h:140:15: note: expected 'apply_func_
args_t' but argument is of type 'int (*)(struct zend_internal_function *,
int,   struct __va_list_tag *, struct zend_hash_key *)'
make: *** [runkit.lo] Error 1
ERROR: `make' failed
```

This means the version that PECL tried to install is not compatible with your PHP version. In this case, you need to tell PECL that you want to install the latest version of runkit directly from its GitHub repository:

```
>sudo pecl install https://github.com/downloads/zenovich/runkit/runkit-
1.0.3.tgz
```

Successful installation should give you an output similar to the one shown in the following screenshot:

```
vagrant@precise64: ~                                              _ □ X
install-runkit-1.0.3
131524    4 drwxr-xr-x 3 root root    4096 Nov  2 15:26 /tmp/pear/temp/pear-build-root9eowUh/
install-runkit-1.0.3/usr
131525    4 drwxr-xr-x 3 root root    4096 Nov  2 15:26 /tmp/pear/temp/pear-build-root9eowUh/
install-runkit-1.0.3/usr/lib
131526    4 drwxr-xr-x 3 root root    4096 Nov  2 15:26 /tmp/pear/temp/pear-build-root9eowUh/
install-runkit-1.0.3/usr/lib/php5
131527    4 drwxr-xr-x 2 root root    4096 Nov  2 15:26 /tmp/pear/temp/pear-build-root9eowUh/
install-runkit-1.0.3/usr/lib/php5/20090626
131523 232 -rwxr-xr-x 1 root root  234017 Nov  2 15:26 /tmp/pear/temp/pear-build-root9eowUh/
install-runkit-1.0.3/usr/lib/php5/20090626/runkit.so

Build process completed successfully
Installing '/usr/lib/php5/20090626/runkit.so'
install ok: channel://__uri/runkit-1.0.3
configuration option "php_ini" is not set to php.ini location
You should add "extension=runkit.so" to php.ini
vagrant@precise64:~$
```

Now, you need to enable the extension in your php.ini file, or add the config file to /etc/php/conf.d — it depends on your OS. To check if the extension is loaded, run the following command line:

```
>php --re runkit
```

Now you should see an output similar to the following screenshot:

```
vagrant@precise64: ~                                              _ □ X
vagrant@precise64:~$ php --re runkit
Extension [ <persistent> extension #45 runkit version 1.0.3 ] {

  - INI {
    Entry [ runkit.superglobal <PERDIR,SYSTEM> ]
      Current = ''
    }
    Entry [ runkit.internal_override <SYSTEM> ]
      Current = '1'
    }
  }

  - Constants [15] {
    Constant [ integer RUNKIT_IMPORT_FUNCTIONS ] { 1 }
    Constant [ integer RUNKIT_IMPORT_CLASS_METHODS ] { 2 }
    Constant [ integer RUNKIT_IMPORT_CLASS_CONSTS ] { 4 }
    Constant [ integer RUNKIT_IMPORT_CLASS_PROPS ] { 8 }
    Constant [ integer RUNKIT_IMPORT_CLASS_STATIC_PROPS ] { 16 }
    Constant [ integer RUNKIT_IMPORT_CLASSES ] { 30 }
    Constant [ integer RUNKIT_IMPORT_OVERRIDE ] { 32 }
    Constant [ string RUNKIT_VERSION ] { 1.0.3 }
```

If runkit is installed, you should see information about this extension.

But what exactly can you do with runkit? We can do the following tasks:

- Create a sandbox—a PHP virtual machine where dangerous or tested code can be executed
- Change a class inheritance
- Add/redefine/remove a constant
- Add/copy/redefine/remove/rename a function
- Add/copy/redefine/remove/rename a method
- Validate PHP code syntax

I can imagine that when you see this, you will say to yourself, "Oh dear". But now, think about your legacy code, and, yes, it is possible to imagine when it could be useful.

We can go back to WordPress as it's a really good source of untestable legacy code. As a random piece of code, we can choose the `WP_User` class, which was mentioned earlier (`https://github.com/WordPress/WordPress/blob/master/wp-includes/capabilities.php`).

Just calling the constructor triggers a chain of calls when almost half of the WordPress is loaded—tons of global variables are needed and the database is called. To be able to run tests, it is necessary to isolate the code. In this case, we really need heavy weapons. Again, this approach should be used only as a last resort, but it demonstrates what you can do with runkit. Now we can use runkit to redefine functions as follows:

```php
<?php
require_once WORDPRESS_LOCATION. DIRECTORY_SEPARATOR .
   'wp-includes' . DIRECTORY_SEPARATOR . 'capabilities.php' ;
require_once WORDPRESS_LOCATION. DIRECTORY_SEPARATOR .
   'wp-includes' . DIRECTORY_SEPARATOR . 'cache.php' ;
require_once WORDPRESS_LOCATION. DIRECTORY_SEPARATOR .
   'wp-includes' . DIRECTORY_SEPARATOR . 'wp-db.php' ;

class WP_UserTest extends PHPUnit_Framework_TestCase
{
    public function setUp()
    {
        $GLOBALS['wpdb'] = $this->getMockBuilder('wpdb')
           ->disableOriginalConstructor()->getMock();
        $GLOBALS['wpdb']->prefix = 'xx';
```

```
runkit_method_redefine('WP_User', 'get_data_by', '',
    'return (object) array(\'ID\'=>99);', RUNKIT_ACC_PUBLIC
    | RUNKIT_ACC_STATIC);
runkit_method_redefine('WP_User', '_init_caps', '', '',
    (RUNKIT_ACC_PUBLIC));
runkit_function_redefine('wp_cache_get', '$key, $group',
    'return 1;');

}

public function tearDown()
{
    unset($GLOBALS['wpdb']);
}

public function testConstructById()
{
    $wpUser = new WP_User();
    $this->assertNotEquals(1, $wpUser->get('ID'));
    $this->assertEquals(99, $wpUser->get('ID'));
}
}
```

The setUp() method contains all the magic tricks. As the first step, we created a global object wpdb that handles database queries. In our case, it's just a fake object; all methods will be there, but will return just NULL. For the purpose of this test, this is ok; we don't want to call the database.

Then, there is another problem with code inside the Wp_User constructor: the static method self::get_data_by(). Stubbing static methods is a problem, or to be precise, you can do it when late static binding is used:

```
$class = $this->getMockClass(
    'MyClass', array('myMethod'));

$class::staticExpects($this->any())->method('myMethod')
    ->will($this->returnValue(true));
```

However, legacy code does not use static::myMethod but self:myMethod. This means we have to use runkit to redefine the get_data_by() method:

```
runkit_method_redefine('WP_User', 'get_data_by', '', 'return
    (object) array(\'ID\'=>99);', RUNKIT_ACC_PUBLIC |
    RUNKIT_ACC_STATIC);
```

This way, we redefine the `WP_User` class and the `get_data_by()` method to return an object with an ID of 99.

Then another step is to redefine the function `wp_cache_get()`:

```
runkit_function_redefine('wp_cache_get', '$key, $group', 'return
    1;');
```

We redefine the `wp_cache_get()` function just to return 1.

This test is not really useful; it just shows how you can stop propagation and isolates a piece of code that you want to test.

With runkit, you can redefine even internal PHP functions. In the previous chapter, we created a simple client to call an API:

```
public function sendRequest($url)
{
    $curl = curl_init($url);
    // Include header in result? (0 = yes, 1 = no)
    curl_setopt($curl, CURLOPT_HEADER, 0);
    // Should cURL return or print out the data? (true =
      return, false = print)
    curl_setopt($curl, CURLOPT_RETURNTRANSFER, true);
    curl_setopt($curl, CURLOPT_TIMEOUT, 10);
    curl_setopt($curl, CURLOPT_ENCODING, "gzip");

    $response = curl_exec($curl);
    curl_close($curl);

    if (!$response || !$jsonResponse = json_decode($response)) {
        throw new \Exception('Invalid response');
    } else {
        return $jsonResponse;
    }
}
```

Then, we created a mock to return a defined response:

```
$curlClient = $this->getMockBuilder('\CurlClient')
  ->setMethods(array('sendRequest'))->getMock();

    $curlClient->expects($this->once())->method('sendRequest')
      ->will($this->returnValue(json_decode
      (file_get_contents(dirname(__FILE__) .
      '/../messages/search.json'))));
```

With runkit, you can redefine the internal `curl_exec` function:

```
public function testRunkitSearch()
{
    runkit_function_redefine('curl_exec', '$curl', 'return
        file_get_contents(dirname(__FILE__) .
        "/messages/search.json");');

    $curlClient = new CurlClient();
    $client = new \StackOverFlow\Client($curlClient);
    $response = $client->search('phpunit');
    $this->assertNotNull($response);
    $this->assertFalse(isset($response->error_id));
}
```

By default, you can't redefine internal functions, but you can change this by adding the following line to the `php.ini` file or the `runkit.ini` configuration file:

```
runkit.internal_override = 1
```

Then, when you execute the test, it works and it's really fast. What we did was, instead of the stubbing method, we forced `curl_exec` to return a prerecorded message. This could be very useful when you have API/database calls buried somewhere deep inside the code, and you actually don't care much about how it works internally. You just need to simulate how the code will behave in certain situations, that is, black box testing.

Summary

Testing legacy code is not easy, but it's possible. In this chapter, we saw several different approaches, from the lightweight use of reflection and changing methods' visibility, to redefining functions with a third-party library, mocking the filestream, and then using runkit and changing anything that we wanted and needed to change.

It's up to you to decide when these methods are appropriate and when they are not. However, working with dirty code requires dirty methods. There are other libraries and extensions that do more or less the same things (for example, TestIt and ext/test_helpers).

This chapter explained to you the possibilities of what you can do when you want to write unit/integration tests for legacy code.

In the next chapter, we will see functional tests that were mentioned as another way to test legacy code—Selenium. It's something different and definitely something that you should know—you are running tests in the web browser, mimicking user behavior but still working with PHP code and PHPUnit tests.

12
Functional Tests in the Web Browser Using Selenium

In the previous chapter, we mentioned Selenium as one of the options for testing legacy code. Also, we have seen a few tricks that might help us to test legacy code. However, all of the suggested methods were just ways of overcoming problems with badly written code.

There is one method that will test any web application—old or new, legacy or latest development—and it doesn't matter how it works, but rather what it does. Yes, this is functional testing where we are not even trying to isolate the tested code but are trying to test it as it is.

To get as close as possible to a real user experience, you can run tests in the web browser and simulate user activity. As we are writing web applications, it would be good to involve everything affecting the web application, not only PHP—populating the HTML and validating it—but also JavaScript or even CSS. As modern web applications are heavily dependent on JavaScript and Ajax calls, testing this functionality might be as important as testing the PHP code.

So, what exactly is this Selenium? How can it help us?

There are several components that allow us to write and execute tests; all such components are listed as follows:

- **Selenium Server**: This server is used for launching and executing tests
- **Selenium IDE**: This is a Firefox extension used to record and replay tests
- **PHPUnit Selenium extension**: This extension allows us to write and execute tests and PHPUnit tests
- **Selenium Grid**: This allows parallel test execution on different machines and browsers

There is one significant difference between Selenium Server versions 1 and 2 that also affects PHPUnit tests. Version 1 used Selenium RC (Remote Control). Selenium behaved as a proxy server passing commands between the test and the web browser. This was done through JavaScript. It still works but it's just maintained (not actively developed anymore).

The change came with Selenium 2, which started to use the WebDriver API. Instead of using JavaScript to tell the browser what to do, it talks directly to the web browser application API. In this way, it's a more robust solution to overcome some JavaScript problems and is also faster.

When you think about PHP, the first thing that comes to mind is that you can't access the application API directly (as it doesn't mix with the Server API over HTTP). The trick is to start the Selenium Server and use JsonWireProtocol, which is a REST web service that accepts JSON over HTTP. The Selenium Server is a launching browser that sends commands to the browser and returns responses to us when required. This way, you can check whether an element on the page exists or that message was displayed.

Installing Selenium

To be able to play with Selenium, we need to install everything we will need later. To write and run tests, we need the following:

- **Selenium IDE**: This Firefox extension is used to record tests
- **Selenium Server**: This server is used to execute tests
- **PHPUnit Selenium extension**: This extension is used to write tests

The Selenium IDE

As was previously mentioned, Selenium is a Firefox extension, which means you have to use Firefox. If you are using Chrome, Internet Explorer, or any other browser, then you can use it just for executing (and not recording) the tests. This is what the extension does: it "watches" what you are doing and records these steps; you can replay them later or export them to the PHPUnit test case.

However, this is an optional component; you can write tests on your own and don't necessarily need this extension. This extension is handy when you start with Selenium testing because it allows you to quickly record tests and export them to PHP, and you can also see how to select elements, trigger events, and so on. Also, it's handy that tests can be recorded by somebody for you: a client, a project manager, or a tester. A disadvantage is that the exported tests are not perfect, and they will probably require manual tweaking.

Instead of downloading and installing it from the Mozilla site, as you would expect from a Firefox extension, you have to download it from the Selenium site at `http://docs.seleniumhq.org/download/`.

After clicking on the link to the XPI file (Firefox-packed extensions), you will be asked to allow the extension installation; this is shown in the screenshot that follows:

Then, you have to install the extension and various programming language formatters as follows:

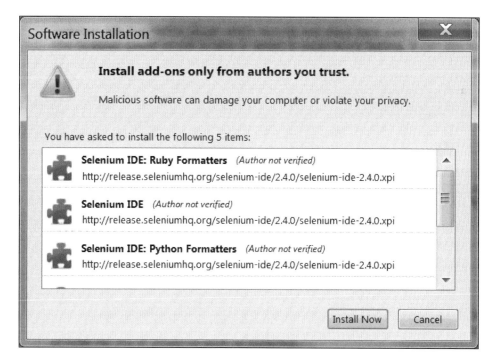

After the extension installation, Firefox needs to be restarted. If you scrolled through the list of formatters, you may have noticed that PHP is missing in the list. Here, I have to be honest—PHP support is not the best. You can find the *Selenium IDE: PHP Formatters 1.3.2* extension, but unfortunately this extension only supports Selenium 1 tests (`PHPUnit_Extensions_SeleniumTestCase`). This works really well (and is well-documented), but as was described, it's not recommended for use anymore; it's for legacy tests using Selenium Server 1.

What we need is a formatter that is able to export to the `PHPUnit_Extensions_Selenium2TestCase` class or a class extending this class. It's a bit unfair that PHP, being such a popular language, is not included in the default installation, but hopefully this will change soon. If this formatter is missing, there is one available that you can use. It's available as a project on GitHub at `https://github.com/suzuki/PHP-Formatter-PHPUnit_Selenium2`.

From the build folder, download the `phpformatter@zatsubun.com.xpi` file (as raw) and drop it into Firefox (drag-and-drop) to install it.

Then, you will be asked to confirm the extension installation as seen in the following screenshot:

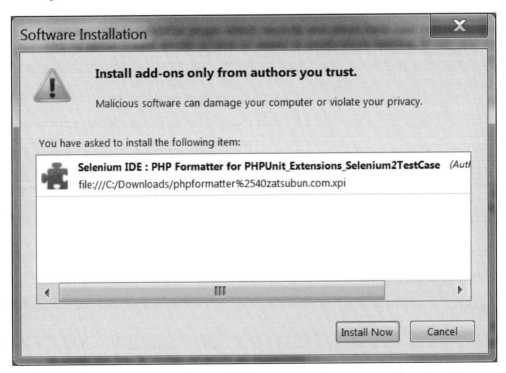

If the extension was installed correctly, you should see the Selenium IDE item in **Menu | Tools**, or you can press *Ctrl + Alt + S* on Linux and Windows to open the Selenium dialog window, as shown in the following screenshot:

When you navigate to **File | Export Test Case As**, the last item should be **PHP / PHPUnit / PHPUnit Selenium2TestCase**. If you see it, the Selenium IDE is ready.

The Selenium Server

The Selenium Server installation is quite easy. You need to have Java installed on your machine because the Selenium Server is a Java application. To test whether you have Java installed, just run `java -version` on the command line and you should see an output similar to the following:

```
java version "1.7.0_51"
Java(TM) SE Runtime Environment (build 1.7.0_51-b13)
Java HotSpot(TM) 64-Bit Server VM (build 24.51-b03, mixed mode)
```

You can download the Selenium Server from `http://docs.seleniumhq.org/download/`. It's important to have the latest version; when the web browser is upgraded, you will possibly need a newer version of the Selenium Server; otherwise, it might stop working or you may see strange error messages. Remember that this might save you from hours of debugging tests that suddenly stop working.

The Selenium Server is just one `.jar` file, which is a Java package, and is similar to a PHP PHAR file. Store the downloaded file wherever it suits you. There is no installation required. To launch the server, just run the following command:

```
>java -jar selenium-server-standalone-2.41.0.jar
```

The `.jar` file needs to be the one that you just downloaded (the version number could be different). When you run the preceding command, you should see a similar output and because it's a Java application, it will work on Linux, Windows, and OS X.

If everything worked properly, then the Selenium Server has started and is listening on port **4444**.

In this case, the installation on Windows might be an advantage because to be able to run the tests in Internet Explorer, you will need a machine or machines with this browser installed.

Installing drivers

To use web browsers other than Firefox for testing, you need to download their respective drivers from `http://code.google.com/p/selenium/downloads/list`.

Drivers for Internet Explorer are available and there is a link to the Chrome driver. There are also other drivers available (such as Android and iOS), but they are provided by a third party—see the Selenium documentation.

The driver installation is simple. Unzip the file and copy it to any location on the system path or add the path where there are drivers stored; you can also start the Selenium Server with an extra parameter where you specify the driver's location as follows:

```
-Dwebdriver.chrome.driver=chromedriver.exe
```

When you use a different browser, the Selenium Server checks whether the driver is available. If it is, it launches tests in this browser; if it isn't, it throws an error.

The PHPUnit Selenium extension

PHPUnit Selenium is an extension. It can be installed in the same way as we installed DBUnit, which was another PHPUnit extension. If you used the Composer installation, you need to add a required dependency into your `composer.json` file as follows:

```
{
    "require": {
        "phpunit/phpunit": "3.7.*",
        "phpunit/phpunit-selenium": "1.3.*"
    }
}
```

Then, just run the following command to install the extension:

```
>php composer.phar update
```

For the PEAR installation, run the following command:

```
>pear install phpunit/PHPUnit_Selenium
```

All it does is just add a few extra classes to the PHPUnit installation.

Testing in the browser

When we have installed these three components—the Selenium IDE, the Selenium Server, and the PHPUnit Selenium extension—we will write simple tests and see how they all work together.

Let's start with an example that might look simple and is a nice real-world example. We can use Google to search for the PHPUnit term. Expect a link to the PHPUnit manual to be returned as the first link, go to the PHPUnit manual page, click on the Selenium chapter link, and verify that the Selenium chapter is displayed.

This might sound simple, but we are jumping between two sites; Google uses Ajax to display the search response, so we know that JavaScript is definitely involved. This is the point of Selenium testing—to simulate user behavior and to test the output in the browser.

Where do we start from? You can start by manually writing tests where the class extends `PHPUnit_Extensions_Selenium2TestCase`, but then you need to know how to send commands to the Selenium Server. This is the moment when the Selenium IDE can really help us. It allows you to record all your activity, replay it, or even export it to the PHPUnit test.

Recording Selenium tests

Recording Selenium tests is really easy. Open the Selenium IDE from **Menu** | **Tools** or press *Ctrl + Alt + S* on Windows and Linux; you will get a window similar to the one in the following screenshot:

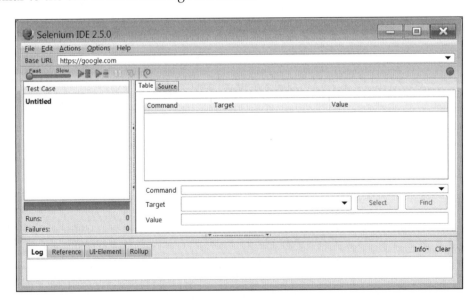

The base URL is where your test starts, then you can set the test speed delay between each command, replay the test, and the record button switches on/off the recording.

When the recording is on, we start with the `www.google.com` page, type in `PHPUnit`, go to PHPUnit manual, find **Chapter 13, PHPUnit and Selenium**, and verify the content of the H1 element.

On the visited page in the PHPUnit manual, select the heading, and right-click in the browser to display the context menu. Here, you can see additional Selenium commands such as **verifyValue** to verify what and where is on the page or in testing language asserts. This is shown in the following screenshot:

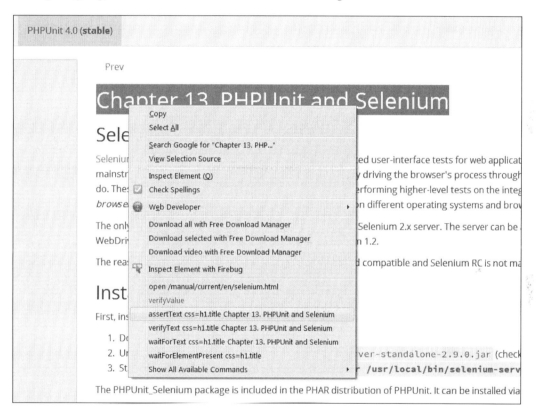

If you completed all of these steps in the Selenium IDE, you should see an output similar to the following:

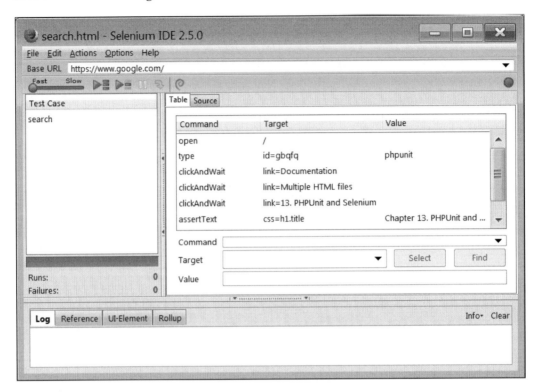

As you can see, there are six commands. Open the Google search page, type in PHPUnit, click on the link to the PHPUnit documentation, select **Multiple HTML files**, click on the link to PHPUnit and Selenium, and then verify the H1 element content. This is the whole point of Selenium testing: sending commands and verifying the output. Now, you can try to replay the recorded test by pressing the play arrow button.

Here, the first problem might arise—Google uses Ajax to return search results as you type. As we can see from the following screenshot, the test will fail:

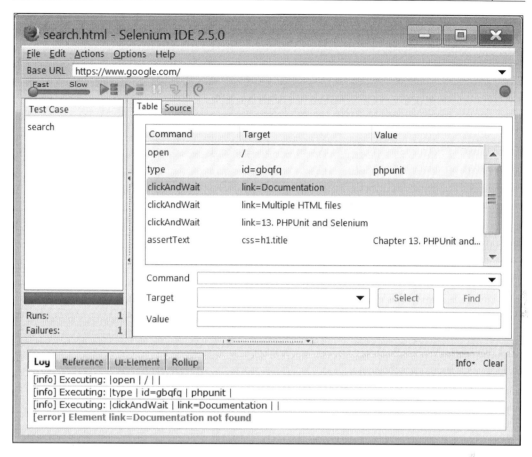

Ajax poses as a problem when you write Selenium tests. Ajax code is executed after the page is loaded and you don't know when the result is going to be available. In our case, the link to the PHPUnit manual is not available yet. The Selenium IDE is very handy and can help you but as with all automated things, it sometimes needs a small manual tweak. We need to add a line to wait for the link to appear. You can use the context menu when clicking on the link to the documentation and select **waitForElementPresent link=Documentation**. Then you need to move this command after you type it; place it before **clickAndWait link=Documentation**.

When talking about commands, there are quite a few available—you can see them when you click on the **Command** dropdown. Each command is executed against a target, which is an HTML element, and you can even pass parameters there. This is very similar, for example, to jQuery—you select an element and then call an action.

The Selenium IDE stores tests internally in the HTML format. This is a part of our recorded test, and you can see it when you click on **Source tab**.

Now, when we have the first test ready, we can export it to the PHPUnit format by navigating to **File | Export Test Suite As... | PHP / PHPUnit / PHPUnit Selenium2TestCase**.

PHPUnit Selenium2TestCase

Now we have exported the test suite that extends the `PHPUnit_Extensions_Selenium2TestCase` class, and this is the base class for Selenium tests installed as a PHPUnit_Selenium extension.

The exported test suite looks like the following:

```php
<?php

class SeleniumFirstTest extends PHPUnit_Extensions_Selenium2TestCase
{
    /**
     * Setup
     */
    public function setUp()
    {
        $this->setBrowser('firefox');
        $this->setHost('127.0.0.1');
        $this->setPort(4444);
        $this->setBrowserUrl('https://www.google.com/');
    }
```

The basic setup indicates where the Selenium Server is listening, which browser to use, and the test's URL.

```php
    /**
     * Method testSeleniumFirst
     * @test
     */
    public function testSeleniumFirst()
    {
        $this->url("/");
        $this->byId("gbqfq")->value("phpunit");
        // ERROR: Caught exception [TypeError: WDAPI.Utils.
          isElementPresent is not a function]
```

```
$this->byLinkText("Documentation")->click();
$this->byLinkText("Multiple HTML files")->click();
$this->byLinkText("13. PHPUnit and Selenium")->click();
$result = $this->byCssSelector("h1.title")->text();
$this->assertEquals("Chapter 13. PHPUnit and Selenium",
    $result);
    }

}
```

As you can see from the preceding code, testSeleniumFirst is not difficult to read. It finds an element on the page and triggers an event. The following is an odd line:

```
// ERROR: Caught exception [TypeError:
    WDAPI.Utils.isElementPresent is not a function]
```

The recorded test in the Selenium IDE is not correctly translated by the PHP formatter when exported. A quick solution, for now, is to delete this line and give it more time to wait for the element to exist. This can be done easily by increasing implicitTimeout. This increased timeout is one of the tricks to handling dynamically loaded content. If an element doesn't exist, Selenium will try to call it again and again during the 10-second interval as shown in the following code:

```
public function testSeleniumFirst()
    {
        $this->timeouts()->implicitWait(10000);
        $this->url("/");
        $this->byId("gbqfq")->value("phpunit");
        $this->byLinkText("Documentation")->click();
        $this->byLinkText("Multiple HTML files")->click();
        $this->byLinkText("13. PHPUnit and Selenium")->click();
        $result = $this->byCssSelector("h1.title")->text();
        $this->assertEquals("Chapter 13. PHPUnit and Selenium",
            $result);
    }
```

To be able to execute the test, you need to start the Selenium Server and then just run the test:

```
>phpunit SeleniumFirstTest.php
PHPUnit 3.7.30 by Sebastian Bergmann.


.


Time: 30.16 seconds, Memory: 5.50Mb

OK (1 test, 1 assertion)
```

You can see the magic when you open the Firefox window where the test was executed. What is interesting to watch is the Selenium Server window, as all the commands are passed there. Sometimes, when you have problems with tests, it might give you some answers. The following screenshot shows the commands sent from the PHPUnit Selenium extension to the Selenium Server:

```
C:\Windows\system32\cmd.exe

]] at URL: /session)
23:13:30.473 INFO - Creating a new session for Capabilities [{browserName=firefo
x}]
23:13:38.109 INFO - Done: /session
23:13:38.133 INFO - Executing: [implicitly wait: 10000] at URL: /session/e575e48
4-e32d-4aef-9377-3b1cfb6dc63e/timeouts/implicit_wait)
23:13:38.144 INFO - Done: /session/e575e484-e32d-4aef-9377-3b1cfb6dc63e/timeouts
/implicit_wait
23:13:38.150 INFO - Executing: [get: https://www.google.com/ncr] at URL: /sessio
n/e575e484-e32d-4aef-9377-3b1cfb6dc63e/url)
23:13:53.088 INFO - Done: /session/e575e484-e32d-4aef-9377-3b1cfb6dc63e/url
23:13:53.092 INFO - Executing: [find element: By.id: gbqfq] at URL: /session/e57
5e484-e32d-4aef-9377-3b1cfb6dc63e/element)
23:13:53.868 INFO - Done: /session/e575e484-e32d-4aef-9377-3b1cfb6dc63e/element
23:13:53.876 INFO - Executing: [send keys: 0 [[FirefoxDriver: firefox on XP (a44
c5bb3-c2a1-4b7b-b13f-cf103996cd93)] -> id: gbqfq], [p, h, p, u, n, i, t]] at URL
: /session/e575e484-e32d-4aef-9377-3b1cfb6dc63e/element/0/value)
23:13:53.965 INFO - Done: /session/e575e484-e32d-4aef-9377-3b1cfb6dc63e/element/
0/value
23:13:53.978 INFO - Executing: [find element: By.linkText: Documentation] at URL
: /session/e575e484-e32d-4aef-9377-3b1cfb6dc63e/element)
23:13:54.658 INFO - Done: /session/e575e484-e32d-4aef-9377-3b1cfb6dc63e/element
23:13:54.663 INFO - Executing: [click: 1 [[FirefoxDriver: firefox on XP (a44c5bb
3-c2a1-4b7b-b13f-cf103996cd93)] -> link text: Documentation]] at URL: /session/e
575e484-e32d-4aef-9377-3b1cfb6dc63e/element/1/click)
```

If you want to use a different browser, navigate to the following line:

```
$this->setBrowser('firefox');
```

The preceding line has to be changed to the following:

- `iexplore`: This is for Internet Explorer
- `chrome`: This is for Google Chrome

To be able to run tests in another browser, you have to install a driver for this browser—as was described previously.

Writing Selenium tests

We saw how to use the Selenium IDE to record tests and export them to the PHPUnit tests. This could be very handy. For example, a tester can record and maintain an HTML version of the tests. This allows you to quickly create a backbone for your tests—but don't expect it to be perfect; manual tweaking will be necessary.

Now, let's have a closer look at how these tests work.

As mentioned earlier, the main class that you have to extend is `PHPUnit_Extensions_Selenium2TestCase`. The PHPUnit Selenium extension is not documented very well—most of the documentation that you find is for `PHPUnit_Extensions_SeleniumTestCase`, which uses the legacy Selenium RC server.

As it sometimes happens, the best documentation is the source code. When you look into the `PHPUnit_Extensions_Selenium2TestCase` class, there are some methods documented by the PHPDoc annotations. PHPDoc uses a magic `__call` method. Personally, I don't like magic methods; they make code less transparent and more difficult to read and debug.

A good starting point might be to look again at our first tests and the generated code:

```
public function setUp()
{
    $this->setBrowser('chrome');
    $this->setHost('127.0.0.1');
    $this->setPort(4444);
    $this->setBrowserUrl('https://www.google.com/');
}
```

The method calls from the preceding code are defined as follows:

- `setBrowser`: This sets the browser we are using for the test
- `setHost` and `setPort`: These are located where the Selenium Server is listening
- `setBrowserUrl`: This is the URL where the tests start

The `setBrowserUrl` method call is important because the tests start there. This might be enough even when another site is involved. In the tests, you usually use `link.click` or `form.submit` to go to another page—even if it's on a different domain, tests will handle it; it's just like another page. If you need to open a different URL, simply use the `$this->url($newUrl)` method. The `$newUrl` variable can be a relative address. Then, it's a relative address to a browser's URL ("/") or absolute and it can point to a different domain (`http://phpunit.de/manual/3.7/en/installation.html`).

That's all for the basic `setUp` function. For the first step, the code looks like the following:

```
public function testSeleniumFirst()
{
    $this->timeouts()->implicitWait(10000);
    $this->url("/");
    $this->byId("gbqfq")->value("phpunit");
    $this->byLinkText("Documentation")->click();
    $this->byLinkText("Multiple HTML files")->click();
    $this->byLinkText("13. PHPUnit and Selenium")->click();
    $result = $this->byCssSelector("h1.title")->text();
    $this->assertEquals("Chapter 13. PHPUnit and Selenium",
        $result);
}
```

The `$this->timeouts()->implicitWait(10000)` statement was just a trick that we used to give the page more time to execute all the Ajax calls. It provides the access to the `PHPUnit_Extensions_Selenium2TestCase_Session_Timeouts` object where you can manipulate all timeout for tests.

The `url` method was mentioned, but then comes the most important part. I expect that as a PHP developer, you should know HTML well. Here, it is necessary because without any knowledge of how HTML works, it might be very difficult to write tests as you will not know what to test. The core part of each test is to access the elements on the page and perform a certain action—trigger an event or check their content or position on the page.

To select the correct element is the first step. There are a few different ways in which you can do this, and you can see some of them in our test. If you know jQuery and its selectors, you will find it very similar.

The following are the available selectors. To demonstrate how they work, let's use this simple HTML element: `<a id="link_element" class="link_class" name="link_name">Link</a>`.

- `byId`: This selector sorts by an element's ID, that is, by its unique identifier. An example of its usage is `$this->byId("link_element");`.
- `byClassName`: This selector sorts by the CSS class name. An example of its usage is `$this->byClassName("link_class");`.
- `byCssSelector`: This selector sorts by the CSS selection (elements and class styles used in CSS files). An example of its usage is `$this->byCssSelector("a.link_class");`.
- `byLinkText`: This selector sorts by link text. An example of its usage is `$this->byLinkText("Link");`.

- `byname`: This selector sorts by name; it is usually for form elements. An example of its usage is `$this->byName("link_name");`.

- `byTag`: This selector finds an element by its tag name. An example of its usage is `$this->byTag("a");`.

- `byXPath()`:This selector uses a powerful XPath expression to select an element. An example of its usage is `$this->byXPath("//a[@id = 'link_name']");`.

For the selected element (`PHPUnit_Extensions_Selenium2TestCase_Element`), the following methods are available:

- `attribute`: This method retrieves the element attribute value

- `value`: This method returns/sets an element's value

- `text`: This method returns an element's content

- `clear`: This method clears an element's content

- `click`: This method performs a click action

- `submit`: This method submits a form

- `css`: This method returns the CSS property value

- `displayed`: This method checks whether an element is displayed

- `enabled`: This method checks whether an element is enabled

- `selected`: This method checks whether an element is selected

- `equals`: This method checks whether two elements are the same (on the same page)

- `location`: This method returns an element's position

- `size`: This method returns an element's width and height

Again, if you are familiar with how jQuery works, you will find the logic here to be the same.

In addition to these, there are other methods available to manipulate the page or force the web browser to perform a certain action. The following are the most important methods. For the rest, go through the documentation:

- `acceptAlert`: Press OK on JavaScript dialog (`alert` and `confirm`)

- `dismissAlert`: Dismiss by clicking on **Cancel** or **No** on the JavaScript dialog

- `moveto`: This method moves the mouse to a position or an element

- `click`: This method performs a mouse button click

- `clickOnElement`: This method performs a click on an element
- `currentScreenshot`: This method returns the current screenshot — exactly what you see in the browser
- `execute`: This method executes JavaScript
- `forward`: This method indicates the forward action
- `backward`: This method indicates the backward action
- `refresh`: This method refreshes the page
- `source`: This method returns the page source
- `title`: This method returns the page title
- `url`: This method returns/sets the page URL
- `frame`: This method changes the frame focus; it is handy when iframe is used
- `window`: This method changes the focus to another window
- `keys`: This method simulates a key press
- `close`: This method closes the window and the session

This was a bit of theory, but now, let's see another example in order to imagine how we can use it. In this case, let's create a sandbox page that is going to be a simple form of a mathematical operation on two input numbers:

```html
<!DOCTYPE html>
<html lang="en">
<head>
    <title>Sandbox</title>
    <link
      href="//netdna.bootstrapcdn.com/bootstrap/3.0.2/css/
      bootstrap.min.css" rel="stylesheet">
</head>
<body>
<div class="container" style="width:500px">
    <div style="width:250px; float: right;">
        <h1 class="page-header">Selenium Sandbox</h1>

        <h2>Input</h2>

        <form method="post" action="" role="form">
            <div class="form-group">
                <label for="number_a">Number A</label>
                <input name="number_a" id="number_a" type="number"
                  class="form-control" />
                <br/>
```

```
                    <label for="number_b">Number B</label>
                    <input name="number_b" id="number_b" type="number"
                       class="form-control" />
                </div>
                <div class="form-group">
                    <label for="addition">Addition</label>
                    <input type="checkbox" value="addition"
                       id="addition" name="operation[]"/>
                    <label for="subtraction">Subtraction</label>
                    <input type="checkbox" value="substitution"
                       id="substitution" name="operation[]"/>
                    <label for="multiplication">Multiplication</label>
                    <input type="checkbox" value="multiplication"
                       id="multiplication" name="operation[]"/>
                    <label for="division">Division</label>
                    <input type="checkbox" value="division"
                       id="division" name="operation[]"/>
                </div>
                <div class="form-group">
                    <input type="submit" value="Calculate"
                       class="btn"/>
                </div>
            </form>
        </div>
```

This is a simple HTML page with one form. To make it prettier than plain HTML, a Bootstrap CSS framework is used. Now follows some short PHP code:

```php
        <div style="width:200px;">
        <h2>Result</h2>
<?php
if ($_SERVER['REQUEST_METHOD'] === 'POST')
{
    if (!isset($_POST['number_a'])
      || !isset($_POST['number_b'])
      || !isset($_POST['operation']))
    {
        throw new InvalidArgumentException('Missing required
           argument');
    }

    $number_a = floatval($_POST['number_a']);
    $number_b = floatval($_POST['number_b']);
```

```php
        echo "<p>Number A: {$number_a}<br/>Number B:
          {$number_b}</p>";
        foreach ($_POST['operation'] as $operation)
        {
            switch ($operation)
            {
                case 'addition':
                  echo 'Addition = <span id="result_addition">'
                  . ($number_a + $number_b) . '</span><br />';
                    break;
                case 'substitution':
                  echo 'Subtraction = <span
                  id="result_substitution">' . ($number_a -
                  $number_b) . '</span><br />';
                    break;
                case 'multiplication':
                  echo 'Multiplication = <span
                  id="result_multiplication">' . ($number_a *
                  $number_b) . '</span><br />';
                    break;
                case 'division':
                  echo 'Division = <span id="result_division">'
                  . ($number_a / $number_b) . '</span><br />';
                    break;
            }
        }
        ?>
        </div>
    </div>
    </body>
    </html>
```

Just to keep things simple, everything is stored in a single file—no MVC.

When you try executing this PHP script, you will see one form and then the displayed result after submitting the form:

Now we can write simple PHPUnit Selenium functional tests verifying the returned numbers. To make our life easier, we can use the Selenium IDE, record tests, and export them. A simple result could look similar to the following:

```php
<?php

class SeleniumSandboxTest extends PHPUnit_Extensions_Selenium2TestCase
{
    public function setUp()
    {
        $this->setBrowser('firefox');
        $this->setHost('127.0.0.1');
        $this->setPort(4444);
        $this->setBrowserUrl('http://localhost/');
    }

    public function testSeleniumSandbox()
    {
        $this->url("/sandbox.php");
```

```
        $this->assertEquals("Selenium Sandbox",
            $this->byCssSelector("h1.page-header")
            ->text());

        $this->byId("number_a")->value("1");
        $this->byId("number_b")->value("1");

        $this->byId("addition")->click();
        $this->byId("multiplication")->click();
        $this->byId("subtraction")->click();
        $this->byId("division")->click();

        $this->byCssSelector("input.btn")->click();

        $this->assertEquals(2, $this->byId("result_addition")
            ->text());
        $this->assertEquals(0, $this->byId("result_subtraction")
            ->text());
        $this->assertEquals(1, $this->byId("result_multiplication")
            ->text());
        $this->assertEquals(1, $this->byId("result_division")
            ->text());
    }
}
```

This code is really easy to read, and as you can see, it performs the following:

1. It opens the `sandbox.php` page.
2. It verifies the page header, that is, verifies whether the correct page is loaded.
3. It enters numbers for the `number_a` and `number_b` inputs (1 and 1).
4. It selects all the checkboxes.
5. It clicks on the submit button.
6. All the results are stored in span elements (`<span id="result_addition">`); it compares the content of these elements with the expected values.

As you can see, we can nicely verify the page content without any need to know how it works. Also, our tests are completely isolated from the tested code; in this way, we can test any code, and the type of legacy code doesn't matter.

This is easy and straightforward, but because it's PHP code and a PHPUnit test, you can handle it as any other code, and if you want to test the same thing more than once, then `dataProvider` is a nice solution:

```
/**
 * @dataProvider dataProvider
```

```
 * @param $testedValue
 * @param $expectedResult
 */
public function testSeleniumSandbox($testedValue,
  $expectedResult)
{
    $this->url("http://localhost/sandbox.php");
    $this->assertEquals("Selenium Sandbox",
      $this->byCssSelector("h1.page-header")
      ->text());

    $this->byId("number_a")->value($testedValue[0]);
    $this->byId("number_b")->value($testedValue[1]);

    $criterion = new
      PHPUnit_Extensions_Selenium2TestCase_ElementCriteria
      ("xpath");
    $criterion->value("//input[@type='checkbox']");

    $checkboxes = $this->elements($criterion);

    for($i=0;$i<count($checkboxes);$i++)
    {
        $checkboxes[$i]->click();
        $this->assertTrue($checkboxes[$i]->selected());
    }

    $this->byCssSelector("input.btn")->click();

    $this->assertEquals($expectedResult[0],
      $this->byId("result_addition")
      ->text());
    $this->assertEquals($expectedResult[1],
      $this->byId("result_substitution")
      ->text());
    $this->assertEquals($expectedResult[2],
      $this->byId("result_multiplication")
      ->text());
    $this->assertEquals($expectedResult[3],
      $this->byId("result_division")
      ->text());
}
```

```php
    public function dataProvider()
    {
        return array(
            array('input' => array(1,0), 'result' => array(2,0,1,1)),
            array('input' => array(20,10), 'result' =>
            array(30,10,200,2)),
            array('input' => array(1000,100), 'result' =>
            array(1100,900,100000,10)),
        );
    }
```

In this test, we used one extra feature and it's `PHPUnit_Extensions_Selenium2TestCase_ElementCriteria`. Together with the XPath expression, it allows us to select multiple elements on a page (in our case, all the checkboxes), click on them, and verify that they are selected:

```php
$criterion = new
    PHPUnit_Extensions_Selenium2TestCase_ElementCriteria("xpath");
        $criterion->value("//input[@type='checkbox']");

    $checkboxes = $this->elements($criterion);

    for($i=0;$i<count($checkboxes);$i++)
    {
        $checkboxes[$i]->click();
        $this->assertTrue($checkboxes[$i]->selected());
    }
```

One set of problems you might want to tackle is capturing all the PHP errors and warnings displayed on the page. I think you will agree that when the page returns **PHP Fatal error:**, the game is over and the test should fail.

However, very often, failing tests are useful if you know on which line and URL the test failed. However, Selenium offers even more; you can capture the screenshot where the test failed, with the exact browser displayed. This is really handy when you are debugging failing tests or something unexpected is happening.

Let's take a look at how we can improve our test to detect PHP error messages and capture screenshots when a test fails.

To make it a bit nicer, we can create a parent class that will handle all the extra bits for all our tests, as shown in the following code:

```php
<?php

abstract class SeleniumParentTestCase extends
    PHPUnit_Extensions_Selenium2TestCase
{
    protected $screenShotsDir;
```

```php
public function setUp()
{
    $this->setBrowser('firefox');
    $this->setHost('127.0.0.1');
    $this->setPort(4444);
    $this->setBrowserUrl('http://localhost');

    if(defined('SCREENSHOT_DIR'))
    {
        $this->screenShotsDir = SCREENSHOT_DIR;
    }
    else
    {
        $this->screenShotsDir = __DIR__ . DIRECTORY_SEPARATOR
            . 'screenshots';
    }

    if(!file_exists($this->screenShotsDir))
    {
        mkdir($this->screenShotsDir);
    }
}

/**
 * Captures screenshot when tests fails
 * @param   Exception              $e
 * @throws PHPUnit_Framework_Error
 */
public function onNotSuccessfulTest(Exception $e)
{
    $fileName = $this->screenShotsDir . DIRECTORY_SEPARATOR .
      get_class($this) . '_' . date('Y-m-d\TH-i-s') . '.png';
    file_put_contents($fileName,
      $this->currentScreenshot());

    parent::onNotSuccessfulTest(
      new PHPUnit_Framework_Error('Url: '.$this->url() . '; 
      Screenshot saved to: '.$fileName,
      $e->getCode(), $e->getFile(), $e->getLine(), $e));
}

/**
 * checks page for PHP errors
 */
```

```php
        protected function checkPage()
        {
            $pageSource = $this->source();

            if(strpos($pageSource,'Fatal error:') !== false)
            {
                $this->fail('Fatal error');
            }

            if(strpos($pageSource,'Warning:') !== false)
            {
                $this->fail('Warning:');
            }

            if(strpos($pageSource,'Parse error:') !== false)
            {
                $this->fail('Parse error:');
            }
        }
    }
```

How will it help our tests? The `screenshotsDir` variable in `setUp` is just a simple way to denote where the screenshots should be stored.

The `onNotSuccessfulTest` method is called every time a test fails. In our case, when the test failed, there was something wrong and we wanted to see what was in the displayed browser. The `$this->currentScreenshot()` method returns the current screenshot as binary data that we store in the file.

The `checkPage` method is a simple but important one that takes the page source (HTML) and checks whether there is a PHP warning or error.

Then, with a simple modification of our test, we can have the advantage of checking every page for errors and also capturing screenshots when there is something wrong, that is, if the test fails. The modification is as follows:

```php
<?php

class SeleniumSandboxTest extends SeleniumParentTestCase
{
    /**
     * @dataProvider dataProvider
     * @param $testedValue
     * @param $expectedResult
     */
```

```php
    public function testSeleniumSandbox($testedValue,
      $expectedResult)
    {
        $this->url("http://localhost/sandbox.php");
        $this->checkPage();
        $this->assertEquals("Selenium Sandbox",
          $this->byCssSelector("h1.page-header")->text());

        $this->byId("number_a")->value($testedValue[0]);
        $this->byId("number_b")->value($testedValue[1]);

        $criterion = new
          PHPUnit_Extensions_Selenium2TestCase_ElementCriteria
          ("xpath");
        $criterion->value("//input[@type='checkbox']");

        $checkboxes = $this->elements($criterion);

        for($i=0;$i<count($checkboxes);$i++)
        {
            $checkboxes[$i]->click();
            $this->assertTrue($checkboxes[$i]->selected());
        }

        $this->byCssSelector("input.btn")->click();
        $this->checkPage();

        $this->assertEquals($expectedResult[0],
          $this->byId("result_addition")->text());
        $this->assertEquals($expectedResult[1],
          $this->byId("result_substitution")->text());
        $this->assertEquals($expectedResult[2],
          $this->byId("result_multiplication")->text());
        $this->assertEquals($expectedResult[3],
          $this->byId("result_division")->text());
    }

    public function dataProvider()
    {
        return array(
          array('input' => array(1,0), 'result' => array(2,0,1,1)),
          array('input' => array(20,10), 'result' =>
          array(30,10,200,2)), array('input' => array(1000,100),
          'result' => array(1100,900,100000,10)),
        );
    }
}
```

Apart from extending `SeleniumParentTestCase` instead of `PHPUnit_Extensions_ Selenium2TestCase`, the rest of the test is the same. However, `$this->checkPage()` is important — place it everywhere a new page is opened to be sure that no errors are displayed on the page.

 Don't forget that the errors and warnings reported depend on your PHP configuration. For development and testing, you should set it as sensitive as possible. To do this, you can use `E_ALL & ~E_NOTICE` or even better `E_ALL | E_STRICT`.

The advantage of the shown approach is that not only is a screenshot taken in the event of an error, but also, if any test fails and something is not right according to the standard PHPUnit response, you get handy extra information as shown:

```
>phpunit --bootstrap bootstrap.php SeleniumSandboxTest.php
PHPUnit 3.7.30 by Sebastian Bergmann.


E..


Time: 24.88 seconds, Memory: 4.75Mb


There was 1 error:


1) SeleniumSandboxTest::testSeleniumSandbox with data set #0
(array(1, 0), array(2, 0, 1, 1))
Url: http://localhost/sandbox.php; Screenshot saved to:
C:\tmp\screenshots\SeleniumSandboxTest_2014-04-28T22-27-43.png


SeleniumParentTestCase.php:59
SeleniumSandboxTest.php:31


Caused by
Warning:


SeleniumParentTestCase.php:59
SeleniumSandboxTest.php:31
FAILURES!
Tests: 3, Assertions: 23, Errors: 1.
```

PHP-SeleniumClient

We have seen the PHPUnit-Selenium extension usage. It works pretty well, but I have to say that the `PHPUnit_Extensions_SeleniumTestCase` legacy was better documented and offered more features than the current `PHPUnit_Extensions_Selenium2TestCase`.

So, to give you the full picture, there are alternatives you can use. Some of them are mentioned on `seleniumhq.org`. There are quite a few available for PHP now. As an example, we can check one called **PHP-SeleniumClient**. I like this one because it uses the same API as Selenium clients for C# or Java. This is an advantage because you can write tests that will almost look the same in many different languages.

The library installation is very easy. As before, we need Composer and a required dependency:

```
{
    "require": {
        "php": ">=5.3.8"
    },
    "require-dev": {
        "nearsoft/php-selenium-client": "*"
    },
    "autoload": {
        "psr-0": {
            "": "src/"
        }
    }
}
```

To see the difference and its usage, let's simply update our first Selenium tests to use this library rather than the PHPUnit-Selenium extension, as shown in the following code:

```
<?php

use Nearsoft\SeleniumClient\By;
use Nearsoft\SeleniumClient\WebDriver;
use Nearsoft\SeleniumClient\WebDriverWait;
use Nearsoft\SeleniumClient\DesiredCapabilities;
```

```php
class SeleniumClientTest extends PHPUnit_Framework_TestCase
{
    /** @var WebDriver */
    private $_driver = null;

    public function setUp()
    {
        $desiredCapabilities = new DesiredCapabilities("chrome");

        $this->_driver = new WebDriver($desiredCapabilities);
        $this->_driver->setScreenShotsDirectory(__DIR__ .
          DIRECTORY_SEPARATOR . 'screenshots');
    }

    public function tearDown()
    {
        if ($this->_driver != null) { $this->_driver->quit(); }
    }

    public function testSeleniumFirst()
    {
        $this->_driver->get("https://www.google.com");
        $this->_driver->findElement(By::id("gbqfq"))
          ->setValue("phpunit");
        $this->_driver->findElement(By::id("gbqfba"))->click();

        $wait = new WebDriverWait(8);
        $documentationLink = $wait->until(
          $this->_driver,"findElement",array
          (By::linkText("Documentation"),true));
        $documentationLink->click();

        $this->_driver->findElement(
          By::linkText("Multiple HTML files"))->click();
        $this->_driver->findElement
          (By::linkText("13. PHPUnit and Selenium"))->click();
        $result = $this->_driver
          ->findElement(By::cssSelector("h1.title"))->getText();
        $this->assertEquals("Chapter 13. PHPUnit and Selenium",
          $result);
        $this->_driver->screenshot();
    }
}
```

As you can see, the code is very similar. The following shows an interesting difference:

```
$wait = new WebDriverWait(10);
        $documentationLink = $wait->until(
          $this->_driver,"findElement",array
          (By::linkText("Documentation"),true));
        $documentationLink->click();
```

This is another solution to handle dynamic content, and it's a cleaner solution than the implicit wait that we used before. This way, you specify an element that is loaded dynamically, and by specifying the wait, you can check even the performance. For example, a call needs to be executed in 2 seconds; otherwise, a visitor might leave the page before seeing the result.

A test case is a standard class extending PHPUnit_Framework_TestCase, and then you can use the library to create a client to communicate with the browser. The API seems to be richer than the PHPUnit-Selenium extension, and things such as "wait for Ajax call" or "take screenshot" are also easier to implement with this client.

However, other than this, the logic and functionality are the same. So, it's up to you to choose the one that suits you.

Organizing Selenium tests

When thinking about functional tests, they should follow the same rules as unit tests. However, they still work slightly differently—mainly because we are not testing one small, isolated piece of code. We can even test the whole complex web application where we want to perform an end-to-end testing, from user registration and account activation to making payments and closing of the account. This can be really complex, and we may need to share data between tests. In this case, I would say it might even be necessary that you take the risk where your tests might not be isolated.

What you should try is to group tests into TestCases by their functionality. For example, registering and activating an account becomes TestCase one. Selecting the latest user account and ordering an item with this account becomes TestCase two. Then, you approve and dispatch the order. For TestCase three, you raise and pay an invoice for the latest order.

This way, you can split tests into logical groups that can run in isolation from each other. Inside the test case, you can share data by using global variables—to be sure you are working with an existing user account. Obviously, this is going to be more fragile than completely isolated unit tests. However, for testing legacy code, it can act as "real life" or at least a job saver.

The problem with this approach is that you will create more and more data in your test system. The solution might be to use a DBUnit extension to bring the database to a known state in the beginning, or to wipe out the old test data if you like.

Also, you might want to specify the order in which the tests have to run to ensure that you will have some data for the tests.

For the given example, we can specify in `phpunit.xml` how the test will run:

```xml
<?xml version="1.0" encoding="UTF-8"?>
<phpunit convertErrorsToExceptions="true"
         convertNoticesToExceptions="true"
         convertWarningsToExceptions="true"
         processIsolation="true"
         stopOnFailure="false" bootstrap="./bootstrap.php">
  <testsuites>
    <testsuite name="MyTestSuite">
      <file>DbUnitDataTest.php</file>
      <file>CreateAccountTest.php</file>
      <file>MakeOrderTest.php</file>
      <file>MakePaymentTest.php</file>
      <file>CloseAccountTest.php</file>
    </testsuite>
  </testsuites>
</phpunit>
```

Summary

Selenium became the standard in functional testing in the browser, and it doesn't matter which programming language you use as there are clients for almost all modern languages. Of course, there is also support for PHP. Installation could be a bit tricky, but when you overcome these problems and understand the logic of how the tests work, then you will see that it's one of the best ways to write functional tests. Of course, you should write unit and integration tests, but functional tests can be another layer providing a guarantee of quality. Another massive advantage is cross-browser testing. You can run end-to-end tests everyday in all the major browsers easily — this is something that even the best tester can't do. The difference between Selenium on other solutions such as headless browsers is that Selenium uses a real web browser and gets you as close as possible to the real user experience.

In the next chapter, we are going to see "the cherry on top": continuous integration servers. These are tools that help you to automate tests, report problems, and much more. When you put everything together, suddenly the whole thing will make perfect sense.

13
Continuous Integration

You have code and you have tests, but now you need to take complete advantage of them in order for them to really help you. What you need to do is run these tests, process the results, and then receive a notification if they fail. This is where we are heading, and there are a few really good open source or free solutions available that can help you.

This chapter is named **Continuous Integration**; so, what exactly does this mean? You can find many long definitions, but to put it simply, it is a process where you integrate your code with code from other developers and run tests to verify the code functionality. You are aiming to detect problems as soon as possible and trying to fix problems immediately. It is always easier and cheaper to fix a couple of small problems than create one big problem.

This can be translated to the following workflow:

1. The change is committed to a version control system repository (such as Git or SVN).
2. The **Continuous Integration (CI)** server is either notified of, or detects a change and then runs the defined tests.
3. CI notifies the developer if the tests fail.

With this method you immediately know who created the problem and when.

For the CI to be able to run tests after every commit point, these tests need to be fast. Usually, you can do this with unit tests for integration, and with functional tests it might be better to run them within a defined time interval, for example, once every hour.

You can have multiple sets of tests for each project, and another golden rule should be that no code is released to the production environment until all of the tests have been passed.

It may seem surprising, but these rules and processes shouldn't make your work any slower, and in fact, should allow you to work faster and be more confident about the developed code functionality and changes. Initial investment pays off when you can focus on adding new functionality and are not spending time on tracking bugs and fixing problems. Also, tested and reliable code refers to code that can be released to the production environment more frequently than traditional big releases, which require a lot of manual testing and verification. There is a real impact on business, and it's not just about the discussion as to whether it is worthwhile and a good idea to write some tests and find yourself restricted by some stupid rules anymore.

What will really help and is necessary is a CI server for executing tests and processing the results; this is also called **test automation**. Of course, in theory you can write a script for it and test it manually, but why would you do that when there are some really nice and proven solutions available? Save your time and energy to do something more useful.

In this chapter, we will see what we can do with the most popular CI servers used by the PHP community:

- Travis CI
- Jenkins CI
- Xinc

For us, a CI server will always have the same main task, that is, to execute tests, but to be precise, it includes the following steps:

1. Check the code from the repository.
2. Execute the tests.
3. Process the results.
4. Send a notification when tests fail.

This is the bare minimum that a server must handle. Of course, there is much more to be offered, but these steps must be easy to configure.

Using a Travis CI hosted service

Travis is the easiest to use from the previously mentioned servers. Why is this the case? This is because you don't have to install it. It's a service that provides integration with GitHub for many programming languages, and not just for PHP. Primarily, it's a solution for open source projects, meaning your repository on GitHub is a public repository. It also has commercial support for private repositories and commercial projects.

What is really good is that you don't have to worry about server configuration; instead, you just have to specify the required configuration (in the same way you do with Composer), and Travis does everything for you. You are not just limited to unit tests, and you can even specify which database you want to use and run ingratiation tests there.

However, there is also a disadvantage to this solution. If you want to use it for a private repository, you have to pay for the service, and you are also limited with regard to the server configuration. You can specify your PHP version, but it's not recommended to specify a minor version such as 5.3.8; you should instead use a major version, such as 5.3. On the other hand, you can run tests against various PHP versions, such as PHP 5.3, 5.4, or 5.5, so when you want to upgrade your PHP version, you already have the test results and know how your code will behave with the new PHP version.

Travis has become the CI server of choice for many open source projects, and it's no real surprise because it's really good!

Setting up Travis CI

To use Travis, you will need an account on GitHub. If you haven't got one, navigate to `https://github.com/` and register there. When you have a GitHub account, navigate to `https://travis-ci.org/` and click on **Sign in with GitHub**.

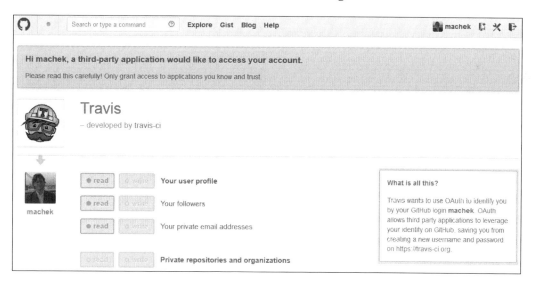

As you can see in the preceding screenshot, there will be a Travis application added to your GitHub account. This application will work as a trigger that will start a build after any change is pushed onto the GitHub repository. To configure the Travis project, you have to follow these steps:

1. You will be asked to allow Travis to access your account.

2. When you do this you will go back to the Travis site, where you will see a list of your GitHub repositories.

3. By clicking on **On/Off**, you can decide which project should be used by Travis.

4. When you click on a project configuration, you will be taken to GitHub to enable the service hook. This is because you have to run a build after every commit, and Travis is going to be notified about this change.

5. In the menu, search for Travis and fill in the details that you can find in your Travis account settings. Only the username and token are required, and the domain is optional.

For a demonstration, you can refer to my sample project, where there is just one test suite, and its purpose is to test how Travis works (navigate to `https://github.com/machek/travis`):

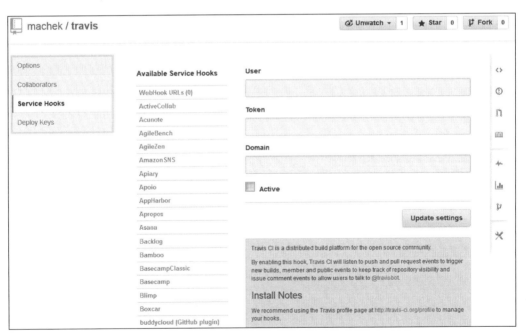

Using Travis CI

When you link your GitHub account to Travis and set up a project to notify Travis, you need to configure the project.

You need to follow the project setup in the same way that we did in the previous chapters. To have classes, you are required to have the test suites that you want to run, a bootstrap file, and a `phpunit.xml` configuration file.

You should try this configuration locally to ensure that you can run PHPUnit, execute tests, and make sure that all tests pass.

If you cloned the sample project, you will see that there is one important file: `.travis.yml`.

This Travis configuration file is telling Travis what the server configuration should look like, and also what will happen after each commit.

Let's have a look at what this file looks like:

```yaml
# see http://about.travis-ci.org/docs/user/languages/php/ for more
  hints
language: php

# list any PHP version you want to test against
php:
  - 5.3
  - 5.4

# optionally specify a list of environments
env:
  - DB=mysql

# execute any number of scripts before the test run, custom env's
  are available as variables
before_script:
  - if [[ "$DB" == "mysql" ]]; then mysql -e "create database IF
  NOT EXISTS my_db;" -uroot; fi

# omitting "script:" will default to phpunit
script: phpunit --configuration phpunit.xml --coverage-text

# configure notifications (email, IRC, campfire etc)
notifications:
  email: "your@email"
```

As you can see, the configuration is really simple, and it shows that we need PHP 5.3 and 5.4, and a MySQL database to create a database, execute the PHPUnit with our configuration, and send a report to my e-mail address.

After each commit, PHPUnit executes all the tests. The following screenshot shows us an interesting insight into how Travis executes our tests and which environment it uses:

You can view the build and the history for all builds.

Even though there are no real builds in PHP because PHP is an interpreted language and not compiled, the action performed when you clone a repository, execute PHPUnit tests, and process results is usually called a **build**.

Travis configuration can be much more complex, and you can run Composer to update dependency and much more. Just check the Travis documentation for PHP at http://about.travis-ci.org/docs/user/languages/php/.

Using the Jenkins CI server

Jenkins is a CI server. The difference between Travis and Jenkins is that when you use Travis as a service, you don't have to worry about the configuration, whereas Jenkins is piece of software that you install on your hardware. This is both an advantage and a disadvantage. The disadvantage is that you have to manually install it, configure it, and also keep it up to date. The advantage is that you can configure it in a way that suits you, and all of the data and code is completely under your control. This can be very important when you have customer code and data (for testing, never use live customer data) or sensitive information that can't be passed on to a third party.

The Jenkins project started as a fork of the Hudson project and is written in Java but has many plugins that suit a variety of programming languages, including PHP. In recent years, it has become very popular, and nowadays it is probably the most popular CI server. The reasons for its popularity are that it is really good, can be configured easily, and there are many plugins available that probably cover everything you might need.

Installation

Installation is a really straightforward process. The easiest method is to use a Jenkins installation package from `http://jenkins-ci.org/`. There are packages available for Windows, OS X, and Linux, and the installation process is well-documented there. Jenkins is written in Java, which means that Java or OpenJDK is required. After this comes the installation, as you just launch the installation and point it to where it should be installed, and Jenkins is listening on port 8080.

Before we move on to configure the first project (or job in Jenkins terminology), we need to install a few extra plugins. This is Jenkins' biggest advantage. There are many plugins and they are very easy to install. It doesn't matter that Jenkins is a Java app as it also serves PHP very well.

For our task to execute tests, process results, and send notifications, we need the following plugins:

- **Email-ext**: This plugin is used to send notifications
- **Git or Subversion**: This plugin is used to check the code
- **xUnit**: This plugin is used for processing the PHPUnit test results
- **Clover PHP**: This plugin is used for processing the code coverage

To install these plugins, navigate to **Jenkins | Manage Jenkins | Manage Plugins** and select the **Available** tab. You can find and check the required plugins, or alternatively use the search filter to find the one you need:

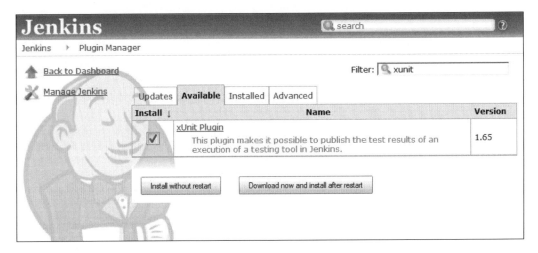

For e-mails, you might need to configure the STMP server connection at **Manage Jenkins | Configure System | E-mail notification** section.

Usage

By now, we should have installed everything that we need, and we can start to configure our first simple project. We can use the same simple project that we used for Travis. This is just one test case, but it is important to learn how to set up a project. It doesn't matter if you have one or thousands of tests though, as the setup is going to be the same.

Creating a job

The first step is to create a new job. Select **New Job** from the Jenkins main navigation window, give it a name, and select **Build a free-style software project**. After clicking on **OK**, you get to the project configuration page.

The most interesting things there are listed as follows:

- **Source Code Management**: This is where you check the code
- **Build Triggers**: This specifies when to run the build
- **Build**: This tests the execution for us
- **Post-build Actions**: This publishes results and sends notifications

The following screenshot shows the project configuration window in Jenkins CI:

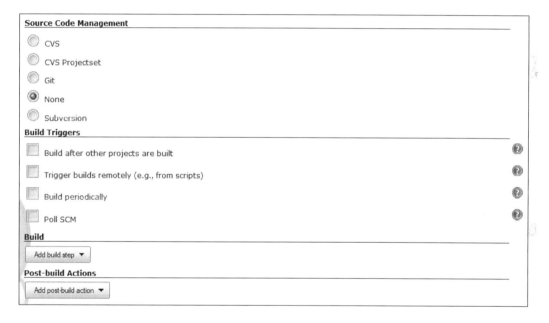

Source Code Management

Source code management simply refers to your version control system, path to the repository, and the branch/branches to be used. Every build is a clean operation, which means that Jenkins starts with a new directory where the code is checked.

Build Triggers

Build triggers is an interesting feature. You don't have to use it and you can start to build manually, but it is better to specify when a build should run. It can run periodically at a given interval (every two hours), or you can trigger a build remotely.

One way to trigger a build is to use post commit hooks in the Git/SVN repository. A post commit hook is a script that is executed after every commit. Hooks are stored in the repository in the /hooks directory (.git/hooks for Git and /hooks for SVN). What you need to do is create a post-commit (SVN) or post-receive (Git) script that will call the URL given by Jenkins when you click on a **Trigger remotely** checkbox with a secret token:

```
#!/bin/sh
wget
  http://localhost:8080/job/Sample_Project/build?
  token=secret12345ABC -O /dev/null
```

After every commit/push to the repository, Jenkins will receive a request to run the build and execute the tests to check whether all of the tests work and that any code change there is not causing unexpected problems.

Build

A build is something that might sound weird in the PHP world, as PHP is interpreted and not compiled; so, why do we call it a build? It's just a word. For us, it refers to a main part of the process—to execute unit tests.

You have to navigate to **Add a build step**—click on either **Execute Windows batch command** or **Execute shell**. This depends on your operating system, but the command remains the same:

```
phpunit --log-junit=result.xml --coverage-clover=clover.xml
```

This is simple and outputs what we want. It executes tests, stores the results in the JUnit format in the file result.xml, and generates code coverage in the clover format in the file clover.xml.

I should probably mention that PHPUnit is not installed with Jenkins, and your build machine on which Jenkins is running must have PHPUnit installed and configured, including PHP CLI.

Post-build Actions

In our case, there are three post-build actions required. They are listed as follows:

- **Process the test result**: This denotes whether the build succeeded or failed. You need to navigate to **Add a post-build action | Publish Junit test result report** and type `result.xml`. This matches the switch `--log-junit=result.xml`. Jenkins will use this file to check the tests results and publish them.

- **Generate code coverage**: This is similar to the first step. You have to add the **Publish Clover PHP Coverage report** field and type `clover.xml`. It uses a second switch, `--coverage-clover=clover.xml`, to generate code coverage, and Jenkins uses this file to create a code coverage report.

- **E-mail notification**: It is a good idea to send an e-mail when a build fails in order to inform everybody that there is a problem, and maybe even let them know who caused this problem and what the last commit was. This step can be added simply by choosing **E-mail notification action**.

Results

The result could be just an e-mail notification, which is handy, but Jenkins also has a very nice dashboard that displays the current status for each job, and you can also see and view the build history to see when and why a build failed.

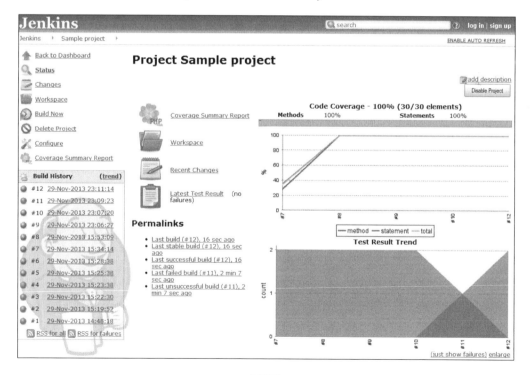

A nice feature is that you can drill down through the test results or code coverage and find more details about test cases and code coverage per class.

If you're not satisfied with the results, you can use the PHPUnit HTML coverage report that we created in *Chapter 5*, *Running Tests from the Command Line*, and navigate to **Post build action | Publish HTML reports** to use the report created with PHPUnit.

> To make testing even more interesting, you can use Jenkins' The Continuous Integration Game plugin. Every developer receives positive points for written tests and a successful build, and negative points for every build that they broke. The game leaderboard shows who is winning the build game and writing better code.

Using the Xinc PHP CI server

Xinc is a CI server written in PHP. What is interesting about this server is that it's in PHP, which means it's going to be a lightweight solution compared to Java applications, and when you have to pay for cloud service, then the amount of memory matters. With Xinc, 512 MB of memory might be enough, whereas for Java you will need at least 1 GB of memory. Another advantage is that it's PHP, so if there is any problem or you want to tweak or extend it, then it's easy.

A disadvantage is that this system is not used as widely as the previous two solutions, and its configuration might also look a bit confusing. Yet, it has pretty good documentation, and so it shouldn't be too difficult to overcome these problems.

Xinc has two parts. The first part is Xinc running as a background process and checking repositories for changes and starting builds, while the second part is a web application that provides an interface to the test results.

Installation

The recommended installation method is to use a PEAR installer. There are a few required dependencies, so manual installation might be a bit tricky.

For installation, you need to discover a few PEAR channels and then run the installation:

```
>pear config-set auto_discover 1
>pear channel-discover pear.phpunit.de
>pear channel-discover pear.elektrischeslicht.de
```

```
>pear channel-discover components.ez.no
>pear install --alldeps xinc/Xinc
```

After installation, you need to run the following post installation script:

```
>pear run-scripts xinc/Xinc
```

This script gives you a few options about where and how Xinc will be installed. You can press the *Enter* key to use the default installation:

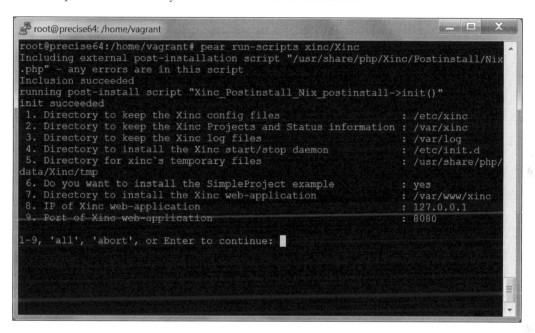

After installation, you will get instructions to enable Xinc to operate on your machine, and they will look similar to this:

```
Xinc installation complete.
- Please include /etc/xinc/www.conf in your apache virtual hosts.
- Please enable mod-rewrite.
- To add projects to Xinc, copy the project xml to /etc/xinc/conf.d
- To start xinc execute: sudo /etc/init.d/xinc start
UNINSTALL instructions:
- pear uninstall xinc/Xinc
- run: /usr/bin/xinc-uninstall to cleanup installed files
[OK] Saved ini settings
Install scripts complete
```

After installation, it is a good idea to check whether Xinc actually works because if there is a problem, it might be really tricky to debug what's going on. You can check it by running the following line of code:

```
>/usr/bin/xinc
```

One of the common problems that you can see now is this error message:

```
PHP Warning:   require(Xinc.php): failed to open stream: No such file
  or directory in /usr/bin/xinc on line 32
PHP Stack trace:
PHP    1. {main}() /usr/bin/xinc:0
PHP Fatal error:   require(): Failed opening required 'Xinc.php'
  (include_path='.:/root/pear/share/pear') in /usr/bin/xinc on line
  32
PHP Stack trace:
PHP    1. {main}() /usr/bin/xinc:0
```

This problem has a simple solution; check whether in your `php.ini` file, PEAR is added to `include_path`.

After these steps, you will have Xinc running as a background task and listening on port 8080 as a web application (you can change it in `www.conf` if you don't like it), and you will have also installed a sample project.

Usage

After installation, we will focus on the aforementioned `Simple Project`. The configuration file is located at `/etc/xinc/conf.d/simpleproject.xml`. Xinc uses Phing (for more information, refer to `http://www.phing.info`). This is a PHP clone of Ant — a building tool that drives processes. You can think of it as a script that says run this and then this. It might sound a bit strange to learn that it uses XML, but when you get used to it, you will realize it's quite an interesting way to go about things.

Ant is far more popular than Phing, but the logic and structure is the same or very similar, and Phing gives you an advantage as there is an option to extend it with PHP if required.

Let's take this simple project and modify it for the example that we used earlier by following the same steps:

1. Check the Git repository.
2. Run the PHPUnit tests.

3. Publish the results.

4. Send notifications.

Almost everything is in place for a sample project, and there are two important files at the location /etc/xinc/conf.d/sampleproject.xml:

```xml
<?xml version="1.0"?>
<xinc>
  <project name="SimpleProject">
    <configuration>
      <setting name="loglevel" value="1"/>
      <setting name="timezone" value="US/Eastern"/>
    </configuration>
    <property name="dir"
    value="/var/xinc/projects/SimpleProject/"/>
    <cron timer="*/4 * * * *"/>
    <modificationset>
      <buildalways/>
    </modificationset>
    <builders>
      <phingBuilder buildfile="${dir}/build.xml"
      target="build"/>
    </builders>
    <publishers>
      <phpUnitTestResults
      file="${dir}/report/logfile.xml"/>
      <onfailure>
        <email to="root"
          subject="${project.name} build
          ${build.number} failed"
          message="The build failed."/>
      </onfailure>
      <onsuccess>
        <phingPublisher
        buildfile="${dir}/publish.xml" target="build"/>
        <artifactspublisher
        file="${dir}/publish.xml"/>
        <artifactspublisher
        file="${dir}/publish.xml"/>
        <deliverable file="${dir}/builds/release-
        ${build.label}.tar.gz" alias="release.tar.gz"/>
      </onsuccess>
      <onrecovery>
      <email to="root"
        subject="${project.name} build
        ${build.number} was recovered"
         message="The build passed after having
          failed before."/>
```

```
        </onrecovery>
      </publishers>
    </project>
  </xinc>
```

This is a project configuration file that checks for modifications every 4 minutes. Run the build, publish the results, and send notifications when the build fails or recovers. The main configuration is in the following line:

```
<phingBuilder buildfile="${dir}/build.xml" target="build"/>
```

The preceding line says the build configuration file is sitting inside the project directory and is called build.xml. Let's have a look at what's there:

```
<?xml version="1.0"?>
<project name="Simple Project Build File"
  basedir="/var/xinc/projects/SimpleProject" default="build">
    <property name="report.dir"
      value="${project.basedir}/report"/>
    <target name="build" depends="prepare, test, tar, generate-
      report">

    </target>
    <target name="prepare">
    <mkdir dir="${report.dir}"/>
    </target>
    <target name="tar">
      <tar destfile="${project.basedir}/release-
      ${xinc.buildlabel}.tar.gz" compression="gzip">
      <fileset dir=".">
        <include name="index.php" />
        <include name="Page.php" />
      </fileset>
      </tar>
    </target>
    <target name="test">
        <phpunit haltonfailure="true" printsummary="true">
            <batchtest>
                <fileset dir=".">
                    <include name="*Test.php"/>
                </fileset>
            </batchtest>
            <formatter type="xml" todir="${report.dir}"
              outfile="logfile.xml"/>
        </phpunit>    </target>
    <target name="generate-report">
```

```
        <phpunitreport infile="${report.dir}/logfile.xml"
            styledir="resources/xsl" todir="report"
            format="noframes"/>
    </target>
</project>
```

This is actually a Phing script. In Phing (Ant) terminology, tasks are called **targets**, and the dependency specifies what tasks need to be executed. For this build, the tasks that are going to be executed are prepare, test, tar, and generate-report targets.

This is what we need with one exception; we need to check the Git repository. The first step is manual, but it could be part of the build. We create/code the directory and clone the GitHub repository we used for previous tests:

git clone https://github.com/machek/travis

To be able to use Git with Phing, we have to install the Git plugin:

>pear install VersionControl_Git-alpha

Now, we need to slightly modify the build script to pull from the Git repository and execute our tests:

```
<?xml version="1.0"?>
<project name="Simple Project Build File"
    basedir="/var/xinc/projects/SimpleProject" default="build">
    <property name="report.dir"
        value="${project.basedir}/report"/>
    <property name="code.dir" value="${project.basedir}/code"/>
    <target name="build" depends="prepare, gitpull, test, tar,
        generate-report">

    </target>
    <target name="prepare">
        <mkdir dir="${report.dir}"/>
     <mkdir dir="${code.dir}"/>
    </target>
<target name="gitpull">
    <echo msg="Getting latest code from ${git.repo}" />
    <gitpull gitPath="git" repository="${code.dir}" all="true" />
</target>
    <target name="tar">
        <tar destfile="${project.basedir}/release-
          ${xinc.buildlabel}.tar.gz" compression="gzip">
          <fileset dir=".">
            <include name="index.php" />
```

```
                <include name="Page.php" />
            </fileset>
        </tar>
    </target>
    <target name="test">
        <phpunit haltonfailure="true" printsummary="true"
            configuration="${code.dir}/phpunit.xml">
            <batchtest>
                <fileset dir="${code.dir}/tests">
                    <include name="*Test.php"/>
                </fileset>
            </batchtest>
            <formatter type="xml" todir="${report.dir}"
                outfile="logfile.xml"/>
        </phpunit>
    </target>
    <target name="generate-report">
        <phpunitreport infile="${report.dir}/logfile.xml"
            styledir="resources/xsl" todir="report"
            format="noframes"/>
    </target>
</project>
```

There is one extra target, `gitpull`, now, and the target tests were also changed to use our tests. This is all that you need to set up a project. When you access the Xinc dashboard served by Apache, you should see a result similar to the following:

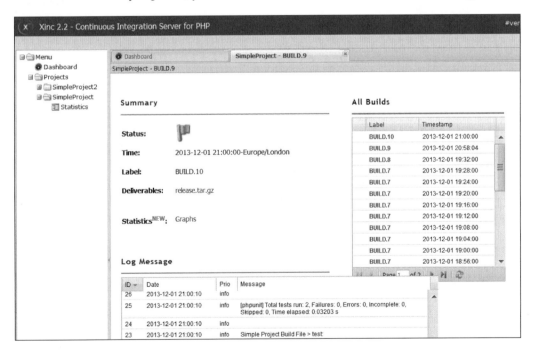

Summary

A continuous integration server is something you really need. You can run PHPUnit tests from a command line, but it's much nicer when it happens automatically, as you have a history of test results and code coverage, and you can notify developers when somebody breaks the tests. It's like a cherry on top, but there is something satisfying when you see that all of your hard work makes sense and you can see its results. Drill through the test results and see the code coverage for each class and method.

We saw three examples, which are probably the most interesting solutions in the PHP world. Travis is very easy to configure and use as a service for open source projects. The king of CI servers is Jenkins, with tons of plugins and easy configuration, and the Xinc CI server is written in PHP. It might depend on your project, but you should try to choose the right one for you. Of course, you can do much more than just run unit tests. You might need a Selenium Server, and then the question is whether your CI server will also host a Selenium Server. You can try to find out more about your code with tools such as PHP CodeSniffer in order to detect if your developers are following coding standards. There is so much more that you can do with CI servers, so just give it a try. You will love them!

In the next and last chapter, we are going to check some PHPUnit alternatives. Even though PHPUnit is a very good tool, there are a few interesting projects available that take a slightly different approach with respect to testing. To gain a complete picture about PHP and writing tests, we are going to look at a few of them, and you will see what **Behavior-Driven Development (BDD)** means.

14
PHPUnit Alternatives, Extensions, Relatives, and BDD

We have seen PHPUnit from the initial steps – installation, basic usage, and so on. We've learned how to write unit tests, how to use test doubles, and almost everything that you can do with PHPUnit. Web development is not an isolated experimental environment, but a very fluid live environment where you have to interact with third-party APIs, databases, use other libraries, and much more. This is the reason why the examples we've used throughout the book were put in the context of modern web application development. PHPUnit is the cornerstone, but sometimes it is not enough. We have seen a few PHPUnit extensions that allow you to do things far beyond the scope of just PHPUnit, such as the Selenium extension. There are thousands of different ways to test code, and that's why we have seen a few alternatives to demonstrate that PHPUnit can be used together with third-party libraries such as Mockery; it's just up to you to decide what suits you best.

To give you the complete picture of testing in PHP, there is one thing left. Testing in PHP doesn't just involve PHPUnit. PHPUnit is the most popular testing framework, but there are others also. In this chapter, we are going to see what other options are available, but more importantly, we will look at the different ways to do it. So far we have talked about **Test-Driven Development (TDD)**, but there is another way to write tests called **Behavior-Driven Development (BDD)**. We are going to see the difference between TDD and BDD and two PHP tools for Behavior-Driven Development.

Unit testing alternatives

PHPUnit is not the only available unit testing framework for PHP. Over the years, a few projects have emerged to provide similar functionality. Some of these are as follows:

- **SimpleTest**: This is a unit testing framework
- **Lime**: This is a Symfony unit testing framework
- **SnapTest**: This is a unit testing framework
- **Testilence**: This is a unit testing library
- **Atoum**: This is a unit test framework

However, PHPUnit has proved to be the most popular and robust unit testing framework, and over the years it has become standard. Except Atoum, none of these alternatives are actively developed anymore, as PHPUnit has emerged from the battle as the winner.

PHPUnit extensions

There are available official PHPUnit extensions such as DBUnit or Selenium, but this doesn't mean that you can't use third-party extensions for the same job. Sometimes PHPUnit provides just a basic set of features, and when you need more features, you may have to look at different ways to get them in the PHPUnit world. In the previous chapters, we saw a few examples showing another approach. One of these examples was test doubles. The PHPUnit approach might look a bit difficult to understand and get used to, so you can use alternative mocking frameworks as follows:

- **Mockery**: This was introduced in *Chapter 8, Using Test Doubles* (`https://github.com/padraic/mockery`)
- **Prophecy**: This is another advanced object mocking framework (`https://github.com/phpspec/prophecy`)
- **TestIt library**: This is an extension library for the PHPUnit mocking engine (`https://github.com/arron0/testit`)
- **Patchwork**: This is a PHP library for redefining user-defined functions (`https://github.com/antecedent/patchwork`)

In *Chapter 9, Database Testing*, we have seen the DBUnit extension usage. However, again, there are other ways to test databases. One of the examples is Doctrine, which is a complex and advanced project where even testing can be done differently without any difficult configuration or code changes. However, as a direct alternative to DBUnit, we can use Phactory, which is a PHP database object factory for unit testing (`http://phactory.org/`).

One last example that we've already seen where alternative solutions might be even better than a PHPUnit default extension is Selenium. PHPUnit Selenium extension is not documented very well, and even the official Selenium site recommends other alternative PHP clients, which are as follows:

- chibimagic / WebDriver-PHP
- php-webdriver-bindings
- facebook / php-webdriver
- Element-34 / php-webdriver
- Nearsoft / PHP-SeleniumClient

To be fair, PHPUnit usually contains everything you need at the beginning, but it's always good to have alternatives available to do things differently when it suits you. It's just up to you to decide the best way for you and for your project.

Behavior-driven development

When it was said that there is no real alternative to PHPUnit, it wasn't exactly true, or to be precise, there is no real alternative in the PHP world for unit testing. However, the reason might be that in recent years, many developers discovered that unit testing has its own challenges and problems. An answer for this came in terms of BDD, which is a different approach in writing tests and testing your code. There are a few projects available that take a different approach to testing, and you might realize that you are better suited to BDD than TDD.

Understanding BDD

To explain what BDD is, we should go back to TDD to examine any potential weaknesses there. As we have seen, you first write a test, and then write the implementation before moving on to refactoring and fixing tests. It's like a circle. However, what if the change is so significant that we break tests completely because it will work differently than we thought. We have to rewrite tests. When we do small refactoring, tests will help to verify that the code still works the same way. When we completely change the code because we didn't implement it according to customer expectations, we then have to rewrite and rethink tests. Our tests are focused on code functionality, and it's almost a one-to-one relationship between code and tests.

For some developers this approach is very limiting. When you do agile software development, you haven't got a definitive product specification where page by page you implement and test required features. You quickly build prototypes, adjust it according to the feedback you get, and refactor it. Sometimes it's a case of stepping back and moving forward and choosing the solution that fits the best.

It might sound weird, but sometimes even you don't know what you are building. Even the customer doesn't have an exactly clear idea of what they want; it's just like a process where you are finding the solution. In this case, the classic TDD approach might be the limitation.

So how is BDD different?

BDD is specified from outside by business needs. It's more focused on features than internal code functionality based around stories. The story is a description of the feature together with acceptance criteria. It's written and driven by a language that's easy to understand by business and business needs.

BDD can be divided into the following two groups:

- **SpecBDD**: This is similar to unit tests; you are testing internal implementation, but you are focused on behavior and not the internal structure of your code, such as classes
- **StoryBDD**: Testing is based on stories written by businesses, and you are testing code from outside, looking at a working block of code/web page, not internal implementation

As PHPUnit is a unit testing tool, to see how BDD works, we have to look at other projects.

At this moment, we have to leave PHPUnit completely, but it's good to see how other testing goes and use different frameworks and tools.

Testing with PHPSpec

PHPSpec (`http://www.phpspec.net`) is a tool that allows you to test code in a way quite similar to unit testing, but instead of writing tests first, you write a spec. It's a description of how your object will behave. What is important in BDD is language. Language should make testing more readable and should allow you to change the way you are thinking about the problem. You are not testing your class and every method, instead you are testing code behavior and what objects will do. This way, you can quickly describe what you are trying to achieve without being too worried about how exactly you are going to implement it. It's about focus, and the most important stories and features that you need to implement. With PHPSpec, you can verify functionality in a similar way to PHPUnit.

Installing PHPSpec

For PHPSpec usage, it's best to start with version 2, and the simplest installation method is to use Composer. The following is the recommended `composer.json` content for the PHPSpec installation:

```
{
    "require-dev": {
        "phpspec/phpspec": "2.0.*@dev"
    },
    "config": {
        "bin-dir": "bin"
    },
    "autoload": {"psr-0": {"": "src"}}
}
```

It will install libraries, create an `/src` directory for your classes, and also install a binary tool to execute tests similar to a PHPUnit script. PHPSpec is not as popular as PHPUnit, so for now, you will have to use just command-line tool, as the IDE support is not so great.

To test installation, simply run the following command line:

```
>phpspec --help
```

You should see an output similar to the following command line:

```
Usage:
 run [-f|--format="..."] [--stop-on-failure] [--no-code-generation]
[spec]


Arguments:
 spec                   Specs to run


Options:
 --format (-f)          Formatter
 --stop-on-failure      Stop on failure
 --no-code-generation  Do not prompt for missing method/class generation
 --help (-h)            Display this help message.
 --quiet (-q)           Do not output any message.
 --verbose (-v|vv|vvv) Increase the verbosity of messages: 1 for normal
output,
2 for more verbose output and 3 for debug
```

```
--version (-V)        Display this application version.
--ansi                Force ANSI output.
--no-ansi             Disable ANSI output.
--no-interaction (-n) Do not ask any interactive question (disables
  code generation).
```

If you get an error message, make sure that bin-dir from composer.json is on your system path.

Using PHPSpec

To demonstrate the PHPSpec usage, let's use some very simple examples. Let's consider a game of football (yeah, some people might call it soccer). We will have two classes, one for the match that we want to play, and a second class for teams playing the match. Functionality actually would be very easy, as each team can score a goal and the winning team gets three points.

Our two classes could look like the following code snippet:

```php
<?php

class Team
{
    private $scoredGoals = 0;
    private $receivedPoints = 0;

    public function scoreGoal()
    {
        return $this->scoredGoals += 1;
    }

    public function getScoredGoals()
    {
        return $this->scoredGoals;
    }

    public function setReceivedPoints($points)
    {
        $this->receivedPoints = $points;
    }

    public function getReceivedPoints()
    {
        return $this->receivedPoints;
    }
}
```

This is the `Team` class. It's just a simple class counting scored goals and received points. The main logic is stored in the `Match` class as shown in the following code:

```php
<?php

class Match
{
    /**
     * @var Team
     */
    public $homeTeam;

    /**
     * @var Team
     */
    public $visitorsTeam;

    public function __construct(Team $homeTeam,
      Team $visitorsTeam)
    {
        $this->homeTeam = $homeTeam;
        $this->visitorsTeam = $visitorsTeam;
    }

    public function getScore()
    {
        return $this->homeTeam->getScoredGoals() . ' : '
          .$this->visitorsTeam->getScoredGoals();
    }

    public function gameOver()
    {
        $this->homeTeam->setReceivedPoints(
          $this->getReceivedPointsHome());
        $this->visitorsTeam->setReceivedPoints(
          $this->getReceivedPointsVisitors());
    }

    private function getReceivedPointsHome()
    {
        if($this->homeTeam->getScoredGoals() >
          $this->visitorsTeam->getScoredGoals())
        {
            return 3;
        }
```

```php
        else if($this->homeTeam->getScoredGoals() <
          $this->visitorsTeam->getScoredGoals())
        {
            return 0;
        }
        else
        {
            return 1;
        }
    }

    private function getReceivedPointsVisitors()
    {
        if($this->homeTeam->getScoredGoals() <
          $this->visitorsTeam->getScoredGoals())
        {
            return 3;
        }
        if($this->homeTeam->getScoredGoals() >
          $this->visitorsTeam->getScoredGoals())
        {
            return 0;
        }
        else
        {
            return 1;
        }
    }
}
```

The match object is constructed with two teams: the home team and the visiting team. All it does is return the current score, and when the match is over, it assigns teams points according to the score.

Our code is stored in an /src directory. Previously, we had tests in the tests directory, and in the same way, spec files are stored in the /spec directory.

For a start, PHPSpec can help us create spec files; just run the following command line from a project root:

```
>phpspec desc Team
```

Now you will have a file in the `spec` directory called `TeamSpec.php`, which will look like the following code snippet:

```php
<?php

namespace spec;

use PhpSpec\ObjectBehavior;
use Prophecy\Argument;

class TeamSpec extends ObjectBehavior
{
    function it_is_initializable()
    {
        $this->shouldHaveType('Team');
    }
}
```

This is the first test, or to be precise, spec. Similar to the Composer autoloader, which we used for PHPUnit tests, in the `/spec` directory, you should have the `bootstrap.php` file with the following lines of code, which uses the Composer autoloader:

```php
<?php
require_once __DIR__ ."/../vendor/autoload.php";
```

You can try to run `TeamSpec` simply by using the following command line:

```
>phpspec run
```

You will get the following output:

```
/ pending: 0%  / passed: 100%  / failed: 0%  / broken: 0%  / 1
examples

1 specs

1 example (1 passed)

68ms
```

This result tells us success. To follow the spec terminology, `TestCase` = `Context` and `test method` = `Example` but it's easy to understand because output is very similar to PHPUnit output. As you can see, we now have one example `TeamSpec`.

When we look at the code, you can see it looks slightly different than the PHPUnit test case. The reason is that both have different logic. We are testing in our `Team` class context, and in there we are testing examples. The `TeamSpec` class extends the `ObjectBehavior` class and allows us to call any method in the class that we are describing. Our example testing how to score goals could look like the following code snippet, where we are calling the `scoreGoal()` method:

```php
function it_scores_goal()
{
    $this->scoreGoal()->shouldReturn(1);
}
```

You can also see the usage of Prophecy\Argument. Prophecy is a mocking framework used by PHPSpec, but it can be used even with PHPUnit.

We saw the spec for the `Team` class, but there was not much happening. A spec for the `Match` class will be more interesting, which could look like the following code snippet:

```php
<?php
namespace spec;

use PhpSpec\ObjectBehavior;

class MatchSpec extends ObjectBehavior
{

    public function let()
    {
        $this->beConstructedWith(new \Team, new \Team);
    }

    public function it_is_initializable()
    {
        $this->shouldHaveType('Match');
    }

    public function it_has_initial_score()
    {
        $this->getScore()->shouldBe('0 : 0');
    }

    public function it_has_score_two_one()
    {
        $this->homeTeam->scoreGoal()->shouldReturn(1);
        $this->homeTeam->scoreGoal()->shouldReturn(2);
        $this->visitorsTeam->scoreGoal()->shouldReturn(1);
```

```
        $this->getScore()->shouldBe('2 : 1');
    }

    public function it_gives_home_team_three_points()
    {
        $this->homeTeam->scoreGoal()->shouldReturn(1);
        $this->gameover();
        $this->homeTeam->getReceivedPoints()->shouldReturn(3);
        $this->visitorsTeam->getReceivedPoints()->shouldReturn(0);
    }
}
```

In this example, we start with the `let()` method. This is equivalent to the `setUp()` method from PHPUnit called before every example. In this case, it's calling the `Match` constructor, but the language is more readable for humans, so it's called the `beConstructedWith` method.

Then you can see a few examples. Each example starts with "it_" similar to "test" in PHPUnit. After each method call matcher is used. Matchers are same thing as the asserts in PHPUnit, just instead of "assert" you say "expect".

As you can see, the syntax is slightly different, but the logic is more or less the same as it would be for PHPUnit tests.

If you execute these specs, you should see an output similar to the following command line:

```
/ pending: 0%  / passed: 100%  / failed: 0%  / broken: 0%  / 6
examples

2 specs

6 examples (6 passed)

80ms
```

Now we have two specs with six examples, all passed.

Functional testing with Behat

Behat (`http://behat.org`) belongs to the second BDD group, storyBDD. As you can see, specBDD is quite similar to unit testing. The storyBDD approach is to test code from outside of code instead of inside. Everything here is driven by a story. A story is something that describes business requirements, such as what is requested, how it should work, and what should be an output. This is done by human readable language. Behat was inspired by Cucumber. Cucumber is Ruby's project, which first used Gherkin—a language that is used to write stories.

When you have a story, you create a feature. A feature is similar to a test suite, but the difference is that it contains implementation of steps from the story. When you execute a story, Behat takes the feature definition and uses steps from there to play scenarios described in the story. This might sound confusing when you compare it to unit tests, but when you see an example, you will agree that it makes sense.

Behat is very often used with Mink. Mink is the bridge between your tests and web browser. It's quite similar to the PHPUnit Selenium extension, which we have seen in *Chapter 12, Functional Tests in the Web Browser Using Selenium*, and indeed Mink can be used together with Selenium. Behat and Mink can be used for functional testing, and depends on the used driver with Selenium. Selenium tests can be in browsers, but headless drivers, such as Goutte Driver, are very handy because they are fast.

Installing Behat

Installing Behat is similar to PHPSpec, and again, Composer is the easiest way. The following is the `composer.json` file content:

```
{
    "require": {
        "behat/behat": "2.4.*@stable"
    },
    "minimum-stability": "dev",
    "config": {
        "bin-dir": "bin/"
    }
}
```

It installs required libraries, and also creates shell script for the Behat execution. When you have Behat installed, just run the following command to initialize the Behat project:

```
>behat --init
+d features - place your *.feature files here
+d features\bootstrap - place bootstrap scripts and static files here
+f features\bootstrap\FeatureContext.php - place your feature related
  code here
```

This is the output that you should see. When you read through, it creates the `features` directory, where you should place your story files with the extension `.feature`.

This is followed by information on where to place scripts that should be loaded, and also creates a `FeatureContext.php` file. This is the file where you put your PHP code, as the extension suggests.

Using Behat

To see how Behat works, we can use the football match example, which we used for PHPSpec. Now comes the important part—Behat begins with a story. We will write a story of how a football match is played. In our case, the football match is going to be the feature, and we will have two scenarios describing how this feature works, as shown in the following code:

```
Feature: Football match

  Scenario: Match starts
    Given New Match
    Then Score should be
    """
    0 : 0
    """

  Scenario: Home teams wins 2 : 1
    Given New Match
    Then Home team scores goal
    And  Visitors team scores goal
    And Home team scores goal
    And Match ends
    Then The Match ends with score
    """
    2 : 1
    """
    And Home team gets points
    """
    3
    """
```

This is the story written in Gherkin. As you can see, it's really easy to understand and there are just a few keywords used, such as `Given`, `Then`, and `And`.

You can find more about Gherkin in the Behat documentation at `http://docs.behat.org/guides/1.gherkin.html`.

Now Behat can help you with an implementation. Just run Behat; it takes the story and suggests an implementation:

```
You can implement step definitions for undefined steps with these
snippets:
    /**
     * @Given /^New Match$/
```

```php
     */
    public function newMatch()
    {
        throw new PendingException();
    }

    /**
     * @Then /^Score should be$/
     */
    public function scoreShouldBe(PyStringNode $string)
    {
        throw new PendingException();
    }

    /**
     * @Then /^Home team scores goal$/
     */
    public function homeTeamScoresGoal()
    {
        throw new PendingException();
    }

    /**
     * @Given /^Visitors team scores goal$/
     */
    public function visitorsTeamScoresGoal()
    {
        throw new PendingException();
    }

    /**
     * @Given /^Match ends$/
     */
    public function matchEnds()
    {
        throw new PendingException();
    }

    /**
     * @Then /^The Match ends with score$/
     */
    public function theMatchEndsWithScore(PyStringNode $string)
    {
```

```
    throw new PendingException();
}

/**
 * @Given /^Home team gets points$/
 */
public function homeTeamGetsPoints(PyStringNode $string)
{
    throw new PendingException();
}
```

As you can see, for each method Behat uses an annotation such as `@Given` or `@Then`. This is a regular expression, which matches lines from the scenario, and this is how Behat detects which method to use for each line of a scenario. These methods are step definitions, and one definition can be called as many times as you like, or to be precise, as many times as it's used in scenarios.

Our example is simple. We want to start a match, score goals, finish a match, and check the score and received goals. In this case, complete implementation could look like the following code snippet:

```php
<?php

use Behat\Behat\Context\BehatContext,
    Behat\Gherkin\Node\PyStringNode;

//
// Require 3rd-party libraries here:

// for PHPUnit 3.7
require_once 'PHPUnit/Autoload.php';
require_once 'PHPUnit/Framework/Assert/Functions.php';

// for PHPUnit 4.x
//include 'phar://phpunit.phar/phpunit/Framework/Assert/Functions.php';
//
```

Here we use PHPUnit because Behat doesn't have its own assertion tool and PHPUnit is the one that suits us well. As PHPUnit 4 is distributed as the PHAR file, there is a slightly different way of how to include the `Functions.php` file for PHPUnit Version 3.7 and version 4.

Now we can look at the feature context of `Feature: Football match`:

```php
/**
 * Features context.
 */
class FeatureContext extends BehatContext
{
    /**
     * @var \Match
     */
    private $match;

    /**
     * Initializes context.
     * Every scenario gets its own context object.
     *
     * @param array $parameters context parameters (set them up
       through behat.yml)
     */
    public function __construct(array $parameters){}

    /**
     * @Given /^New Match$/
     */
    public function newMatch()
    {
        $this->match = new \Match(new \Team, new \Team);
    }

    /**
     * @Then /^Score should be$/
     */
    public function scoreShouldBe(PyStringNode $string)
    {
        assertEquals('0 : 0', $this->match->getScore());
    }

    /**
     * @Then /^Home team scores goal$/
     */
    public function homeTeamScoresGoal()
    {
        $this->match->homeTeam->scoreGoal();
    }
```

```
    /**
     * @Given /^Visitors team scores goal$/
     */
    public function visitorsTeamScoresGoal()
    {
        $this->match->visitorsTeam->scoreGoal();
    }


    /**
     * @Given /^Match ends$/
     */
    public function matchEnds()
    {
        $this->match->gameOver();
    }


    /**
     * @Then /^The Match ends with score$/
     */
    public function theMatchEndsWithScore(PyStringNode $string)
    {
        assertEquals($string->getRaw(), $this->match->getScore());
    }


    /**
     * @Given /^Home team gets points$/
     */
    public function homeTeamGetsPoints(PyStringNode $string)
    {
        assertEquals($string->getRaw(),
          $this->match->homeTeam->getReceivedPoints());
    }
}
```

When we have an implementation, we can run Behat to execute the story, and show which step definition was used, as shown in the following command line:

```
>behat
Feature: Football match

  Scenario: Match start  # features\match.feature:3
    Given New Match       # FeatureContext::newMatch()
    Then Score should be  # FeatureContext::scoreShouldBe()
      """
      0 : 0
      """
```

```
    Scenario: Home teams wins 2 : 1   # features\match.feature:10
      Given New Match                 # FeatureContext::newMatch()
      Then Home team scores goal      # FeatureContext::homeTeamScoresGoal()
      And Visitors team scores goal   # FeatureContext::visitorsTeamScoresGo
al()
      And Home team scores goal       # FeatureContext::homeTeamScoresGoal()
      And Match ends                  # FeatureContext::matchEnds()
      Then The Match ends with score  # FeatureContext::theMatchEndsWithSco
re()
        """
        2 : 1
        """
      And Home team gets points       # FeatureContext::homeTeamGetsPoints()
        """
        3
        """


2 scenarios (2 passed)
9 steps (9 passed)
0m0.474s
```

As you can see, two scenarios were executed and nine steps passed.

Summary

In this last chapter, we saw that PHPUnit became standard in PHP as an xUnit testing tool. However, it doesn't mean you can't extend or replace parts of PHPUnit with alternative solutions. Of course you can; it's just up to you to choose the one that suits you best.

However, PHPUnit and TDD is not the only way. BDD is another way to write tests. It's focused on features and stories. Human readable code makes this task easier and allows developers to focus on important business requirements. It was just a brief introduction, but it should give a glance into the BDD world so that you can imagine what a different approach could look like. We have seen PHPSpec and Behat as two very good projects that introduced the concept of BDD to the PHP world. What hasn't been mentioned in this chapter is another brilliant project, Codeception, which is a modern, full-stack testing framework built on top of PHPUnit, and brings under one roof unit, functional, integration, and acceptance tests. However, this chapter was just an introduction to the concept of BDD, and definitely couldn't answer all questions related to BDD.

And this is it. This book should be an inspiration for you, and now it's up to you to write better code, write tests, and move your programming skills to another level. I hope you understand why you should write tests and how to do them, but there are millions of ways of how exactly to do it. It's up to you which method to choose, and for every project and every developer, there might be a slightly different solution. This book may not always give you definitive answers, but it should give you enough information about PHPUnit to be able to use it effectively and appreciate what a good tool it is.

Index

N

NetBeans
about 27
URL 27
using 27-30

O

ObjectBehavior class 276
Object Oriented Programming. *See* **OOP**
Object Relational Mapping. *See* **ORM**
onNotSuccessfulTest method 240
OOP 56
ORM 61
OrmTestCase class 159

P

Patchwork library
about 201
URL 201, 268
used, for testing legacy code 202-204
PayPal API
testing 177-183
PayPal developer website
URL 178
PDT
about 34
URL 34
PEAR
installing 15
PECL tool
URL 208
Phactory
URL 268
Phing
URL 260
PHP
running, from command line 11, 12
PHP CLI
about 10
PHP, running from command line 11, 12
PHP Development Tools. *See* **PDT**
phpinfo() function 12
PHP-SeleniumClient
about 243

installing 243
using 243-245
PHPSpec
installing 271, 272
testing with 270
URL 270
using 272-277
PhpStorm
about 41
installing 41
URL 41
using 43, 44
PHPUnit
about 10
installing, methods 10
Mockery, comparing to 133, 134
URL 10
PHPUnit installation
Composer, used 13-15
Linux package installation 17, 18
manual installation 18
PEAR, used 15, 16
requirements 10
testing 18-21
testing, Xdebug used 21, 22
PHPUnit Selenium2TestCase 226-228
PHPUnit Selenium extension
about 215
installing 221
PHPUnit test
anatomy 51, 52
functions, testing 53-56
methods, defining 53
methods, testing 56-61
PHPUnit third-party extensions
about 268, 269
Mockery 268
Patchwork 268
Prophecy 268
TestIt library 268
PHPUnit XML configuration file
about 107
attributes 108
code coverage configuration 110
example code 108
<php> elements 108
test listeners 109

Thank you for buying
PHPUnit Essentials

About Packt Publishing

Packt, pronounced 'packed', published its first book *"Mastering phpMyAdmin for Effective MySQL Management"* in April 2004 and subsequently continued to specialize in publishing highly focused books on specific technologies and solutions.

Our books and publications share the experiences of your fellow IT professionals in adapting and customizing today's systems, applications, and frameworks. Our solution based books give you the knowledge and power to customize the software and technologies you're using to get the job done. Packt books are more specific and less general than the IT books you have seen in the past. Our unique business model allows us to bring you more focused information, giving you more of what you need to know, and less of what you don't.

Packt is a modern, yet unique publishing company, which focuses on producing quality, cutting-edge books for communities of developers, administrators, and newbies alike. For more information, please visit our website: www.packtpub.com.

About Packt Open Source

In 2010, Packt launched two new brands, Packt Open Source and Packt Enterprise, in order to continue its focus on specialization. This book is part of the Packt Open Source brand, home to books published on software built around Open Source licenses, and offering information to anybody from advanced developers to budding web designers. The Open Source brand also runs Packt's Open Source Royalty Scheme, by which Packt gives a royalty to each Open Source project about whose software a book is sold.

Writing for Packt

We welcome all inquiries from people who are interested in authoring. Book proposals should be sent to author@packtpub.com. If your book idea is still at an early stage and you would like to discuss it first before writing a formal book proposal, contact us; one of our commissioning editors will get in touch with you.

We're not just looking for published authors; if you have strong technical skills but no writing experience, our experienced editors can help you develop a writing career, or simply get some additional reward for your expertise.

Instant Hands-on Testing with PHPUnit How-to

ISBN: 978-1-78216-958-1   Paperback: 82 pages

A practical guide to getting started with PHPUnit to improve code quality

1. Learn something new in an Instant!
    A short, fast, focused guide delivering immediate results.

2. Discover how to make best use of PHPUnit in your projects.

3. Get started with code testing using PHPUnit in no time.

Backbone.js Patterns and Best Practices

ISBN: 978-1-78328-357-6   Paperback: 174 pages

A one-stop guide to best practices and design patterns when building applications using Backbone.js

1. Offers solutions to common Backbone.js related problems that most developers face.

2. Shows you how to use custom widgets, plugins, and mixins to make your code reusable.

3. Describes patterns and best practices for large scale JavaScript application architecture and unit testing applications with QUnit and SinonJS frameworks.

Please check **www.PacktPub.com** for information on our titles

Learning FuelPHP for Effective PHP Development

ISBN: 978-1-78216-036-6   Paperback: 104 pages

Use the flexible FuelPHP framework to quickly and effectively create PHP applications

1. Scaffold with oil - the FuelPHP command-line tool.

2. Build an administration quickly and effectively.

3. Create your own project using FuelPHP.

Persistence in PHP with Doctrine ORM

ISBN: 978-1-78216-410-4   Paperback: 114 pages

Build a model layer of your PHP applications successfully, using Doctrine ORM

1. Develop a fully functional Doctrine-backed web application.

2. Demonstrate aspects of Doctrine using code samples.

3. Generate a database schema from your PHP classes.

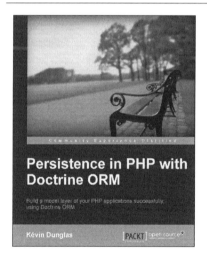

Please check **www.PacktPub.com** for information on our titles

Printed in Germany
by Amazon Distribution
GmbH, Leipzig